ADVANCES IN ACCOUNTING EDUCATION: TEACHING AND CURRICULUM INNOVATIONS

ADVANCES IN ACCOUNTING EDUCATION: TEACHING AND CURRICULUM INNOVATIONS

Series Editor: Bill N. Schwartz

Recent Volumes:

Volume 1:	Edited by Bill N. Schwartz and David E. Stout
Volumes 2–7:	Edited by Bill N. Schwartz and J. Edward Ketz
Volumes 8–9:	Edited by Bill N. Schwartz and Anthony H. Catanach Jr.

ADVANCES IN ACCOUNTING EDUCATION: TEACHING AND CURRICULUM INNOVATIONS VOLUME 9

ADVANCES IN ACCOUNTING EDUCATION: TEACHING AND CURRICULUM INNOVATIONS

EDITED BY

BILL N. SCHWARTZ
Howe School of Technology Management
Stevens Institute of Technology
Hoboken, New Jersey, USA

ANTHONY H. CATANACH Jr.
School of Business, Villanova University, USA

JAI

United Kingdom – North America – Japan
India – Malaysia – China

JAI Press is an imprint of Emerald Group Publishing Limited
Howard House, Wagon Lane, Bingley BD16 1WA, UK

First edition 2008

British Library Cataloguing in Publication Data
A catalogue record for this book is available from the British Library

ISBN: 978-0-7623-1458-4
ISSN: 1085-4622 (Series)

Printed and bound in Great Britain by MPG Books Ltd, Bodmin, Cornwall

CONTENTS

LIST OF CONTRIBUTORS *ix*

TEACHING THE INCOME STATEMENT: FRAMING THE DISCUSSION WITHIN THE CONTEXT OF EARNINGS QUALITY
James F. Sepe and J. David Spiceland 1

USING SEC ENFORCEMENT RELEASES TO TEACH AUDITING AND ETHICS-RELATED CONCEPTS
Jill M. D'Aquila 17

TAX SOFTWARE VERSUS PAPER RETURN: THE EFFECT OF A COMPUTERIZED DECISION AID ON COGNITIVE EFFORT AND STUDENT LEARNING
Rebekah Sheely Heath 57

REVISITING HIRING DECISIONS BY PUBLIC ACCOUNTING: THE IMPACT OF EDUCATIONAL PATH, AGE AND GENDER
Elizabeth Dreike Almer and Anne L. Christensen 77

LEARNING TO INTERPRET AND RECONCILE TAX AUTHORITY
Ernest R. Larkins 95

A NEW APPROACH TO IMPROVING AND EVALUATING STUDENT WORKPLACE WRITING SKILLS
Susan A. Lynn and Thomas E. Vermeer 115

INTEGRATING TAX AND FINANCIAL ACCOUNTING: THREE EXERCISES FOR USE IN TAX AND FINANCIAL ACCOUNTING CLASSES
Sharon Bruns, Diana Falsetta and Timothy J. Rupert 151

GROUPTHINK IN ACCOUNTING EDUCATION
Michael P. Riordan, Diane A. Riordan and E. Kent St. Pierre 189

THE EFFECT OF FRAUD TRIANGLE FACTORS ON STUDENTS' CHEATING BEHAVIORS
Freddie Choo and Kim Tan 205

CURRENT FACTORS AND PRACTICES RELATED TO INSTRUCTIONAL APPROACH IN THE INTRODUCTORY FINANCIAL ACCOUNTING COURSE
Christie L. Comunale, Thomas R. Sexton and Stephen C. Gara 221

DOES ETHICS INSTRUCTION MAKE A DIFFERENCE?
John Delaney and Martin J. Coe 233

USING THE ALBRECHT AND SACK STUDY TO GUIDE CURRICULUM DECISIONS
Steve Johnson, Bunney Schmidt, Steve Teeter and Jonathan Henage 251

USING A TECHNOLOGY-MEDIATED APPROACH TO CREATE A PRACTICE–FEEDBACK–INTERACTION PROCESS FOR USE WITH ACCOUNTING COURSES
Richard E. Lillie 267

STUDENT TURNED CONSULTANT: TEACHING THE BALANCED SCORECARD USING EXPERIENTIAL LEARNING
Noah P. Barsky, Anthony H. Catanach and C. Andrew Lafond 287

A PRELIMINARY STUDY OF LEARNING OBJECTIVES ACROSS THE CURRICULUM: AN ANALYSIS OF VARIOUS ACCOUNTING TEXTBOOKS
Leonard Stokes 307

LIST OF CONTRIBUTORS

Elizabeth Dreike Almer	Portland State University, OR, USA
Noah P. Barsky	School of Business, Villanova University, PA, USA
Sharon Bruns	College of Business Administration, Northeastern University, MA, USA
Anthony H. Catanach	School of Business, Villanova University, PA, USA
Freddie Choo	Department of Accounting, San Francisco State University, CA, USA
Anne L. Christensen	College of Business, Montana State University, MT, USA
Martin J. Coe	Department of Accountancy, Western Illinois University, IL, USA
Christie L. Comunale	School of Professional Accountancy, Long Island University – C.W. Post Campus, NY, USA
Jill M. D'Aquila	Davis College of Business, Jacksonville University, FL, USA
John Delaney	Department of Accounting, Augustana College, IL, USA
Diana Falsetta	Department of Accounting, University of Miami, FL, USA
Stephen C. Gara	School of Accounting, Drake University, IA, USA
Rebekah Sheely Heath	Department of Accounting, Pittsburg State University, KS, USA

Jonathan Henage	Utah Valley State College, UT, USA
Steve Johnson	Utah Valley State College, UT, USA
C. Andrew Lafond	Department of Accounting and Taxation, Philadelphia University, PA, USA
Ernest R. Larkins	School of Accountancy, Georgia State University, GA, USA
Richard E. Lillie	Department of Accounting and Finance, California State University, CA, USA
Susan A. Lynn	Department of Accounting and Management Information Systems, Robert G. Merrick School of Business, University of Baltimore, MD, USA
Diane A. Riordan	School of Accounting, James Madison University, VA, USA
Michael P. Riordan	School of Accounting, James Madison University, VA, USA
Timothy J. Rupert	College of Business Administration, Northeastern University, MA, USA
Bunney Schmidt	Utah Valley State College, UT, USA
James F. Sepe	Accounting Department, Santa Clara University, CA, USA
Thomas R. Sexton	College of Business, State University of New York – Stony Brook, NY, USA
J. David Spiceland	Accounting Department, University of Memphis, Tennessee, USA
Leonard Stokes	School of Business, Siena College, NY, USA
E. Kent St. Pierre	Department of Accounting and Information Systems, University of Delaware, Delaware, USA

Kim Tan	Department of Accounting & Finance, California State University Stanislaus, CA, USA
Steve Teeter	Utah Valley State College, UT, USA
Thomas E. Vermeer	Department of Accounting and Management Information Systems, Robert G. Merrick School of Business, University of Baltimore, MD, USA

TEACHING THE INCOME STATEMENT: FRAMING THE DISCUSSION WITHIN THE CONTEXT OF EARNINGS QUALITY

James F. Sepe and J. David Spiceland

ABSTRACT

This chapter provides an approach for teaching the income statement within an earnings quality framework in an intermediate accounting course. Not only is the approach rich in content, but it also is an engaging pedagogical device. The article provides a broad outline and then fills in the details with discussion, information, and examples.

Those analyzing an income statement receive clues regarding earnings quality from the presentation of the components of net income, and the related supplemental disclosures. Anecdotal evidence, though, suggests that many of us tend to teach the income statement with little regard for the fact that various components of income provide significantly different signals for predicting future profitability. Most financial and intermediate textbooks simply describe income statement presentation without offering much in the way of providing meaning to revenue and expense classifications and

Advances in Accounting Education: Teaching and Curriculum Innovations, Volume 9, 1–15

ISSN: 1085-4622/doi:10.1016/S1085-4622(08)09001-9

without exploring the permanent versus transitory nature of income statement components.

We define the term *earnings quality* to mean the ability of reported earnings (income) to predict future earnings. After all, an income statement simply reports on events that already have occurred. The relevance of any historical-based financial statement hinges on its predictive value. To enhance predictive value, analysts explicitly or implicitly attempt to separate a company's transitory earnings from its permanent earnings. There is a significant body of literature that addresses this question of permanent versus transitory earnings. For example, see Ali, Klein, and Rosenfeld (1992). Transitory earnings result from transactions or events that are not likely to occur again in the foreseeable future, or that are likely to have a different impact on earnings in the future.

Companies often voluntarily provide a *pro forma earnings* number at the same time they announce annual or quarterly earnings determined according to GAAP. These pro forma earnings numbers are controversial as they represent management's biased interpretation of permanent earnings. Standard setters are concerned with the issue of reporting multiple earnings values and the potential for investor confusion. In August 2001, the Financial Accounting Standards Board (FASB) disseminated a proposal for a new project entitled "Reporting Information About the Financial Performance of Business Enterprises."[1] One of the principal reasons an instructor can cite for the project was the increase in the reporting of pro forma earnings. In 2004, the FASB and the International Accounting Standards Board (IASB) decided to combine their respective projects on the reporting of income statement items.

Not only have the FASB's concern over companies' reporting of pro forma earnings and the current requirement to identify the reasons for differences between such numbers and GAAP earnings not stemmed the tide, but also the gap between the two numbers is growing. According to Merrill Lynch, in the second quarter of 2006 the difference between GAAP and pro forma earnings for the 1,600 companies covered by Merrill was the widest observed since 2004 (Lahart, 2006, 1). As an example, in the third quarter of 2004, AT&T reported pro forma net income of $593 million ignoring a charge to write down equipment, but using GAAP for the same period AT&T reported a net loss of $7.1 billion.[2]

The concept of earnings quality attracted significant attention after the turn of the century. *Issues in Accounting Education* devoted an entire issue (November 2002) to the topic. Cases an instructor can use in the classroom are the subject of most of the articles in that issue. Amernic and Robb (2003) offer a way to frame the entire Intermediate Accounting course with an earnings quality theme. Much of the article addresses the issue of framing in general and the definition of earnings quality. However, the article offers little in the way of guidance on how to actually construct a course within this framework and provides neither an outline nor any examples.

This chapter provides faculty with a detailed approach for teaching the income statement within an earnings quality framework in an intermediate accounting course. We have found this approach to be an extremely effective way to present the material to students. Instructors can expect to devote approximately 3½ to 4 h of class time to the topic. We suggest that this coverage come early in the first intermediate course, perhaps in week three. An instructor can then revisit the lessons learned about earnings quality within the context of other intermediate accounting topics.

We offer a brief outline for teaching the income statement in Exhibit 1 of our Income Statement discussion.

COMPREHENSIVE INCOME

Instructors should remind students that the purpose of the income statement is to summarize the profit-generating activities that occurred during a particular reporting period and that it is a *change* statement reporting the changes in shareholders' equity that occurred during the period as a result of revenues, expenses, gains, and losses. Discussion of this concept is an excellent lead-in to a conversation about comprehensive income. First, instructors should make sure students understand the distinction between owner transactions and nonowner transactions that affect equity. Then instructors should define comprehensive income as the total change in equity for a reporting period other than from transactions with owners.

With the concept of comprehensive income consisting of all nonowner changes in equity understood, instructors should emphasize that a few nonowner changes in equity are not included in the determination of traditional net income and that these are referred to as *other comprehensive income*. It is useful to point out the four possible other comprehensive income items. Instructors should indicate that each of these will be covered either later in the intermediate course or in other parts of an accounting major's curriculum, so at this point an instructor needs only to list the items. The items include net unrealized holding gains (losses) on security-available-for-sale investments, gains (losses) on pensions, deferred gains (losses) from derivatives, and foreign currency translation adjustments.

Exhibit 1. Outline of the Income Statement Discussion

I. *Comprehensive Income*
   A. The purpose of the income statement is to summarize the profit-generating activities that occurred during a particular reporting period.
   B. Comprehensive income is the total change in equity for a reporting period other than from transactions with owners.
   C. The presentation of comprehensive income can be included as an extension to the income statement, reported (exactly the same way) as a separate statement of comprehensive income, or included in a statement of changes in equity.

II. *Income from Continuing Operations*
   A. Income from continuing operations includes the revenues, expenses, gains, and losses that probably will continue in future periods.
      1. Distinction often is made between operating and nonoperating income.
      2. A single-step income statement format groups all revenues and gains together and all expenses and losses together.
      3. A multiple-step income statement format includes a number of intermediate subtotals before arriving at income from continuing operations.

III. *Earnings Quality*
   A. Earnings quality refers to the ability of reported earnings (income) to predict a company's future earnings. To enhance predictive value, analysts try to separate a company's *transitory earnings* effects from its *permanent earnings*.
   B. Not all revenue and expense items included in operating income are indicative of a company's permanent earnings.
   C. Some gains and losses included in nonoperating income are not indicative of a company's permanent earnings.

IV. *Separately Reported Items*
   A. Intraperiod tax allocation associates tax expense or tax benefits with ordinary continuing operations as well as with any discontinued operations or extraordinary items.
   B. Discontinued operations involve the disposal or planned disposal of a *component of an entity* whose operations and cash flows can be clearly distinguished from the rest of the entity.
   C. Extraordinary items are material gains and losses that are both *unusual in nature* and *infrequent in occurrence*.

To complete coverage of comprehensive income, instructors should discuss financial statement presentation. In annual and quarterly financial statements, companies must report both net income and comprehensive income and reconcile the difference between the two (FASB, 1997). Students find it difficult to understand that a company must report two separate attributes of other comprehensive income: (a) components of comprehensive income *created during the reporting period* and (b) the comprehensive income *accumulated* over the current and prior periods. We find it useful to relate reporting of the traditional net income component of total comprehensive income to the reporting of other comprehensive income. Instructors should remind them that (a) net income reported in the income statement is an amount *created during the reporting period* and (b) retained earnings, in general, is net income *accumulated* over the current and prior periods (less dividends paid). In a similar manner, we report (a) components of comprehensive income *created during the reporting period* as an extension to the income statement and (b) the *accumulated* comprehensive income as a component of shareholders' equity in the balance sheet as we do retained earnings. Companies can present comprehensive income items (a) as an extension to the income statement, (b) reported (exactly the same way) as a separate statement of comprehensive income, often included in the financial statements as a disclosure note, or (c) in the statement of changes in shareholders' equity.

Instructors may find it useful to show a real-world example of a comprehensive income presentation that includes both net income and components of other comprehensive income as well as the same company's balance sheet that includes both retained earnings and accumulated other comprehensive income. An instructor might even demonstrate how the current year's components of other comprehensive income explain the change from the preceding year in the ending balances of accumulated other comprehensive income in the comparative balance sheets.

INCOME FROM CONTINUING OPERATIONS

It is difficult to overemphasize that the role of accounting is to provide information useful in making decisions about the future. The FASB's *Statement of Financial Accountings Concepts No. 1*, "Objectives of Financial Reporting for Business Enterprises," provides support and we recommend revisiting those objectives at this point in the lecture. One source of information that analysts could use to predict future cash flows is what has occurred in the past. A company's operating transactions that probably will continue into the future frequently are the best predictors of future cash flows. Having students envision themselves in the role of analysts predicting future profitability using income statements that include discontinued operations and extraordinary items helps them see the importance of properly segregating those items from income from ordinary continuing operations. Instructors can help students with this assignment by using a simple example that shows the presentation of an income statement with an extraordinary gain or loss included in continuing operations contrasted with the correct presentation.

Many corporate income statements distinguish between *operating* income and *nonoperating* income within the continuing operations section. Instructors can discuss the distinction with students and then show them a few real-world examples. Then instructors might want to discuss what companies include in operating income, revenues and expenses directly related to their principal revenue-generating activities. For example, operating income for a manufacturing company includes sales revenues from the sale of products and all expenses related to this activity. Instructors should do the same for nonoperating income which includes gains and losses (that are not extraordinary) as well as revenues and expenses that are peripheral or incidental to the main operating activities of the company. For example, companies report income from investments, gains, and losses from the sale of operating assets and from investments, interest and dividend revenue, and interest expense as nonoperating income.

After covering this distinction between operating and nonoperating income, instructors can discuss the usefulness of a multiple-step income statement format rather than a single-step format. Because most corporate income statements are multiple-step, we recommend an instructor do not spend much time on this difference and focus on the multiple-step approach. The most recent edition of Accounting Trends and Techniques (2006, p. 295) reported that of the 600 companies in its survey, 495 used the multiple-step format. Of the 105 that used a single-step format, all of them did show income tax expense as a separate item.

OPERATING INCOME AND EARNINGS QUALITY

With this foundation laid, an instructor can address the concept of earnings quality as it relates to the income statement. Instructors can begin by defining earnings quality as the ability of reported earnings (income) to predict a company's future earnings. They can discuss the concept with the class and provide some simple examples of situations where earnings quality is in question, such as the loss of a major customer near the end of the reporting period. They also can encourage the class to suggest questionable items that might appear in the determination of operating income.

A good question might be: "Should all items of revenue and expense normally included in operating income be considered indicative of a company's permanent earnings?" Of course the answer is no, not necessarily, but students can suggest examples. The class should recognize that operating expenses often include some unusual items that may or may not continue in the future. At an appropriate point in the discourse, show them the upper-half of a corporate income statement that includes some questionable items. For example, Exhibit 2 contains partial income statements for Winn Dixie Stores, Inc. Instructors can ask students if there are any items on the statement that they would like more information about. They should easily identify asset impairment charges and restructuring costs.

Students will encounter several other similar items later in the intermediate course, such as inventory writedowns and asset impairment losses. Instructors should mention these items but might not want to address the measurement issues at this point. Restructuring costs offer a topical, but underutilized, opportunity to demonstrate the issues at this juncture.

Exhibit 2. Partial Income Statements – Winn Dixie Stores, Inc. (Years Ended June 30, 2004 and June 25, 2003, Amounts in Millions)

	2004	2003
Net sales	$10,633	$11,026
Cost of sales	7,819	7,893
Gross profit	2,814	3,133
Operating expenses		
Selling, general and administrative	2,943	2,830
Asset impairment charges	35	–
Restructuring costs	9	–
Operating income (loss)	(173)	303

Restructuring costs appear regularly in corporate income statements, either directly on the face of the statement or in a disclosure note if the costs are included with other line items (FASB, 2002). In fact the most recent edition of Accounting Trends and Techniques (2006, p. 313) reports that of the 600 companies surveyed, 249 (42%) included restructuring costs in their income statements. This is a key financial reporting issue that receives far too little attention in most financial accounting courses but which fits nicely into the discussion of earnings quality.

Classroom conversation can include the ideas mentioned in the following discussion. Restructuring costs include costs associated with the shutdown or relocation of facilities or downsizing of operations. Facility closings and related employee layoffs translate into costs incurred for severance pay and relocation costs. The appearance of restructuring costs in corporate income statements increased significantly in the 1980s and 1990s. Many U.S. companies reacted to increased competition by streamlining their operations.

Prior to 2003, companies often would recognize (expense) restructuring costs in the period they made the decision to restructure, not when the actual activities took place. The SEC became concerned about the frequency with which companies were accruing restructuring costs in this manner. According to Arthur Levitt (1998, p. 16), one of the chief concerns was that some companies purposely expensed large costs in an effort to manipulate future income. For instance, employee relocation costs incurred in conjunction with a restructuring may produce future benefits to a company through greater operating efficiency. If so, accrual prior to any action may result in premature expense recognition of these costs. The discussion of the accounting treatment of restructuring costs presents an ideal opportunity to discuss the concept of earnings management and how it relates to earnings quality. Restructuring costs are an example of what often has been referred to as a "big bath" charge that shifts income from the current period to a future period or periods. *SFAS No. 146* now requires that restructuring costs be recognized only in the period incurred. No longer can a company accrue restructuring costs in the period the company commits to an exit plan, unless the costs actually have been incurred (FASB, 2002).

Once students grasp the nature of restructuring costs, an instructor can address the crucial question: Should financial statement users consider these costs part of a company's permanent earnings stream, or are they transitory in nature? There is no easy answer. Consider the following facts. During the 13-year period from 1991 through 2003, the Dow Jones Industrial 30 companies reported 83 restructuring costs in their collective income statements. That is an average of approximately 2.75 per company, but the average is deceiving. Twelve of the 30 companies reported either one instance or no restructuring costs during that period. However, DuPont reported restructuring costs in 10 of the 13 years, Alcoa in 9 of the years. An analyst must interpret restructuring costs in light of a company's past history in this area. Information in disclosure notes describing the restructuring and management plans related to the business involved also can be helpful. Kemp (2002) presents a case that involves an analyst's downgrade of an otherwise sound investment because of a deterioration of earnings quality caused by an unusual accounting method for restructuring costs.

NONOPERATING INCOME AND EARNINGS QUALITY

The nonoperating components of net income also are worthy of discussion with respect to earnings quality, particularly gains and losses resulting either from the sale of operational assets or from the sale of investments. For example, as the stock market boom reached its height late in the year 2000, many companies recorded huge gains from sale of investments that had appreciated significantly in value. How should those gains be interpreted in terms of their relationship to future earnings? Are they transitory or permanent?

Once again, instructors can begin the discussion by providing students with a real-world example of an income statement that contains at least one significant nonoperating item. For example, we could show them Intel's 1999 and 2000 income statements that are depicted in Exhibit 3 and then ask them if there is anything in the 2000 income statement that would concern an analyst attempting to predict future earnings. In 2000, income before taxes increased by approximately 35% from the prior year, the *gains on investments, net* increased from $883 million to over $3.7 billion, accounting for a large portion of the increase in income. Some analysts questioned the quality of Intel's earnings for the period because of these large gains. Instructors can take the example one step further by showing students Intel's 2001 income statement. In that year, Intel reported a $466 million loss on investments.

Exhibit 3. Partial Income Statements – Intel Corporation (Years Ended December 30, Amounts in Millions)

	2000	1999
Net revenues	$33,727	$29,389
Operating expenses		
Cost of sales	12,650	11,836
Research and development	3,897	3,111
Marketing, general, and administrative	5,089	3,872
Amortization of intangibles	1,586	411
In-process research and development	109	392
Operating expenses	23,331	19,622
Operating income	10,395	9,767
Gains on investments, net	3,759	883
Interest and other, net	987	578
Income before taxes	15,141	11,228

SEPARATELY REPORTED ITEMS

Once that students are more comfortable with the distinction between the permanent and transitory nature of income statement components, it is an easy transition to a discussion of separately reported items. Now they are aware that there are a number of questionable items that a company might include in the income from continuing operations section of an income statement. However, there are two items, discontinued operations and extraordinary gains and losses that require a clear message from the reporting company. The income effects of these events are decidedly not part of our permanent earnings stream; they are transitory in nature.

Until recently, there were three voluntary separately reported items. A recent accounting standard requires that changes in accounting principles be treated retrospectively (FASB, 2005). Instead of including the cumulative effect of the change in current income as a separately reported item, companies must now retrospectively recast prior years' financial statements when they report those statements again (in comparative statements, for example). In other words, those statements are made to appear as if the company had used the newly adopted accounting method in those years. Instructors should discuss the FASB's motivation for this change in reporting. Does the change improve comparability with prior years thus enhancing earnings quality?

Before instructors begin the discussion of the two remaining separately reported items, they should introduce the concept of intraperiod tax allocation. This topic tends to be a difficult one for students, particularly when losses are involved. We suggest that instructors present them with a very simple trial balance containing only income statement items, something similar to Exhibit 4.

Instructors should ask students to help construct a multiple-step income statement assuming that the gain is part of continuing operations. Then the students should recast the income statement assuming that the gain is "extraordinary" in nature and will not likely occur again in the foreseeable future. In the latter case, all of the income effects, including the tax effect, must be reported separately. Once they understand the basic concept, repeat the exercise, but instead of a $20 million gain, assume the company reported a $20 million loss.

Now students should be ready to discuss the two separately reported items. Most textbooks cover these items in depth, so we are not going to discuss them further here. We recommend showing real-world examples of actual income statement presentations of both items, including disclosure notes. Later in this chapter we provide some resources that make this task easier for the instructor.

Exhibit 4. Partial Trial Balance – XYZ Corporation (Amounts in Millions)

Revenues		80,000
Cost of goods sold	42,000	
General and administrative expenses	10,000	
Gain		20,000
Income tax expense (40%)	19,200	

OTHER TOPICS

An instructor's presentation of the income statement would not be complete without a discussion of earnings per share disclosures and accounting changes. Instructors should discuss simple and diluted EPS. We calculate only simple EPS and then illustrate the presentation of simple EPS with an income statement that contains separately reported items.

As we already mentioned, voluntary changes in accounting principles are no longer accounted for currently, but retrospectively. Instructors should discuss and illustrate accounting for changes in estimates and briefly discuss accounting for a change in reporting entity. We try never to miss an opportunity to relate accounting treatment and disclosure to the concept of earnings quality. For example, why does GAAP require a company to disclosure a material income effect of a change in accounting estimate in a disclosure note?

EXAMS

What we describe in this chapter is a method of teaching the content of the income statement. This approach should not have a significant impact on how instructors test students on the concepts learned. However, we suggest that short cases or online activities are a good way to reinforce the concept of earnings quality and the distinction between permanent and transitory earnings. For example, ask students to go online and find an earnings announcement that provides both a company's GAAP earnings and its pro forma earnings. They can share what they found, and the class can discuss the reason why adjustments from GAAP to pro forma earnings found might be appropriate for an analyst attempting to predict future profitability.

RESOURCES

Hypothetical illustrations and examples certainly have pedagogical value. However, real-world examples offer additional advantages in the classroom. Because students see the actual application of issues being discussed, they are more acutely engaged in the learning process. The classroom offers the opportunity to present extensive, current disclosure notes that are impractical for inclusion in a textbook. This chapter indicates several points in the presentation of the income statement where such examples can provide an essential real-world perspective. An instructor can use them liberally throughout the Intermediate course.

The most important source of financial statements and disclosures for publicly traded companies is the SEC's EDGAR (Electronic Data Gathering, Analysis, and Retrieval) database. The SEC makes this information available on the Internet at http://www.sec.gov/edgar/searchedgar/webusers.htm. Company websites are another source for financial statements and disclosure notes.

10-K wizard (www.tenkwizard.com) is a nice tool that allows instructors to search the EDGAR database to identify filings that contain specific items for which they are searching. For instance, we could perform a key word search of all 10-Ks filed within a certain time period that contain the term "discontinued operations." Also, the SEC recently added a similar engine that searches EDGAR's company filings for the last two years (www.sec.gov/edgar/searchedgar/webusers.htm).

EARNINGS QUALITY AND OTHER INTERMEDIATE TOPICS

Instructors can draw upon the earnings quality framework established in the income statement presentation numerous times in the remainder of the intermediate course when teaching topics such as revenue recognition, LIFO liquidations, impairment writedowns, accounting method choice, and many others. For example, when covering inventory, an instructor might ask students why it is important for a company to disclose the amount of any LIFO liquidation profit or loss that occurred during the period. A LIFO liquidation profit or loss reduces earnings quality because these "paper" profits or losses are unlikely to occur again in the future. The inventory method choice also affects earnings quality, particularly in periods of rapidly changing prices. Revenue recognition offers many opportunities for an instructor to use the earnings quality framework. For example, an instructor could introduce the practice of "channel stuffing" and ask students how this practice affects earnings quality.

We find that students often ask questions about the role of the auditor as it relates to what we have discussed in this chapter, particularly when the discussion moves to earnings management issues. Instructors should be prepared to deal with these questions without getting into areas that belong in the audit course. For example, an instructor could briefly discuss discretionary accruals, and then provide an example such as the warranty liability or the allowance for uncollectible receivables. Yes, a company could manage its earnings by over or underestimating these accruals, but only within a limited range. A number outside of that range should trigger a response from the auditor.

SUMMARY

In our classrooms we tend to teach the income statement in the intermediate accounting course with little regard for the fact that various components of income provide distinctly different signals for predicting future profitability. Students are better served by our teaching them the income statement within an earnings quality framework. This approach is essential to a decision-makers' perspective. By encouraging students to think critically about the analytic value of income statement components they not only become more actively engaged in the learning process, but also gain an essential decision-makers' perspective.

NOTES

1. "Reporting Information About the Financial Performance of Business Enterprises," *Proposal for a New Agenda Project* (Norwalk, CT: FASB, 2001).
2. AT&T Online news release (October 21, 2004).

REFERENCES

Accounting Trends and Techniques-2006. (2006). New York: AICPA.

Ali, A., Klein, A., & Rosenfeld, J. (1992). Analysts' use of information about permanent and transitory earnings components in forecasting annual EPS. *The Accounting Review*, January, pp. 183–198.

Amernic, J.H., & Robb, S.W. (2003). Quality of earnings as a framing device and unifying theme in intermediate financial accounting. *Issues in Accounting Education*, February, pp. 1–22.

FASB. (1997). *Reporting comprehensive income*, Statement of Financial Accounting Standards No. 130. Norwalk, CT: FASB.

FASB. (2002). *Accounting for costs associated with exit or disposal activities*, Statement of Financial Accounting Standards No. 146. Norwalk, CT: FASB.

FASB. (2005). *Accounting changes and error corrections – a replacement of APB Opinion No. 20 and FASB Statement No. 3*, Statement of Financial Accounting Standards No. 154. Norwalk, CT: FASB.

Kemp, B. (2002). Earnings quality assessment by a sell-side financial analyst. *Issues in Accounting Education*, November, pp. 361–368.

Lahart, J. (2006). Ahead of the Tape: Fore! *The Wall Street Journal Online*, September 26, p. 1.

Levitt, A., Jr. (1998). The numbers game. *The CPA Journal*, December, p. 16.

USING SEC ENFORCEMENT RELEASES TO TEACH AUDITING AND ETHICS-RELATED CONCEPTS

Jill M. D'Aquila

ABSTRACT

I have presented an inventory of Accounting and Auditing Enforcement Releases (AAERs) by the Securities and Exchange Commission (SEC) for accounting educators to incorporate into their auditing, accounting, ethics, or financial accounting courses. I have organized the AAERs by audit issues in a manner consistent with the order of topics typically covered in a financial auditing class. Accounting educators can bring a dimension of realism into the classroom by using AAERs to discuss issues concerning audit planning, audit testing, accounting ethics, fraud, and financial accounting.

Accounting scandals at companies such as Enron, WorldCom, and Tyco, as well as the enactment of the Sarbanes–Oxley Act (SOX, 2002), have heightened the focus on ethics in the business world and, therefore, in the classroom. Jennings (2004, p. 24) states that

> To recover from the moral failures of the past decade, accounting firms and businesses are reviewing their conduct, processes, and procedures. As business leaders and accounting professionals seek to implement meaningful changes that could prevent these

Advances in Accounting Education: Teaching and Curriculum Innovations, Volume 9, 17–55

ISSN: 1085-4622/doi:10.1016/S1085-4622(08)09002-0

> types of ethical collapses, business schools and schools of accountancy also have the opportunity to do some introspection on the content and delivery mechanisms for ethics training.

Accordingly, some have voiced a need for accounting educators to critically evaluate ethics education in a post SOX era. Madison and Schmidt (2006, p. 99) believe that ethics education is "of great importance" to accounting educators. In fact, numerous researchers indicate a need for accounting educators to incorporate more ethical issues in the classroom (Earley & Kelly, 2004, p. 54; Gaa & Thorne, 2004, p. 1; Haywood, McMullen, & Wygal, 2004, p. 85; Jennings, 2004, p. 7; Madison & Schmidt, 2006, p. 99; Peterson & Buckhoff, 2004, p. 64; PricewaterhouseCoopers, 2003; Thomas, 2004, p. 27). Peterson and Buckhoff (2004, p. 64) caution that educators who fail to incorporate fraud in their curriculum "will continue to graduate students who are ill prepared to meet the challenges of an increasingly unethical business world."

If accounting educators have more ethics-related resources available to them, perhaps educators will be more likely to incorporate ethics in their courses. Securities and Exchange Commission (SEC) enforcement releases are a particularly useful source of ethics-related material and could help students to understand how and why fraudulent financial reporting occurs based on real stories. Accordingly, I have compiled current materials based on recent Accounting and Auditing Enforcement Releases (AAERs) to augment the resources that are already available to accounting educators.

My aim is to provide resources to help the instructor tailor assignments for their specific instructional needs and, ultimately, to increase the availability of helpful resources to accounting educators who wish to incorporate ethics in the classroom. Specifically, I have provided an index of relevant teaching topics, based on actual and recent SEC enforcement releases, specifically known as AAERs, for use in an auditing course. I have organized the enforcement releases by specific audit topics to facilitate topical access and have arranged the topics in a manner consistent with the order of topics typically covered in an auditing class.

The material is particularly appropriate for an introductory or advanced auditing course. I presently incorporate AAERs in a three-credit introductory financial auditing course that I teach to undergraduate students. Accordingly, I have included specific guidance in incorporating enforcement releases in the classroom based on my experience. I believe that accounting educators also could use the material in financial accounting, fraud, and business ethics courses.

LITERATURE REVIEW

An increase of ethics-related educational material is apparent by Thomas' (2004) comprehensive inventory of books, articles, videos, and websites, among other resources. Thomas' inventory of resources includes brief descriptions of each item, as well as sources for obtaining these resources. An increase in available materials is indicated by the textbooks that are devoted entirely to such cases (see Beasley, Buckless, Glover, & Prawitt, 2006; Cullinan & Wright, 2003; Knapp, 2007; Thibodeau & Freier, 2007) or incorporate cases within other educational materials (see Albrecht et al., 2006 or Mintz & Morris, 2008). I provide an additional type of resource to accounting educators who wish to integrate ethics within their courses.

Given that accounting educators have more ethics-related resources available to them, it is not surprising that accounting chairs believe the amount of ethics covered in accounting courses has actually increased (Madison & Schmidt, 2006, p. 108). Accounting chairs do want more ethics coverage in courses, especially accounting courses. Furthermore, they believe accounting educators should integrate ethics throughout the curriculum for accounting majors.

Licata, Bremser, and Rollins (1997, p. 538) advocate the integration of SEC material in the accounting curriculum and specifically state that "Educators need access to information on actual incidences of fraudulent financial reporting to be able to help their students understand why and how this type of fraudulent financial reporting occurs." The SEC has made the AAERs available on its website (www.sec.gov/divisions/enforce/friactions.shtml). Licata et al. imply that accounting educators underutilize SEC enforcement releases as they contain a wealth of information based on actual scenarios which can be incorporated in the classroom. Furthermore, by requiring students to locate enforcement releases, accounting educators can help students develop research skills.

Stice and Stocks (2000, p. 184) support the use of real-world examples in class. Respondents to their survey identified the use of real-world examples as one of the most important factors affecting the perceived effectiveness of a teacher. Thibodeau and Freier (2007, p. xii) point out that the use of real-world examples may impart critical auditing skills, including technical skills, interpersonal relations, and ethical analysis. Earley and Kelly (2004, p. 61) also seem to support the use of real-world scenarios, as they indicate that students can relate better to context-specific ethics scenarios versus general issues. They believe that such context-specific scenarios have the potential to improve students' context-specific moral reasoning. Licata et al.'s (1997) materials, which cover the period from 1982 to 1995, are particularly useful since they provide the opportunity to use real-world scenarios in an auditing course.

Clikeman (2000, p. 114) integrates research studies, as opposed to real-world examples, into a first year auditing course. He explains that his goal is to "... describe the rich environment in which auditing is practiced." Furthermore, Clikeman indicates such benefits as making presentations more stimulating, updating course content, influencing accounting practice, and improving students' critical thinking skills. Although I have focused on SEC enforcement releases, as opposed to research studies, in my initial auditing course, I believe that the use of such enforcement releases share the same benefits stated by Clikeman.

I have organized the remaining parts of this chapter as follows. In the next section, I include a description of the AAERs, as well as the framework used to categorize the enforcement releases. Next, I discuss appropriate enforcement releases within each of the four major areas in an auditing course. I also provide specific guidance in incorporating enforcement releases in the classroom, including sample discussion questions. Finally, I discuss the overall value of the resources, as well as suggestions for other potential pedagogical issues.

COMPILATION OF AAERS

I compiled pertinent AAERs pursued by the SEC since July 31, 1997, from information publicly available on the SEC's website (www.sec.gov/divisions/enforce/friactions.shtml). This time frame coincides with an SEC (2003) review, as a result of section 704 of the Sarbanes–Oxley Act (2002), of all enforcement releases involving violations of reporting requirements imposed under the securities laws during the five years preceding the enactment of the Sarbanes–Oxley Act (July 31, 1997 through July 30, 2002). The SEC had identified the frequency of audit issues in enforcement matters against auditors to determine specific areas where auditors have been deficient. I extended the period of the SEC study by three years to reflect more current enforcement releases. Furthermore, I selected those enforcement releases that appeared to be most descriptive about the nature of audit deficiencies and relevant to the topics presented. Accordingly, I included approximately 50 percent of the total enforcement releases involving auditors during this period.

I used the four overall categories used by Licata et al. (1997, p. 539) to form a framework, as most traditional auditing texts cover these topics. The areas are (1) the auditing profession; (2) the auditing process; (3) applications of the auditing process; and (4) completing the audit. I developed the specific subcategories based on the nature of the specific AAERs. The chapter includes both tables for quick referencing, based on the four topical areas, as well as guidance in incorporating the enforcement releases in class.

THE AUDITING PROFESSION

Table 1 discloses the details of AAERs that are particularly suited for the overall discussion of the auditing profession which typically takes place during the first few weeks of class.

Independence and Professional Ethics

The AICPA Code of Professional Conduct provides a guide to professional accounting issues. In this section, I have included AAERs relating to bookkeeping, investments, non-audit fees, employment relationships, joint business relationships, threatened litigation, and contingent fees, among other areas. Some of the enforcement releases relate to releases preceding SOX. Accordingly, I use these in class to point out that some actions, while acceptable in the past, are no longer acceptable post SOX and I discuss the reason for the changes in the auditor/client relationship over time.

Prior to discussing the AICPA Code of Professional Conduct, I divide AAERs relating to a number of the above topics among my students and have them summarize the issues involved. I find that AAER Nos. 1363, 1491, 1584, and 1596 work well here since they cover a variety of topics, including bookkeeping, investments, jointly marketed services, and contingent fees, respectively. The latter three enforcement releases involve three of the Big 4 firms. Since many students already have accepted offers from each of these three firms, I try to assign the enforcement releases according to their future employment plans to stimulate their interest. These AAERs, as well as many of the AAERs in this section, are fairly brief and, therefore, easy to incorporate in one class discussion.

Table 1. AAERs Relating to the Auditing Profession.

AAER No.	Client	Date	Auditor	Description	Additional Topics
Independence and professional ethics					
Bookkeeping					
983	Members Service Corp.	11/7/97	O'Neal & White	The auditor maintained the client's books, was a principal of a company in which the client owned, and was a shareholder	Training and experience
1339	Monarch Investments (Iron Holdings)	10/31/00	Horton & Co.	A staff auditor served as a bookkeeper	
1363	Am-Pac International	1/25/01	Swart, Baumruk & Co	Numerous independence issues are discussed. The auditor maintained the client's general ledger on their own accounting software and prepared the financial statements, among a number of other accounting tasks, since the client had no accounting experience	
Investment relationships					
1073	Visual Cybernetics	9/9/98	Scarano & Lipton	The auditor offered and sold securities, as well as solicited other clients to purchase securities while serving as auditor	
1491	Aim Funds	1/14/02	KPMG	A Big 4 firm had an investment in the client via mutual funds. There were inadequate procedures to prevent or detect independence. This case can be especially helpful when discussing a firm's procedures to prevent and detect independence problems	

1556	Misc.	5/16/02	Moore Stephens, PC	The auditor was a trustee who owned securities in clients, made loans to clients, and had other investment relationships with clients	
Comprehensive					
1405	Waste Mgmt	6/19/01	Andersen	The auditor received significant non-audit fees. Finance employees had previously been employed by the auditors.	Red flags and risk assessment, completing the audit
2234	Xerox	4/19/05	KPMG	The auditor received significant non-audit fees. The auditors maintained offices at the client's location	Due professional care and skepticism
Other					
1241	Underwriters' Financial Group	3/29/00	Chadbourne & Miller	The auditor issued an unqualified opinion despite threatened litigation upon possible withdrawal due to suspicions of illegal conduct	
1584	Baen Company	6/27/02	Moret E&Y	The auditor had joint business relationships relating to software with the client and jointly marketed their services to potential customers. On numerous occasions, the auditors functioned in a capacity identical to that of the client's own employees. Furthermore, the auditors relied on internal audit work performed by an affiliated accounting firm	
1596b	Misc.	7/17/02	PWC	The auditor charged contingent fees to numerous clients for investment banking services. This case is particularly helpful when discussing Rule 302 of the AICPA Code of Professional Conduct	

Table 1. *(Continued)*

AAER No.	Client	Date	Auditor	Description	Additional Topics
Training and experience					
1643/1672	ACLN, Ltd	10/8/02	BDO Cyprus	An international company with a lack of training/experience in applying US GAAP or GAAS	
1846	Rockies	8/20/03	KPMG	A New Zealand audit manager was not experienced in applying US GAAP or GAAS. This case demonstrates the need for additional supervision given an audit team with virtually no prior experience with a client or its business	
983	Members	11/7/97	O'Neal & White	The concurring partner lacked training and proficiency. This case points out the importance of an adequately trained and proficient concurring partner in recognizing audit deficiencies	Independence
Due professional care and skepticism/illegal acts					
1823	California Micro Devices	7/29/03	Price WaterhouseCoopers	This case describes the auditor's duty to exercise professional skepticism for large and unusual transactions, particularly those occurring at year-end, as well as for management estimates. The client in this case was a high-tech company vulnerable to rapid changes in technology with difficulty maintaining revenue linearity and historically reported 70–90% of its sales in the third month of each quarter. The	Analytical review, red flags and risk assessment, confirmations

				auditors were aware of erroneous revenue recognition, as revenue was recorded when inventory was ready for shipping. There was a write-off of $12 million of accounts receivable at year-end. Information about the write-off in a press release conflicted with information given to the auditors. Furthermore, there was a shareholder lawsuit about such write-offs. Yet, when the client failed to submit detailed analysis setting forth reasons for the write-offs, the auditors did not perform any further investigation
1794	CUC International/ Cendant	6/4/03	Ernst & Young	The auditors failed to recognize evidence about reserves that were not in conformity with GAAP. For instance, when the auditors questioned a client schedule to support an assertion about the timing of $109 million of pre-tax income, the client revised the schedule and changed the nature and amounts of items included. However, the aggregate amount of scheduled items remained the same and the revisions were contradictory and inconsistent. The auditors relied on management's representations and accepted all but $23 million and posted this amount as an audit difference that was not deemed to be material

Table 1. *(Continued)*

AAER No.	Client	Date	Auditor	Description	Additional Topics
1762/2229	Chancellor	4/24/03 4/11/05	BKR Betcalf Davis	The auditors failed to design audit procedures to determine senior management fraud. The predecessor auditors had been fired after refusing to report the financial results. Although the auditors were suspicious of fabricated documents, they did not appropriately follow-up. Rather, the auditors relied on management's representations and failed to inform the audit committee of possible management fraud. There was no support for a fabricated consulting fee from a related party that had been reversed in the prior year since the fees were not supportable	Predecessor auditors
2234	Xerox	4/19/05	KPMG	This is a well known case involving a client who improperly accelerated the recognition of revenue by over $3 billion and increased earnings by approximately $1.5 billion. The auditors had performed the audit for approximately 40 years. Despite numerous warnings, the auditors did not sufficiently test these accounting actions, even when the client declined to test the appropriateness of such practices. When a partner questioned these actions, the partner was replaced on the audit. Although the auditors raised concerns about illegal acts with the client, they did not inform the	Independence

				client's board of directors or audit committee. This case is helpful when discussing extending audit procedures given the risk of material misstatement due to fraud, as well as "whistle-blow" channels of communication when issues are not appropriately addressed at the engagement team level	
Audit reports					
1037	Perry Drugstores	5/19/98	Andersen	This case provides a helpful discussion about the auditor's role in forming an opinion when there is substantial doubt. In this case, the auditors had issued an unqualified opinion, as opposed to a qualified opinion or disclaimer despite the lack of evidence to resolve a $20 million inventory discrepancy	Red flags and risk assessment, inventory
1452	EMB	9/19/01	Harlan & Boettger	This is a helpful case to use when discussing going concern issues. In this case, the client inappropriately recorded an asset from a joint venture investment that was not yet finalized and the auditors issued an unqualified opinion	Workpapers
955	Ponder Industries	9/10/97	Hairston, Kemp, Sanders & Stich	This case discusses the appropriateness of a qualified opinion with an emphasis paragraph. The client materially misstated net income. Although the audit report and the footnotes to the financial statements disclosed uncertainties, the actual financial statements did not properly reflect these uncertainties. The case emphasizes that supplemental disclosure in the audit report or in footnotes cannot justify the use of improper accounting	

Table 1. *(Continued)*

AAER No.	Client	Date	Auditor	Description	Additional Topics
1278	DCI Communications	6/23/00	Schnitzer & Kondub	The auditors inappropriately issued an unqualified opinion with emphasis when the client improperly recorded a $1.7 million intangible asset resulting from an incomplete acquisition	
Workpapers					
1377	Panworld	3/14/01	Orton & Co.	Audit work and planning was not sufficiently documented (e.g., the audit program was not signed or dated). Generic audit programs were used	Predecessor auditor, audit programs, internal control
1452	Madera Int'l	9/19/01	Harlan & Boettger	The audit program and overall planning were not sufficiently documented (e.g., workpapers were incomplete, undated, and unsigned)	Audit reports
1787	SmarTalk	5/22/03	Price Waterhouse Coopers	The auditors made undocumented changes to prior year workpapers and discarded documents during a post audit review when considering resigning given a class action shareholder lawsuit alleging accounting fraud. The post audit revisions were not dated to indicate that they had been made as part of a post audit review. The auditors had discarded most post audit reviewer notes, as well as numerous other documents	Red flags and risk assessment

1871	NextCard	9/25/03	Ernst & Young	The auditors went to great lengths to alter prior year workpapers upon concern about an examination by regulatory agencies. To ensure that revised documents appeared to have been created at the time of the audit, the auditors re-set the date on the computer when preparing revised workpapers and later deleted a number of documents and e-mails from the hard drive that were inconsistent with the altered versions
1884	North Face	10/1/03	Deloitte & Touche	The auditors replaced prior year workpapers with newly created workpapers disclosing a different conclusion when a client had refused to make an adjustment. This case points to AU Section 338 and a discussion of the role of workpapers, as well as modifications to working papers after they have been finalized
2053	Sport-Haley	7/9/04	Levine, Hughes, and Mitheun	The auditors revised workpapers and disposed of client documents at the same time as an SEC review

I have the students download the enforcement releases and prepare a brief (e.g., two-page) written assignment outside of class (see Appendix A). The students then collaborate in class for approximately 10 minutes with the other students assigned to the same enforcement action to discuss the issues. The groups take turns describing the enforcement action to the class. Students seem more willing to discuss the enforcement action after convening in small groups. In fact, I find that students reveal more information during the discussion than they reveal in their written assignments. I then use this discussion as a springboard for presenting the specific rules of the AICPA Code of Professional Conduct. Since the students are already familiar with the concepts after discussing the "stories" I am able to discuss the complete set of rules fairly quickly. The stories seem to elicit the students' interest in knowing more about the AICPA Code of Professional Conduct.

Training and Experience

Several enforcement releases point out the auditor's lack of training and experience. AAER Nos. 1643/1672 and 1846 are helpful when discussing international issues, as they involve auditors from overseas. AAER No. 983, on the other hand, is helpful when discussing the purpose of the concurring partner review.

Due Professional Care and Skepticism/Illegal Acts

Although lack of due professional care by auditors has caused practically all enforcement releases, I have found that a few enforcement releases are especially good examples for classroom discussion. AAER Nos. 1794, 1823, and 2234 are excellent comprehensive case studies. In addition, AAER Nos. 1762/2229 and 2234 discuss the auditors' responsibilities when they become aware of information regarding a possible illegal act. I have described several of these AAERs during class to explain more clearly what it means for auditors to "exercise due professional care." I believe the students more clearly understand the phrase when they have a frame of reference.

Audit Reports

Students should determine when conditions warrant an opinion other than unqualified. While enforcement releases typically arise as a result of an inappropriate opinion provided by the auditor, a few such releases specifically focus on the auditor's incorrect decision to issue an unqualified opinion. AAER No. 1037 discusses the appropriateness of qualified opinions and disclaimers, whereas AAER No. 1452 specifically focuses on going concern issues. In addition, AAER Nos. 955 and 1278 are both helpful when discussing the distinction between an unqualified opinion and a qualified opinion with an emphasis paragraph. I have found it interesting to describe a particular client situation to the students and then solicit their ideas about the appropriate type of opinion to issue. We then can discuss the inappropriateness of the auditors' actual opinion.

Workpapers

Workpaper deficiencies cited in enforcement releases relate primarily to either insufficient documentation or, more seriously, to altered workpapers. The topic of altered workpapers became a particularly newsworthy topic given the obstruction of justice charges imposed on Arthur Andersen when they altered workpapers in the case of Enron. Two enforcement releases (AAER Nos. 1377 and 1452) relate to insufficient documentation, whereas the other enforcement releases (AAER Nos. 1787, 1871, 1884, and 2053) relate to the more serious issue of altered workpapers. In class, I make reference to AAER Nos. 1787, 1871, and 1884, as they all occurred within the same period and they relate to three of the Big 4 firms. Students seem to be particularly interested in knowing that Andersen is joined by three of the other large firms in being sanctioned by the SEC for altering workpapers. I make reference to AAER No. 1871 to point out the measures auditors have taken in altering workpapers.

THE AUDITING PROCESS: PLANNING

This section incorporates such topics as communicating with the predecessor auditor, obtaining an understanding about the client's business, developing audit programs, considering the extent of reliance on internal controls versus substantive testing, and performing analytical review procedures. Prevalent throughout this process is the concept of risk assessment and identification of red flags. The AAERs that relate to these topics appear in Table 2.

Predecessor Auditors

AAER Nos. 1377, 1510, 1587, 1762 all deal with problems between the client and the predecessor auditors. In AAER No. 1510, the auditors failed to communicate with the predecessor auditors whereas, in the other AAERs, the auditors failed to consider the audit implications of the resignation of predecessor auditors.

Other Planning Issues: Knowledge of the Client's Business; Audit Programs; Control Testing versus Substantive Testing; and Analytical Review Procedures

In AAER Nos. 1261 and 1488, the auditors did not obtain an appropriate level of knowledge of the client's business. AAER Nos. 1261 and 1377 involve inappropriately developed audit programs. AAER No. 1676 would be an appropriate case to discuss the extent of reliance on internal controls versus substantive testing. Finally, AAER No. 1823 discusses the importance of analytical review procedures.

Although AAER No. 2234, which is described in other sections, does not make specific reference to analytical review, I use it in class to demonstrate the importance of examining financial statement relationships. Specifically, I distribute the financial statements for Xerox, the subject of AAER No. 2234, for the period 1996–1999.[1] I also distribute financial statements for a close competitor, Canon Corp., as well as published ratios for each of these companies for the same period. Without revealing the identity of either company, I ask the students to examine the data and try to determine which company experienced the fraud. Most students are able to correctly identify Xerox. In class, I have the students reveal the "clues" that lead them to their conclusion, most of which tend to relate to significant increases in profitability. It is important to point out that Xerox sold receivables to a third party in 1999 for $1,495 million. If students eliminate this amount from Operating Cash Flow, they will obtain a negative amount. Since students tend to ignore the Statement of Cash Flows, I point out

Table 2. AAERs Relating to the Audit Process – Planning.

AAER No.	Client	Date	Auditor	Description	Additional Topics
Predecessor auditors					
1377	Panworld	3/14/01	Orton & Co.	The auditors failed to consider the implications of the resignations of four predecessor auditors. In addition, the auditors had relied on a memo relating to an asset valuation that had been written five years prior to the audit by a predecessor auditor who had withdrawn the audit report	Workpapers, audit programs, internal control
1510	Itex Corp.	3/5/02	Kevin R. Andersen	Despite questions raised by the predecessor auditors concerning the valuation of certain transactions, the auditors did not communicate with the predecessor auditor. Rather, the auditor relied on management's explanation that the prior auditors had not finished as a result of a fee dispute	Red flags and risk assessment
1587	Cronos Group	7/2/02	Moore Stephens Chartered Acct	This case discusses the concept of a "clearance letter," or written confirmation by the predecessor audit that there are no concerns that require the successor auditor to not accept the engagement. The auditors accepted an audit engagement despite obtaining a qualified clearance letter, an explanation from the predecessor auditors about a possible management defalcation, a forged confirmation, and other evidence of false statements by management. In fact,	

Table 2. (*Continued*)

AAER No.	Client	Date	Auditor	Description	Additional Topics
				resignation of the predecessor auditor had been prompted by the refusal of the Board of Directors to investigate a possible management defalcation	
1762	Chancellor	4/24/03	BKR Betcalf Davis	Predecessor auditors were fired after refusing to report financial results	Due professional care
Understanding the business					
1261	Dynamic American Corp.	5/25/00	Jensen, Jones	The auditors had insufficient knowledge of the client's business	Audit programs
1488	California Software Corp./CSPI	1/7/02	James E. Slayton	The auditors failed to obtain an understanding of the revenue recognition method used by the client and, therefore, the overstatement of revenue and assets	
Audit programs					
1261	Dynamic American Corp.	5/25/00	Jensen, Jones	The auditors did not develop appropriate audit programs	Understanding the business
1377	Panworld	3/14/01	Orton & Co.	The auditors used generic audit programs and did not consider internal control weaknesses. As a result, the auditors did not address areas of greatest audit exposure	Workpapers, predecessor auditors, internal control
Internal control					
1377	Panworld	3/14/01	Orton & Co.	Auditors failed to consider internal control weaknesses	Workpapers, predecessor auditors, audit programs

1676	Golden Bear Golf (Paragon Construction)	11/26/02	Andersen	Auditors chose not to rely on internal control, but did not perform enough substantive testing to obtain sufficient evidence	Red flags and risk assessment
Analytical review					
1823	California Micro Devices	7/29/03	Price Waterhouse Coopers	The client had difficulty maintaining revenue linearity and historically reported 70–90% of its sales in the third month of each quarter. Although an analytical review of sales returns and allowances amounts pointed to questions and although the amounts conflicted with supporting details and with a press release, the auditors failed to investigate the discrepancies. This case examines the issue of recklessness	Due professional care, red flags and risk assessment, confirmations
Risk assessment/red flags					
1037	Perry Drugstores	5/19/98	Andersen	The auditors identified the client as a moderate risk despite $17 million in inventory discrepancies, the client's failure to explain or appropriately record such discrepancies, and the auditor's risk management group's conclusion that the inventory systems might not provide accurate values	Audit reports, inventory
1839	Tyco	8/13/03	Price Waterhouse Coopers	The auditors failed to continually re-assess audit risk throughout the audit given repeated and consistent acts about the lack of management integrity. Numerous red flags are described in detail	
2008	Warnaco Group, Inc.	5/11/04	Price Waterhouse Coopers	This is a comprehensive case about a high-risk client and aggressive accounting. The auditors had internally assessed the risk of fraudulent financial reporting as a five out of six and had identified significant risk factors. Such risks included aggressive/unrealistic forecasts, management	Inventory

Table 2. (*Continued*)

AAER No.	Client	Date	Auditor	Description	Additional Topics
				dominated by a single person without counterbalancing controls (e.g., effective board oversight); excessive interest in the stock price; and excessive interest in delaying losses	
2076	MCA Financial Corp.	8/5/04	Grant Thornton/ Doeren Myhew & Co.	This case involves a high-risk client in terms of operating characteristics and financial stability (e.g., accounts based on estimates; significant related party transactions; and unusual highly complex transactions close to year-end). Numerous red flags are described	
2237	Adelphia	4/26/05	Deloitte & Touche	This is an excellent case to use when discussing risk management programs employed by auditors, as well as categories of risk factors. This was a massive fraud involving senior management and the transfer of billions of dollars of liabilities to off balance sheet affiliates, among other fraudulent practices. A much greater than normal audit risk was identified and the auditors identified numerous pervasive risk factors posed by the audit as a whole (e.g., management dominated by one strong personality), as well as specific risks with particular accounts. The auditors did not appropriately tailor the audit approach and	

				did not implement follow-up procedures to make sure the audit tests mitigated audit risk. Numerous red flags are discussed	
1010	National Trade Trust	1/30/98	Bloomington	The client was dominated by one individual with an attitude toward financial reporting that was unduly aggressive. The predecessor auditor had identified related party issues and a going concern issue	
1271	Firstmark	6/8/00	Edwards, Faust & Smith	The auditors were aware of management's plan to apply for listing on the NASDAQ National Market or the American Stock Exchange, which required a minimum earnings threshold	
1220	CEC	2/7/00	Clancy & Co	This was a public company controlled by two individuals with no core business and no source of recurring revenue. The employees had no accounting experience and there were assets that were difficult to value. Yet, the audit program did not consider such risks	
1405	Waste Mgmt	6/19/01	Andersen	The client had been identified as a "high-risk client" that "actively managed reported results," had a "history of making significant fourth-quarter adjustments," and was in an industry that required "highly judgmental accounting estimates or measurements"	Independence, completing the audit
1510	Itex Corp.	3/5/02		The client had difficult to value assets and a material portion of the client's assets consisted of artwork with pieces appraised at identical values. There were significant and unusual transactions at year-end;	Predecessor auditor issues

Table 2. *(Continued)*

AAER No.	Client	Date	Auditor	Description	Additional Topics
				unusual purchases, sales, and repurchases of assets within a short period of time; and transactions with an offshore entity with a post office box	
1676	Golden Bear Golf (Paragon Construction)	11/26/02	Andersen	The client's revenue recognition was aggressive and subjective. There was a large unbilled revenue balance, lack of profitability, and an unreliable cost accounting system. The auditors were aware of red flags, but failed to follow up on significant year-end adjustments, a change in revenue recognition, related party issues, recording unbilled costs at year-end, among other issues	Internal control
1787	SmarTalk	5/22/03	Price Waterhouse Coopers	The client had an excessive interest in strong earnings and aggressive accounting and was unable to generate cash despite earnings growth. There were subjective estimates and an inexperienced staff	Altered workpapers
1823	California Micro Devices	7/29/03	Price Waterhouse Coopers	A comprehensive case that discusses numerous red flags, as more fully described under Due Professional Care and Skepticism	Due professional care, confirmations

the usefulness of comparing net income with cash flows from operating activities, which, in this case, is not consistent.

I use the discussion of these clues as a springboard to discuss horizontal, vertical, and cross-sectional analysis. Thus, the students actually use the techniques before I formally introduce these topics in class. I use the graphics in the actual enforcement action to show the students the extent of topside adjustments used by Xerox to meet Wall Street's expectations of earnings per share.

Risk Assessment/Red Flags

Accounting educators are likely to focus particularly on this section, especially given the recently adopted new standards (SAS Nos. 104–111) relating to assessing and responding to risks in a financial statement audit (American Institute of Certified Public Accountants, 2006a–h). Five cases that specifically discuss risk assessment are AAER No. 1037, 1839, 2008, 2076, and 2237. AAER Nos. 2008, 2076, and 2237 involve high-risk clients, whereas AAER No. 1037 describes an inappropriate risk assessment made by the auditors.

After introducing the concept of audit risk, I use AAER No. 1037 in class to have the students arrive at their own risk assessment based on the circumstances in this case. I also particularly like to discuss AAER No. 2237 since it points to the need to tailor audit procedures based on risk assessment. Given a high-risk client, I ask the students what they would change about the audit procedures for this client. I like to point out the risk management program described in this case since it offers specifics about how one firm handles high-risk clients. This case is helpful since it also discusses pervasive risk factors as well as risks specific to particular accounts. AAER No. 1839 is helpful in pointing out the need to continually re-assess audit risk throughout the audit. Educators could use any one of the remaining cases (i.e., AAER No. 1010, 1271, 1220, 1405, 1510, 1676, 1787, or 1823) for illustrative purposes when discussing specific red flags to look for in an audit.

APPLICATIONS OF THE AUDITING PROCESS

Once the student understands the overall nature of the accounting profession and the steps involved in planning the audit, the student is ready to learn the specific steps involved in testing the reliability of the financial statement amounts. Such steps involve numerous areas. I have identified several enforcement releases since they appear to be particularly appropriate for discussing two major areas of the auditing process – confirmations of accounts receivable and cash, as well as physical inventory observation and other tests of inventory. These AAERs appear in Table 3.

Confirmations

AAER No. 1823 is a comprehensive case fully discussed under due professional care and skepticism. I use this case (see Appendix B) in class to discuss issues the auditors should consider when testing accounts receivable and the need to follow up on discrepancies and non-confirming responses for positive confirmations. It provides a logical transition to the discussion of alternative procedures. AAER No. 10044 discusses the auditor's responsibility for confirming material year-end transactions. Several enforcement releases discuss confirmation of information other than accounts receivable balances. AAER Nos. 1389 and 1984 involve forged bank confirmations, whereas AAER No. 1835 involves significant contracts with customers.

Inventory

Two cases (AAER Nos. 1037 and 2008) are particularly helpful when discussing inventory. Since they both also address red flags and risk assessment, I suggest using either one to cover both of these topics.

COMPLETING THE AUDIT AND EVALUATING FINDINGS

The audit, as well as the course, typically culminates with the evaluation of audit findings. This step is, perhaps, the most important step in the audit since it provides the basis for determining the type of opinion on the fairness of the financial statements. Therefore, students need to realize the critical nature of the thought process in arriving at an audit conclusion. I have included the details of two AAERs that are particularly suited for this topic in Table 4.

Table 3. AAERs Relating to Applications of the Auditing Process.

AAER No.	Client	Date	Auditor	Description	Additional Topics
Confirmations					
1823	Calif. Micro Devices	7/29/03	Price Waterhouse Coopers	This is a comprehensive case involving the failure to follow up on discrepancies and a high rate of non-confirming responses. In fact, more than half of the customers did not reply to confirmation requests for account receivable balances. The case explains the auditor's responsibilities when evidence provided by confirmations alone is not sufficient to reduce audit risk to an acceptably low level. Examples of alternative procedures are explored	Due professional care, analytical Review, red flags and risk assessment
10044	Styles on Video	6/17/98	Kellogg & Andelson	The auditors confirmed accounts receivable balance, but failed to confirm details given two material year-end transactions with high risk	
1389b	Sky Scientific Inc.	5/4/01		The auditors accepted faxed confirmations	
1984	Powerball	4/1/04	Thomson	The auditors failed to confirm cash, which comprised of two-thirds of the total assets. A faxed bank statement had been altered by the president	
1835	Microstrategy	8/8/03	Coopers	The auditors failed to adequately confirm contracts, despite information from management that contradicted such contracts. Despite the auditor's belief that the contracts were "convoluted and self-contradictory," the auditor placed almost exclusive reliance on management's representations	

Table 3. *(Continued)*

AAER No.	Client	Date	Auditor	Description	Additional Topics
Inventory					
1037	Perry Drugstores	5/19/98	Andersen	The client disclosed $20 million in inventory shrinkage and recorded the shrinkage as an asset. The auditors accepted this practice and relied on the results of various analytical tests, as opposed to data revealed from the physical inventory and other testing. In fact, physical counts at five stores, as well as extensive month-long testing performed on one additional store disclosed large discrepancies consistent with physical counts at other stores. The case more fully describes the specific procedures performed. The auditors had identified a moderate risk in this area despite the significant discrepancies, the client's failure to explain or record these discrepancies, and a conclusion made by the auditor's computer risk management group that the systems might not provide accurate inventory values. In the subsequent year, the client disclosed a non-cash charge of $33.4 million relating to, among other things, an adjustment of store inventory. With the auditors' consent, the client inappropriately categorized the adjustment as a "change in estimate," and did not restate its financial statements until a later time	Audit reports, red flags and risk assessment
2008	Warnaco Group, Inc.	5/11/04	Price Waterhouse Coopers	The client filed an annual report that contained a $145 million restatement of the prior three years' financial results due to a material inventory	Red flags and risk assessment

overstatement caused by an antiquated and defective accounting system. The report, however, was misleading since it explained that the misstatement was a result of a write-off of previously deferred "start-up related" costs identified in connection with the company's adoption of a new accounting pronouncement. This misleading explanation was also included in a press release touting "record earnings." When the auditors recommended the reclassification of costs, the client became upset and, as a result, a new audit team and partner were assigned to the audit. The auditors not only failed to object to such a mischaracterization in the restated financial statements, but they also included this misleading explanation in their own audit report. They had concluded during their audit that the inventory overstatement most likely resulted from internal control deficiencies and accounting errors

Table 4. AAERs Relating to Completing the Audit and Evaluating Findings.

AAER No.	Client	Date	Auditor	Description	Additional Topics
1405	Waste Mgmt	6/19/01	Andersen	The auditors allowed the client to continue for numerous years, a series of improper accounting practices. For several years, the auditors had quantified significant (e.g., \$163 million) misstatements for which they prepared proposed adjusting journal entries. In one year, these adjustments represented 11.7% of pre-tax income. In another year, they represented 7.2% of pre-tax income, which was below the 8% materiality threshold. The client not only refused to book these entries, but also continued to engage in accounting practices that gave rise to the proposed entries. The auditors ultimately concluded that these proposed adjustments were not material. In addition, the auditors identified accounting practices that gave rise to known and likely misstatements for which the auditors did not prepare any adjusting journal entries and, therefore, did not quantify other known and likely	Independence, red flags and risk assessment

				misstatements. Although the auditors expressed their concerns to the audit committee, they continued to express unqualified audit reports. The SEC point out a number of critical issues with respect to materiality (e.g., as the aggregate misstatements increase, the risk of "further misstatement remaining undetected" also increases)
1706	Sunbeam	1/27/03	Andersen	When management refused to make adjusting journal entries for \$3 million in revenue and \$2.9 million for inventory, the auditors passed on the entries after quantitative materiality analysis
2125	Gemstar-TV Guide	10/20/04	KPMG	This case discusses issues relating to the withdrawal of a previously issued audit report. Although potential misstatements of financial statements involving senior management came to light after the audit report was issued when the audit committee commenced an investigation, the auditors did not perform adequate procedures or consider qualitative materiality issues.

AAER No. 1405 is a comprehensive case mentioned in other sections of this chapter. I use this case to discuss evaluating audit findings in terms of analyzing known and likely misstatements, as well as standing up to management. I particularly use it to point out the importance of judgment in evaluating materiality. Without revealing the identity of the company or the fact that the company was the subject of an SEC enforcement action, I present facts relating to the known and likely misstatements identified by the auditors, as well as materiality for the years involved. Interestingly, during one year (i.e., 1996), misstatements actually fell slightly below materiality. After the students make their own conclusions about the appropriate type of opinion, I reveal the identity of this company, as well as the circumstances of the case. I hand out to the students the "Legal Conclusions" section of this enforcement action since it provides a particularly helpful discussion about using judgment in evaluating materiality. A main benefit of this case is that it provides a good example of a concept (i.e., judgment) that is often difficult for students to truly grasp.

AAER No. 2125, as well as AAER No. 1405 discussed previously, emphasize the importance of making sure that assessments of materiality are not purely mechanical (e.g., quantifying the magnitude of a misstatement in percentage terms only), as well as considering qualitative issues. AAER No. 2125 is a good case for discussing subsequent events, among other issues.

INCORPORATING AAERS IN THE CLASSROOM

I have based my discussion of using AAERs in class on the present three-credit introductory auditing course I teach to undergraduate students. The accounting program presently requires students to take only one three-credit auditing course and, therefore, the content of this course is fairly extensive. Accordingly, instructors teaching advanced or graduate auditing courses most likely will have more flexibility in using AAERs in class. I try to be creative by integrating the cases throughout the semester via classroom discussion. In addition, I vary class assignments by including two or three written AAER assignments in addition to textbook exercises and an auditing simulation project. Depending on the extent and level (e.g., undergraduate or graduate) of auditing coverage in the accounting program, instructors can incorporate the materials in this chapter into the classroom in a number of ways. I have discussed pedagogical issues that I have come across when using enforcement releases in my class.

Vignettes or Written/Oral Assignments

I often make reference to the alleged audit failures when presenting audit topics. Thus, I use the enforcement releases as vignettes. When I use this approach, I do not require the students to read the enforcement action on their own. Accordingly, I am able to integrate numerous enforcement releases throughout the semester by using minimal class time. I also have students download specific enforcement releases and prepare a written assignment outside of class. Alternatively, instructors may wish to have students do classroom presentations in place of (or in addition to) written assignments.

When making reference to the enforcement releases in class, I focus particularly on the summary section and legal conclusion section of the AAER to highlight the main points. Similarly, most textbooks also make reference to actual scenarios at the start of a chapter or within a chapter via the margin or a textbox. By discussing enforcement releases prior to starting a topic, I seem to capture the students' attention more fully. Using a conversational approach, I am able to cover many of the textbook topics before making actual reference to the textbook or my teaching notes.

During the semester, I also typically assign enforcement releases for the students to complete outside of class. Many students in my class have reported a preference to the written assignments over class discussion alone since the written assignments encourage them to think on their own and grasp the concepts more fully. Students have said they found it helpful to look up concepts in the text or in their notes to compare to the case before coming to class.

I limit the written assignments to only two or three during the semester since it is an undergraduate auditing course and I use a variety of other types of assignments in class. Instructors teaching a graduate auditing course may wish to consider expanding the number or the comprehensiveness of written assignments, as I have discussed later. Licata et al. (1997, p. 555) points out that a benefit of written assignments is the exposure to enforcement releases without the use of in-class time.

Although the students prepare individual written assignments, I often discuss these assignments in class as well. Some students in my class have reported that the class discussion has helped them to interpret the cases more clearly. The classroom discussion tends to be more thorough than the individual written assignments. Given time constraints, however, instructors may choose to eliminate classroom discussion of the written assignments.

Specific or Comprehensive Assignments

Instructors also have the option of assigning fairly brief AAERs for a particular topic or assigning more comprehensive AAERs (e.g., AAER Nos. 1405 and 2234) that they can use throughout the semester for a variety of issues. Both of these approaches seem to work well. The latter approach would be particularly suited for a graduate level auditing course. When I have used a comprehensive case for my undergraduate course, I have assigned specific topics and questions within the case to highlight the key points for the students. Students believed they understood the key topics more clearly since they focused on certain portions of the enforcement release, as opposed to the entire case. Furthermore, instructors could assign the same enforcement release or could assign multiple enforcement releases among groups of students, as I have described in the "Independence and Professional Ethics" section of this chapter. Assigning multiple enforcement releases is effective if the instructor wishes to cover a variety of topics within one class session.

Licata et al. (1997, p. 554) offer numerous other helpful suggestions for student applications. For instance, students could select several enforcement releases relating to a particular topic and prepare a more comprehensive written analysis. The instructor also could expand these writing assignments to include library research on the accounting and auditing standards involved, as well as relevant articles. Licata et al. provide a more detailed discussion of each of these approaches, as well as guidance for grading such assignments.

Other Pedagogical Issues

Given the variety of assignments described above, the grading system will vary. Based on the brevity of the two or three written assignments in my class, I weigh the assignments approximately 10–15 percent of the students' course grade. When grading the individual assignments, I use a simple scale (e.g., check plus, check, or check minus) based on the students' ability to identify the key points and relate these points to relevant auditing concepts, as well as their overall written (and, if applicable, verbal) skills. I have found that, overall, the students seem to summarize most of the key points and that a simple grading scheme appears to sufficiently differentiate the quality of submissions. This scale would most likely not be appropriate for more comprehensive assignments, especially in a graduate course.

There are a number of sources available to help guide instructors in preparing appropriate discussion questions when assigning a comprehensive analysis of enforcement releases to students. In fact, there are several textbooks devoted entirely to such cases, as discussed earlier in this chapter. This chapter aims to provide resources to help the instructor tailor assignments for their specific instructional needs. I have included a number of discussion questions I have used in these cases that can be especially helpful for instructors who wish to assign any one of the enforcement releases in this chapter, as disclosed in Table 5. Some discussion questions are general and instructors can use them with almost any enforcement action. Other questions are more specific to certain auditing topics.

When assigning enforcement releases, I have used a number of general discussion questions along with a few questions that specifically relate to the enforcement action assigned. I often incorporate one or more of my own discussion questions (instructors can use the sample questions in this chapter as a guide). I have also had students develop some of their own questions. Previous experience indicates that students can be perceptive and creative in developing their own questions. Having the students develop their own questions also reveals the areas on which students are focusing. Of course, instructors may use a combination of these approaches.

The instructor also may wish to expand upon any one of the suggested discussion questions. For instance, one of the discussion questions requires the students to prepare common-sized financial statements for the financial statement period and compute applicable ratios to determine financial statement items that should have been of particular interest to the auditors during the audit. When covering the topic "analytical review," the instructor may wish to have the students obtain their own copy of the financial statements in question and prepare such analytical review. Alternatively, the instructor may try the exercise I have described in the "Other Planning Issues" section of this chapter. This "solve the puzzle" type approach tends to make it more interesting for the student and is, therefore, likely to facilitate learning.

Based on classroom observation and student feedback, my experience indicates that such "stories" do elicit student attention and illustrate realism. When asked, at the end of the semester, to describe the most important concept learned in the course, students often make reference to the ethics-related stories discussed during the semester.

Table 5. Suggested Discussion Questions.

General questions

1. What are the auditing deficiencies in this case? Discuss in detail the specific GAAS standards the auditors violated. (L, C)
2. What are the accounting standards for this area? (L)
3. Give a detailed explanation of the accounting problem. (C)
4. Identify the alternative courses of action available to the auditor when he/she became aware of the accounting fraud. Assume the role of the auditor. Which of these alternatives would you have chosen? Why? (K)
5. What should the auditor have done differently? (L)
6. If the auditor adequately examined this account, what important audit evidence should have been discovered? (L)
7. What factors about the audit engagement and the client may have affected the auditor's judgment? (L)
8. What special problems do fraud cases pose for the auditors? (L)
9. What responsibility does an auditor have to uncover fraud perpetrated by client management? Discuss factors that mitigate this responsibility and factors that compound it. Relate this discussion to this case. (K)
10. Define the terms ethics. Using a scale from highly unethical to highly ethical, evaluate the conduct of each individual involved in this case. (K)
11. Is it likely that the fraud could occur without involvement/knowledge of top management? (C)
12. People who study instances of financial reporting fraud often note that three conditions are generally present for fraud to occur: incentive, opportunity, and attitude. Describe examples of these three conditions that were present in this situation. (B) [Note: Students could be referred to SAS No. 99 (American Institute of Certified Public Accountants, 2003) to obtain a description of the fraud triangle components and how to apply these components to specific situations.]
13. Was the board of directors' response to problems timely and adequate? Why or why not? (C)
14. What are the responsibilities of a client's board of directors? Could the board of directors – especially the audit committee – have prevented the problems? Should they have known about the risks? What should they have done about them? (B)
15. Do you believe that the individuals who behaved unethically in this case were appropriately punished? Defend your answer. (K)
16. Identify the client's major business risks and describe how those risks may increase the likelihood of material misstatements. (B)
17. Assume that you were the manager on this audit engagement. Contrary to your advice, the engagement partner is inclined to allow the financial reporting practice in question. What are your options and what do you do? (C)
18. How should disagreements between members of an audit engagement team be resolved? What mistakes, if any, were made by the auditors in resolving the conflicts that arose during the audit? (K)

Specific topical questions

1. Audit/Client Relationships: Does this case illustrate the appropriate relationship between the auditor and management or the board of directors of a client? (C)
2. Audit/Client Relationships: What are the auditors' responsibilities for ensuring that they are independent? How did the auditor violate these requirements? (C)
3. Planning: Prepare common-sized financial statements for this client for the financial statement period. Compute applicable ratios. Given the data, which financial statement items do you believe should have been of particular interest to the auditors during the audit? (K)

Table 5. (*Continued*)

4. Planning: List non-financial variables that the auditors should consider when planning an audit. For each of these items, briefly describe their audit implications. (K)
5. Planning: Explain why industry knowledge is so important to an auditor. (K)
6. Internal Control: Present your assessment of the client's internal control and its contribution to opportunities for fraud. Be as specific as possible. (C, K)
7. Internal Control: Recommend internal control procedures to strengthen this area. (C, B)
8. Internal Control: What are the incentives for this client's management to commit fraud? (C)
9. Evidence: What type of evidence or what additional procedures should the auditor have considered with this client? (C) Explain the specific audit procedures that might have led to the detection of the accounting irregularities. (K)
10. Evidence: There are five management assertions that underlie a set of financial statements. Comment on the limitations of the evidence that these procedures provide with regard to any one of the management assertions. (K)
11. Evidence: What procedures should the auditors use as a follow-up to management's representations for this particular audit area? (C)
12. Evidence: How might analytical review have assisted the auditor in discovering the fraud? (C)
13. Red Flags/Audit Risk: What key red flags, or audit risk factors, were present during the audit? Did the auditors appropriately consider these factors in planning the audit? Why or why not? (K)
14. Red Flags/Audit Risk: List several factors at this client that would have contributed to a high inherent risk assessment. What conditions, attitudes, and motivations at the client created an environment conducive for fraud and could have been identified as red flags by the auditors? (K, B)
15. Audit Reports: Identify the misstatements and use them to explain the appropriateness of a qualified or adverse, rather than unqualified opinion. (C)

Sources: B, Beasley, Buckless, Glover, Prawitt; C, Cullinan and Wright; K, Knapp; L, Licata, Bremser, Rollins.

CONCLUSION

This chapter addresses the need for more ethics-related materials, as voiced by accounting educators in recent years and, more specifically, the importance of integrating actual incidences of fraudulent financial reporting in the accounting curriculum. Enforcement releases pursued by the SEC appear to be an underutilized resource for accounting educators, as these AAERs contain a wealth of information based on actual scenarios which can be incorporated in the classroom. Accordingly, I have organized alleged audit failures, as described in AAERs, in a manner consistent with the order of topics typically covered in an auditing class. Courses that are particularly suited for such scenarios are undergraduate or graduate auditing. Financial accounting, fraud, and business ethics courses also could benefit from the materials in this chapter.

FUTURE USES

This chapter opens the door to other areas that instructors may find useful. In this chapter, I have limited the enforcement releases to those situations involving auditors and those topics particularly suited for auditing students. These enforcement releases discuss a number of other interesting accounting issues. Also, there are other enforcement releases which do not involve auditors. These enforcement releases may be a valuable source of information. For instance, instructors could categorize these enforcement releases by type of misstatement (e.g., fictitious revenue) or by specific account involved (e.g., inventory). Accordingly, educators should consider these other areas to make the materials accessible for classroom use.

NOTE

1. I do not distribute information for 2000 since the students tend to focus on this particular year at the expense of the prior years, which is when much of the fraud occurred.

ACKNOWLEDGMENT

The author acknowledges gratefully the comments of Bill N. Schwartz and two anonymous reviewers.

REFERENCES

Albrecht, W. S., Albrecht, C. C., & Albrecht, C. O. (2006). *Fraud examination* (2nd ed.). Mason, OH: South-Western.

American Institute of Certified Public Accountants. (2003). Statement on Auditing Standards No. 99: Consideration of fraud in a financial statement audit. New York: AIPCA.

American Institute of Certified Public Accountants. (2006a). Statement on Auditing Standards No. 104: Amendment to Statement on Auditing Standard No. 1, Codification of auditing standards and procedures. New York: AIPCA.

American Institute of Certified Public Accountants. (2006b). Statement on Auditing Standards No. 105: Amendment to Statement on Auditing Standard No. 95, Generally Accepted Auditing Standards. New York: AIPCA.

American Institute of Certified Public Accountants. (2006c). Statement on Auditing Standards No. 106: Audit evidence. New York: AIPCA.

American Institute of Certified Public Accountants. (2006d). Statement on Auditing Standards No. 107: Audit risk and materiality in conducting an audit. New York: AIPCA.

American Institute of Certified Public Accountants. (2006e). Statement on Auditing Standards No. 108: Planning and supervision. New York: AIPCA.

American Institute of Certified Public Accountants. (2006f). Statement on Auditing Standards No. 109: Understanding the entity and its environment and assessing the risks of material misstatement. New York: AIPCA.

American Institute of Certified Public Accountants. (2006g). Statement on Auditing Standards No. 110: Performing audit procedures in response to assessed risks and evaluating the audit evidence obtained. New York: AIPCA.

American Institute of Certified Public Accountants. (2006h). Statement on Auditing Standards No. 111: Amendment to Statement on Auditing Standard No. 39, Audit sampling. New York: AIPCA.

Beasley, M. S., Buckless, F. A., Glover, S. M., & Prawitt, D. F. (2006). *Auditing cases* (3rd ed.). Saddle River, NJ: Pearson Education Inc.

Clikeman, P. M. (2000). Integrating research into the initial auditing course. *Advances in Accounting Education* (2), 113–130.

Cullinan, C. P., & Wright, G. B. (2003). *Cases from the SEC files: Topics in auditing*. Saddle River, NJ: Pearson Education Inc.

Earley, C. E., & Kelly, P. T. (2004). A note on ethics educational interventions in an undergraduate auditing course: Is there an "Enron effect"? *Issues in Accounting Education*, *19*(1), 53–71.

Gaa, J. C., & Thorne, L. (2004). An introduction to the special issue on professionalism and ethics in accounting education. *Issues in Accounting Education*, *19*(1), 1–6.

Haywood, M. E., McMullen, D. A., & Wygal, D. E. (2004). Using games to enhance student understanding of professional and ethical responsibilities. *Issues in Accounting Education*, *19*(1), 85–99.

Jennings, M. M. (2004). Incorporating ethics and professionalism into accounting education and research: A discussion of the voids and advocacy for training in seminal works in business ethics. *Issues in Accounting Education*, *19*(1), 7–26.

Knapp, M. C. (2007). *Contemporary auditing: Real issues and cases* (5th ed.). Mason, OH: South-Western.

Licata, M. P., Bremser, W. G., & Rollins, T. P. (1997). SEC enforcement actions against auditors: Auditing education linked to the pitfalls of audit practice. *Issues in Accounting Education*, *12*(2), 537–560.

Madison, R. L., & Schmidt, J. J. (2006). Survey of time devoted to ethics in accountancy programs in North American colleges and universities. *Issues in Accounting Education*, *21*(2), 99–109.

Mintz, S. M., & Morris, R. E. (2008). *Ethical obligations and decision making in accounting: Text and cases*. New York, NY: McGraw-Hill Irwin.

Peterson, B. K., & Buckhoff, T. A. (2004). Anti-fraud education in academia. *Advances in Accounting Education* (6), 45–67.

PricewaterhouseCoopers. (2003). *Educating for the public trust: The PricewaterhouseCoopers position on accounting education*. New York, NY: PricewaterhouseCoopers.

Sarbanes–Oxley Act (Public Law 107-204). 2002.

SEC. (2003). Report Pursuant to Section 704 of the Sarbanes–Oxley Act of 2002, January 24.

Stice, J. D., & Stocks, K. D. (2000). Effective teaching techniques: Perceptions of accounting faculty. *Advances in Accounting Education* (2), 179–191.

Thibodeau, J., & Freier, D. (2007). *Auditing after Sarbanes–Oxley: Illustrative cases*. New York, NY: McGraw-Hill.

Thomas, C. W. (2004). An inventory of support materials for teaching ethics in the post-Enron era. *Issues in Accounting Education*, *19*(1), 27–52.

APPENDIX A. SAMPLE ASSIGNMENT – SEC ACCOUNTING AND AUDITING ENFORCEMENT RELEASES (AAERS) RELATING TO INDEPENDENCE AND PROFESSIONAL ETHICS

AAERs to be assigned in class.

AAER 1363 Swart, Baumruk & Co/Am-Pac International (bookkeeping)
AAER 1491 KPMG/AIM Funds (investment in mutual fund)
AAER 1584 Moret E&Y/Baan Company (jointly marketed services)
AAER 1596 PWC/Various Clients (Part C-contingent fees)

Download the assigned AAER from the EDGAR website as follows:

- Go to www.sec.gov
- Select "SEC Divisions" – "Enforcement" on the right side of the screen
- Select "Selected Accounting and Auditing Enforcement Releases"
- Select the appropriate AAER.

Address the following questions. Your answer should be typed and should not exceed two pages.

1. Identify the specific rule of the AICPA Code of Conduct that was broken. Explain in detail the nature of the deficiency relating to independence. Your answer should include *your* opinion as to why the deficiency compromised the auditor's independence.
2. Summarize the "Legal Analysis/Standards" section relating to independence.
3. Describe the punishment to the CPAs. Do you believe the punishment was appropriate? Be sure to explain your reasoning.

APPENDIX B. SAMPLE ASSIGNMENT – SEC ACCOUNTING AND AUDITING ENFORCEMENT RELEASES (AAERS) RELATING TO CONFIRMATIONS

Download AAER No. 1823 (Marrie, CPA and Berry, CPA/California Micro Devices) from the EDGAR website as follows:

- Go to www.sec.gov
- Select "SEC Divisions" – "Enforcement" on the right side of the screen
- Select "Selected Accounting and Auditing Enforcement Releases"
- Select AAER No. 1823 (7/29/03)

Read Section II and identify the background issues that the auditors should consider when testing Accounts Receivable:

Read Section III B 2. "Marrie and Berry Recklessly Failed to Comply with Applicable Professional Standards in their Confirmation of CMD's Accounts Receivable." Identify the audit deficiencies. In your explanation, be sure to address the following questions: What specific procedures were performed? Why were these procedures inadequate? What procedures should have been performed? Use the reverse side of this page if necessary.

TAX SOFTWARE VERSUS PAPER RETURN: THE EFFECT OF A COMPUTERIZED DECISION AID ON COGNITIVE EFFORT AND STUDENT LEARNING

Rebekah Sheely Heath

ABSTRACT

This study examines the effect of using a computerized decision aid on student cognitive effort and learning in the first tax course. Students at a mid-western university in the United States prepared a 1040 tax return using either paper or tax software from a given set of taxpayer information. Students using paper forms reported higher levels of cognitive effort than did students using the tax software, however, no association between self-efficacy and cognitive effort was found. A test for association between decision aid type and inferential (higher-level) learning (the third level of Bloom's taxonomy) found cognitive effort to be statistically significant. The study also found a significant interaction between cognitive effort and experience. These results suggest that paper forms, which require students to work through task processes, may be better instructional tools for helping students acquire a deeper understanding of subject matter. Although tax software provides potential

Advances in Accounting Education: Teaching and Curriculum Innovations, Volume 9, 57–76

ISSN: 1085-4622/doi:10.1016/S1085-4622(08)09003-2

benefits of increased accuracy and speed, practitioners should be aware of its limitations as a learning tool.

A debate exists within the academic community as to the best way to help students learn tax accounting. One group of instructors does not require students to prepare tax returns during the educational process, preferring instead to focus on concepts. A second group requires students to use software in preparing tax returns to teach tax law and increase student exposure to current technology. A final group requires students to prepare paper tax returns believing that students acquire more knowledge in this manual process. Consequently, understanding learners' cognitive processes as they work through steps in completing a task successfully (e.g., tax return preparation) is important to educators. Since computerized decision aids are increasingly being used in public accounting, practitioners also will find this study useful for its insights regarding the potential limitations of these tools, particularly with inexperienced staff members who are still learning their jobs.

Prior research assumes that preparing paper returns requires more cognitive effort than using tax software. This study argues that students exert more cognitive effort when preparing paper tax returns than when using software, and that increased levels of cognitive effort are associated with higher levels of inferential learning. This study measures self-reported cognitive effort, and its results suggest that students exert more cognitive effort when they prepare tax returns without a computerized decision aid. Additionally, increased levels of cognitive effort are found to be associated with higher levels of inferential learning (e.g., the ability to apply technical principles, ideas, and theories in particular situations), after controlling for ability, experience, and efficacy with respect to tax return preparation. The study's results also confirm that inexperienced preparers put forth less cognitive effort than do experienced preparers when using a computerized decision aid. Finally, the study finds evidence of undue reliance on tax software (i.e., reduced levels of cognitive effort) by inexperienced users. This provides additional evidence of the potential behavioral problems associated with the use of computerized decision aids by inexperienced users.

The remainder of the chapter is organized as follows. First, a brief review of the relevant literature is provided, which is followed by the hypotheses development section. Next, the research methodology and results are discussed. The chapter concludes with a discussion of its implications and limitations.

LITERATURE REVIEW

Cognitive Effort as a Function of Perceptions Regarding the Decision Aid

Educational technology research suggests a link between cognitive effort and students' perceptions of technology (i.e., easy or difficult to use) (Bryant & Hunton, 2000, p. 140). Clark (1982, pp. 92–101) showed that high-ability students perceived well-structured instruction to be less demanding. Therefore, they invested less effort when instructed in a highly structured manner, and as a result, they learned less than the lower ability students.

Salomon (1984, pp. 647–658) explored how learners' a priori perceptions of message categories related to their perceived self-efficacy in handling them, and how these perceptions related to the amount of cognitive effort and learning. His findings showed that the amount of cognitive effort that an individual expends may depend on the way the stimulus, the task, or the context is perceived.

Self-efficacy is an individual's estimate of his or her ability to attain a certain level of performance in a specific task. Conceptions of ability affect how effectively people use the cognitive skills they possess (Bandura, 1990, p. 333). In a series of studies, Todd and Benbasat (1993, p. 82) found that when subjects were provided with a decision aid, they behaved as if effort minimization was an important consideration.

Learning as a Function of Cognitive Effort

Inferential learning is a higher order of learning, corresponding most closely to the third level of Bloom's taxonomy: *application.* Application refers to the use of technical principles, ideas, and theories in particular and concrete situations. Educational research indicates that students who perform hand calculations outperform computer decision aid users when they are given traditional text-based materials that facilitate a complete solution to experimental problems (Glover, Prawitt, & Spilker, 1997, p. 244). Rose and Wolfe (2000, p. 287) found that students who performed hand calculations with text-based instructions scored higher on a learning performance measure, than did subjects using a decision aid.

The Moderating Effect of Experience

Glover et al. (1997, p. 232) argue that the use of structured decision aids may influence relatively *inexperienced* decision-makers to approach computer aided tasks mechanistically (i.e., mindlessly), without becoming actively involved in the task or judgment. Other research also has found that the more expertise a decision-maker has in making a judgment, the less likely it is that the decision-maker will rely solely on a decision aid (Whitecotton, 1996, p. 111).

HYPOTHESES DEVELOPMENT

This section develops the research hypotheses to be tested in this study. Perceptions regarding the ease of software use may hinge on a learner's attitude toward computers. Jennings and Onwuegbuzie (2001, pp. 367–384) examined whether age and various other individual-specific variables were significantly related to four dimensions of computer attitude: anxiety, confidence, liking, and usefulness. They found that the youngest group of undergraduate subjects (22 years or less) reported less computer anxiety and higher levels of confidence, than did the other older age groups. Therefore, students might be expected to be more confident (i.e., self-efficacy) that they can prepare accurate returns using tax software. Consequently, this study tests the following hypothesis:

H1. On average, students will possess higher levels of self-efficacy with respect to preparing accurate returns using tax software, as compared to self-efficacy with respect to preparing accurate returns using paper forms.

Learners are likely to possess preconceived ideas regarding the tax return preparation process. If learners believe that tax software is easy to use and that it does not make mistakes, they are more likely to process a tax return mindlessly, and less likely to invest a large amount of cognitive effort in the return preparation process. This leads to the following hypothesis:

H2. Students will exert more cognitive effort when preparing paper returns than when using tax software to prepare tax returns.

Previous research suggests that larger amounts of cognitive effort (i.e., more time and/or increased intensity) should be associated with higher measures of task performance. In fact, Cloyd (1997, pp. 232–255) found that increases in effort duration improved search effectiveness regardless of the level of prior knowledge. Thus, I test the following hypothesis:

H3a. There is a positive association between cognitive effort and higher-level (inferential) learning.

This study exposes students to factual knowledge (e.g., exemptions, standard versus itemized deductions, filing status) during two weeks of tax return preparation training using materials provided by the Internal Revenue Service (IRS). Since I cannot predict whether the process of preparing an actual tax return will add to students' knowledge of basic tax facts, the following null hypothesis is tested:

H3b. There is no association between cognitive effort and lower-level (factual) learning.

Cognitive theory suggests that cognitive effort will vary between experienced and inexperienced decision-makers because of differences in their general knowledge structures. Prior studies indicate that inexperienced decision-makers put in less effort when using a computerized decision aid (Glover et al., 1997, p. 232). This may cause them to rely more heavily on a computerized decision aid than would experienced decision-makers (Whitecotton, 1996, p. 111). Therefore, I test the following hypothesis:

H3c. The less experience possessed, the less effort employed when software is utilized.

Finally, I examine the accuracy of the tax returns prepared. The IRS encourages taxpayers to e-file their tax returns. One reason is the increased accuracy associated with software-generated tax returns compared to manually prepared paper returns (Internal Revenue Service, 2005). Prior research also has found increased accuracy when computerized decision aids are utilized (Glover et al., 1997, p. 249). As such, the following hypothesis is tested:

H4. Software-generated returns will be more accurate than paper returns.

In summary, it is expected that the use of paper forms in preparing tax returns will require more cognitive effort, which in turn, will be associated with increased learning. However, tax software is expected to produce more accurate returns.

RESEARCH METHODOLOGY

This study uses a quasi-experimental design and survey methodology to test its research hypotheses. Specifically, it relies on two surveys to collect student perception data on computers and self-efficacy, as well as measures of cognitive effort. Two problems and an exam also were used to evaluate student learning. All of these instruments are available from the author upon request. A description of the experiment follows.

Survey Administration

The sample consisted of 140 students taking the first course in federal income tax offered at a mid-western university in the United States. Student subjects were enrolled in three different Spring semesters between 2003 and 2005, and all were taught by the same instructor.

Prior to delivery of the first survey instrument, students were exposed to the Volunteer Income Tax Assistance (VITA) materials provided by the IRS. During the first two weeks of the semester (i.e., six 50-min class periods), they received a quick overview of the tax return process for individuals as outlined in the VITA training materials, including a 30-min introduction to TaxWise return preparation software. After completing VITA training, student subjects completed a written questionnaire that surveyed their attitudes toward computer usage, as well as their self-confidence with respect to preparing accurate tax returns both manually and with software. Surveys were administered during a regular classroom period.

After completion and collection of the survey, students from the 2003 and 2004 semesters were randomly assigned to either a paper tax return group or a software tax return group. In addition to the paper and software groups, the 2005 semester students also were randomly assigned to a control group that did not prepare a tax return. After receiving their group assignments, students in the paper and software groups then were required to prepare an individual tax return for a married couple with dependents, wage and investment income, capital gains, and itemized deductions. Students assigned to software groups prepared the return using TaxWise software as a decision aid. Students were told that the purpose of the tax return assignment was to both familiarize them with current tax forms and help them learn the tax law, since problem solvers need to know that learning is a task goal for knowledge acquisition to occur (Bernardo, 1994, pp. 379–395).

No major changes in the individual income tax law occurred during this time period which might affect the problem solution.

Students had 1 week to complete the assignment. To encourage students to take the task seriously, I weighted the assignment equal to one of three exams administered during the course. Students also were instructed to complete the assignment individually, without collaboration with others. To reduce incentives to collaborate, I told the students that I would provide feedback on their returns and give them an opportunity to make corrections before a final grade would be assigned. After final grading, all tax returns were collected and retained by the instructor to reduce the likelihood that the solution could be passed from one class to another.

After collecting the tax return assignment, I distributed a second survey instrument to collect measures of cognitive effort in preparing the return. Two days later, I distributed a third instrument which asked students to identify relevant tax issues posed by two specific fact patterns and to suggest appropriate tax treatments. I evaluated student responses to develop a measure of their ability to apply technical principles in particular situations. A graduate student also evaluated the same student responses and an inter-rater reliability of 91 percent was achieved.

The following week students received their first exam which tested basic tax facts that were presented in their VITA training. Since the tax issue identification problems were administered only several class periods before the first exam, any learning that was captured by the tax issue identification instrument was most likely gained as a result of class lectures and the tax return preparation process, and not as a result of studying for the exam. This increases the internal validity of the study.

Model Specification

The following set of functional relations defines the research design used to examine each hypothesis:

H1. Mean of Efficacy with Software > Mean of Efficacy with Paper (assuming students possess favorable Computer Attitudes)

H2. Cognitive Effort $= f$ (Decision Aid Efficacy, Type of Decision Aid)

H3a. Higher-Level Learning $= f$ (Decision Aid Efficacy, Type of Decision Aid, Experience, Ability, Cognitive Effort, Effort $\times$ Experience)

H3b. Lower-Level Learning = f (Decision Aid Efficacy, Type of Decision Aid, Experience, Ability, Cognitive Effort)

H3c. Mean of Cognitive Effort (Experienced Subjects utilizing Software) > Mean of Cognitive Effort (Inexperienced Subjects utilizing Software)

H4. Accuracy = f (Cognitive Effort, Efficacy with Decision Aid, Ability, Experience, Type of Decision Aid)

Measures

Computer Attitude

This study measures subjects' attitudes toward computers by using the Nickell and Pinto (1986, pp. 301–306) Computer Attitude Scale (short form). This 10-question survey assesses a very broad concept of computer attitude that includes the following four factors: anxiety, confidence, liking, and usefulness. To determine a score for the respondent's attitude toward computers, answers for negative questions are first reversed, and then the scores for the 10 questions are averaged. A score of one indicates an extremely negative attitude toward computers, a score of five an extremely positive attitude, and a score of three is neutral. A principal components factor analysis yielded four components corresponding to anxiety, confidence, liking and usefulness, and the alpha coefficient for the scale was 0.6552.

Efficacy with Paper Return

Paper return self-efficacy was measured using a Likert-scale version of Bandura's (1990) scale. The survey required student responses (one for strongly agrees and five for strongly disagrees) to five questions to determine their perceived confidence in preparing a paper return accurately (100 percent, 80 percent, 60 percent, 40 percent, and 20 percent). After summing the question responses, low totals indicated a high level of confidence in preparing accurate paper returns. A principal component factor analysis suggested the existence of a second possible construct related only to the fifth question of the survey. Nevertheless, the alpha coefficient for this scale was 0.7606.

Efficacy with Software

Students also were surveyed to determine their perceived confidence in preparing a tax return accurately using software. These questions were similar to those used to measure efficacy with paper returns. As before, low-response totals indicated a high level of confidence in preparing accurate tax returns using software. A principal factor analysis once again extracted two components, however, in this case it was only the first question that measured a second possible construct. The alpha coefficient for this scale was 0.8805.

Cognitive Effort

The amount of cognitive effort invested by a student when preparing the tax return was measured using a two-question version of Salomon's (1984, pp. 647–658) Amount of Invested Mental Effort (AIME) scale. The first question asked "How hard did you try when preparing this tax return?" and was answered using a 4-point Likert scale (one being "Not at all," two being "Hardly at all," three being "Somewhat," and four being "Very Hard"). The second question asked was "How much did you concentrate when preparing the tax return?" and was answered using the same 4-point scale. After responses to both questions were averaged, low (high) scores indicated low (high) levels of cognitive effort. A principal components factor analysis extracted one component, and the alpha coefficient of the scale was 0.6912.

Experience

Students who had never previously prepared a tax return were assigned a value of zero. Students with prior tax return preparation experience were assigned a value equal to their self-reported years of experience in preparing tax returns.

Factual Learning

The percentage score on the subject student's first exam (a test of the basic tax return preparation process as presented in the VITA training materials) was included as a measure of factual knowledge.

Inferential Learning

To assess inferential learning, this study adopted an approach consistent with the measure of schema acquisition which was used by Low and Over (1992, pp. 62–69). Keywords were identified in the solutions to the two tax issue identification problems previously assigned to the subjects. A student answer that included all of the keywords received a score of five for each question. An answer that failed to include one keyword received a score of four, missing two keywords a score of three, etc. If the student response did not identify any relevant tax issues, then the answer was scored zero. If a student answer included all of the keywords from the solution as well as other relevant tax issues, additional points were awarded. Thus, a perfect score per the solution manual would equal five points, while a score of seven was possible for exceptional answers. The scores for both problems were added together to obtain a measure of inferential learning.

Ability

A control variable for student ability was included in the model specifications for H3 and H4. Ability was measured using the student's grade point average (GPA).

RESULTS

Descriptive Statistics

The final sample yielded 140 students from the three semesters tested: 42 from Spring 2003, 45 from Spring 2004, and 53 from Spring 2005. Fifty-six percent of the sample was female and 47 percent indicated some prior experience with taxes (i.e., prepared their own return or someone else's in the past). Average subject age was 23.82 years, with 33 percent of the sample being 23 or older. Seventy-four percent of the subjects were accounting majors and another eight percent were accounting minors.

An analysis of the means of the pre-treatment measures of efficacy for both paper return and software groups yielded no significant overall differences between the two groups ($t = 0.614$ and 0.094, respectively), nor between the paper return and control groups ($t = 1.594$ and 1.611, respectively), nor between the software and control groups ($t = 1.131$ and 1.474, respectively). There also were no differences between the paper return and software groups with respect to the means for GPA and experience in preparing tax returns ($t = 0.048$ and -0.212, respectively), nor between the paper return and control groups ($t = -0.984$ and -0.792, respectively), nor between the software and control groups ($t = -0.769$ and -0.715, respectively). These results suggest that the two treatment groups and control group were randomly assigned.

Before beginning a statistical analysis of the data, I tested for potential outliers among the independent variables using Mahalanobis distance.

Two outliers were identified and removed from the sample leaving a sample of 138 students for the remaining statistical tests. Additionally, to verify that cognitive effort is not a measure of general ability, or highly correlated with other independent or control variables, correlation analyses were performed. Matrices of the independent, control, and dependent variables for the paper return and software groups are presented in Table 1.

Hypothesis Testing Results

H1 assumes that student subjects possess favorable computer attitudes. Table 2 reveals a mean measure of computer attitude for the sample of 3.73 which suggests that this assumption was valid.

H1 predicted that students would express more confidence in their ability to prepare accurate tax returns using software rather than paper forms. Again, Table 2 appears to support this prediction. Students expressed a mean level of efficacy of 8.30 when using software, but only 10.91 when preparing paper returns. A paired samples t-test of the means finds this difference to be statistically significant ($t = 9.96$).

Since 33 percent of the sample was 23 or older, I conducted further testing to determine if my measure of self-efficacy with respect to software was being driven by the age of the sample. Students 22 years or younger reported a mean level of efficacy of 8.31 in using software and a mean level of efficacy with paper forms of 11.30. A t-test of these means also finds statistically significant differences ($t = 10.19$). Students 23 years or older reported a mean level of efficacy of 8.33 with respect to software and a mean level of efficacy with paper forms of 10.17. Again, the difference is statistically significant ($t = 3.41$). Therefore, age does not appear to affect results as they relate to H1.

Before testing H2–H4 with multiple regressions, I compared the means of the variable measuring inferential learning for the paper return, software, and control groups to ascertain the effectiveness of the study's manipulation. I expected that the control group would possess a lower measure of inferential learning than the paper return and software groups, since it had less required exposure to the tax material. According to Table 2, the inferential learning of the paper group (mean of 6.81) was marginally higher ($t = 1.46$) than that of the control group (mean of 5.88). The mean measure of inferential learning for the software group (mean of 7.12) also was significantly higher ($t = 1.98$) than that of the control group (mean of 5.88). These results suggest that treatment was effective.

Table 1. Correlation Matrices.

	1	2	3	4	5	6	7	8
Panel A: Paper return group								
1. Computer attitude	1.000	0.162	0.018	−0.263	0.249	−0.132	−0.186	0.137
2. Efficacy with paper		1.000	0.653**	−0.232	−0.099	−0.099	−0.370**	0.021
3. Efficacy with software			1.000	−0.349*	−0.270*	−0.005	−0.321*	−0.074
4. Cognitive effort				1.000	0.340*	0.015	0.159	0.071
5. Factual learning					1.000	0.128	0.063	0.531**
6. Inferential learning						1.000	−0.003	0.273*
7. Experience (years)							1.000	−0.067
8. GPA								1.000
Panel B: Software group								
1. Computer attitude	1.000	−0.308*	−0.273*	−0.015	−0.044	0.091	0.254	−0.097
2. Efficacy with paper		1.000	0.497**	0.169	−0.115	−0.141	−0.123	−0.158
3. Efficacy with software			1.000	−0.056*	−0.211	−0.090	−0.233	0.178
4. Cognitive effort				1.000	0.433**	0.328*	0.157	0.167
5. Factual learning					1.000	0.398**	0.050	0.454**
6. Inferential learning						1.000	0.331*	0.567**
7. Experience (years)							1.000	0.119
8. GPA								1.000

*Correlation is significant at the 0.05 level (two-tailed).
**Correlation is significant at the 0.01 level (two-tailed).

Table 2. Descriptive Statistics.

Variable	Range	Minimum	Maximum	Total Sample		Paper Return Group		Software Return Group		Control Group	
				Mean	Standard deviation	Mean	Standard deviation	Mean	Standard deviation	Mean	Standard deviation
Computer attitude	1–5	2.6	4.5	3.73	0.43	3.63	0.41	3.80	0.43	3.80	0.44
Efficacy with paper	5–25	5.0	20.0	10.91	3.19	11.27	3.01	10.89	3.26	9.99	3.38
Efficacy with software	5–25	1.0	25.0	8.30	3.35	8.47	3.22	8.54	3.83	7.20	2.15
Experience	0–5	0.0	5.0	1.41	1.78	1.34	1.78	1.38	1.73	1.68	2.01
Cognitive effort	1–4	2.0	4.0	3.55	0.47	3.61	0.41	3.46	0.43	NA	NA
Factual learning	0–100	50.0	100.0	83.22	11.05	80.01	11.08	83.3	10.58	92.23	7.05
Inferential learning	0–13	2.0	13.0	6.86	2.56	6.81	2.86	7.12	2.26	5.88	3.31
GPA	0–4	1.0	4.0	3.17	0.54	3.16	0.55	3.16	0.54	3.28	0.50

Notes: Computer attitude: 1 = extremely negative attitude toward computers, 5 = extremely positive attitude, and 3 = neutral; efficacy with paper return: a low score indicates a high level of confidence, while a high score indicates low confidence; efficacy with software: a low score indicates a high level of confidence in preparing accurate returns using tax software, while a high score indicates a low confidence; experience: experience in preparing tax returns measured in years; cognitive effort: a low (high) score indicates a low (high) level of cognitive effort while preparing the return; factual learning: the percent correct from the first exam on those portions of the exam testing basis tax law facts; inferential learning: the number of tax issues that a student was able to identify and solve within a set of problems; and GPA: grade point average measured on a 4-point scale.

H2 predicted that paper return group subjects would report using more cognitive effort than the software group. Table 3 appears to support this hypothesis as the Type of Return variable was statistically significant ($t = -3.54$).

H3a predicted a positive association between cognitive effort and inferential learning. Table 4 provides some support for this prediction as Cognitive Effort was positive and marginally significant at the 0.09 level.

Table 3. Results for Test of Hypothesis 2.

$N = 101$ $R^2 = 0.113$ $F = 6.316$	Unstandardized Coefficients			Standardized Coefficients		
	Expected sign	*b*	Standard error	*B*	*t*	Significant value
Constant		3.879	0.163		23.756	0.000
Efficacy	+	−0.020	0.013	−0.152	−1.503	0.136
Type of return	−	−0.352	0.099	−0.358	−3.544	0.001

Notes: Dependent variable = self-reported cognitive effort on a 1–4 scale; efficacy = for software group, efficacy is measured as the student's self-efficacy with respect to preparing accurate tax returns using software. For the paper form group, efficacy is measured as the student's self-efficacy with respect to preparing accurate tax returns manually; and type of return = a dichotomous variable: 0 for a paper return and 1 for software.

Table 4. Results for Test of Hypothesis 3a.

$N = 87$ $R^2 = 0.177$ $F = 2.908$	Unstandardized Coefficients			Standardized Coefficients		
	Expected sign	*b*	Standard error	*B*	*t*	Significant value
Constant		−3.572	3.435		−1.040	0.302
Efficacy	+	−0.025	0.077	−10.036	−0.318	0.715
Type of return	−	0.172	0.578	0.033	0.297	0.767
Experience	+	2.263	1.102	1.548	2.053	0.043
GPA	+	1.719	0.561	0.317	3.063	0.003
Cognitive effort	+	1.393	0.799	0.233	1.743	0.085
Effort × experience	+	−0.587	0.301	−1.491	−1.950	0.055

Notes: Dependent variable = score earned (0–13) on two tax issue identification problems; efficacy = for software group, efficacy is measured as the student's self-efficacy with respect to preparing accurate tax returns using software. For the paper form group, efficacy is measured as the student's self-efficacy with respect to preparing accurate tax returns manually; type of return = a dichotomous variable: 0 for a paper return and 1 for software; experience = subject years of experience in preparing tax returns; GPA = measure of student ability; and cognitive effort = measured using two question version of AIME scale.

The results also indicate that Ability and Experience influence inferential learning, as the two control variables for these factors also were positive and statistically significant. Additionally, the interaction between Experience and Cognitive Effort was negative and statistically significant, thus providing some initial support for the moderating effect of experience, which is further tested in H3c.

H3b predicted no significant difference in the amount of *lower level* (factual) knowledge acquired by the two experimental groups. Since the exams used to test Factual Learning were not identical each year, *z* scores of the test results were calculated and used in the statistical models. Table 5 finds both Ability (GPA) and Cognitive Effort to be significantly and positively associated with Factual Learning. However, since Type of Return is marginally significant at the 0.104 level, it would be overstating the results to suggest that H3b is supported.

H3c predicted that experienced and inexperienced student subjects would behave differently when using a computerized decision aid. Specifically, inexperienced subjects using tax software were expected to act in a mindless or passive manner (i.e., the less experience, the less cognitive effort). Since only 44 students used tax software and provided data for all model variables, a multiple regression was not considered feasible. Instead, I conducted an independent samples comparison of the means of Cognitive Effort based on experience (0 years and greater than 0 years). The results in

Table 5. Results for Test of Hypothesis 3b.

$N = 96$	Unstandardized Coefficients			Standardized Coefficients		
$R^2 = 0.296$ $F = 7.648$	Expected sign	*b*	Standard error	*B*	*t*	Significant value
Constant		−3.859	0.843		−4.576	0.000
Efficacy	+	−0.038	0.025	−0.153	−1.557	0.123
Type of return		0.294	0.179	0.158	1.643	0.104
Experience	+	−0.011	0.049	−0.021	−0.226	0.822
GPA	+	0.786	0.169	0.418	4.657	0.000
Cognitive effort	+	.427	0.182	0.215	2.340	0.021

Notes: Dependent variable = *z* score of number correct out of 100 on first tax exam; efficacy = for software group, efficacy is measured as the student's self-efficacy with respect to preparing accurate tax returns using software. For the paper form group, efficacy is measured as the student's self-efficacy with respect to preparing accurate tax returns manually; type of return = a dichotomous variable: 0 for a paper return and 1 for software; experience = subject years of experience in preparing tax returns; GPA = measure of student ability; and cognitive effort = measured using two-question version of AIME scale.

Table 6. Results for Test of Hypothesis 3c.

	N	Mean	Standard Deviation	Mean Standard Error
Panel A: Cognitive effort for software subject group				
Software				
Experienced users	25	3.630	0.376	0.075
Inexperienced users	25	3.450	0.375	0.075
$t = 1.695$; df = 48; significant value = 0.097 (two-tailed test)				
Panel B: Cognitive effort for paper return group				
Paper				
Experienced users	27	3.694	0.451	0.087
Inexperienced users	23	3.550	0.557	0.116
$t = 0.995$; df = 48; significant value = 0.325 (two-tailed test)				

Table 6 (Panel A) reveal a marginally significant difference between means for inexperienced students using software (3.450) and experienced students using software (3.630). However, no statistically significant differences in the means for cognitive effort were found for the paper return group (Table 6, Panel B). Therefore, these findings provide only modest support for previous research that suggests that inexperienced students rely too much on computerized decision aids by exerting a reduced level of cognitive effort (Glover et al., 1997, p. 245).

H4 addressed the effect of tax return preparation mode on return accuracy. Students preparing paper returns averaged 3.55 mistakes on the tax return problem, while tax software subjects averaged only 2.22 mistakes. The errors resulted primarily from incorrectly transferring amounts between forms or using an incorrect amount in the tax calculation. Multiple regression results reported in Table 7 indicate that both Type of Return and Ability (GPA) are positively associated with tax return accuracy. It is interesting to note that before this study's experiment, students were more confident in their ability to prepare accurate software-generated returns compared to paper returns (Table 2). These findings suggest that they were correct in those beliefs.

RESULTS AND IMPLICATIONS

On average, students possessed favorable attitudes toward computers and were more confident that they could accurately prepare a tax return when

Table 7. Results of the Test of Hypothesis 4.

$N = 35$ $R^2 = 0.325$ $F = 2.890$	Unstandardized Coefficients			Standardized Coefficients		
	Expected sign	*B*	Standard error	*B*	*t*	Significant value
Constant		2.397	7.177		0.334	0.741
Type of return	+	2.970	1.320	0.383	2.250	0.034
Experience	+	0.206	0.382	0.101	0.539	0.595
GPA	+	2.697	1.320	0.362	2.044	0.052
Cognitive effort	+	0.204	1.681	0.022	0.121	0.904

Notes: Dependent variable = number of mistakes (reverse coded); type of return = a dichotomous variable: 0 for a paper return and 1 for software; experience = subject years of experience in preparing tax returns; GPA = measure of student ability; and cognitive effort = measured using two-question version of AIME scale.

using software. Students did indeed prepare more accurate tax returns when using tax software. However, student confidence was not associated with either a higher- or lower-level learning. Practitioners who use tax software will find these findings interesting as they support the widely held belief that tax software improves accuracy in the tax return preparation process.

Additionally, I find that students who prepare tax returns using paper forms reported higher levels of cognitive effort. However, their efficacy with a particular type of decision aid did not appear to impact their cognitive effort. While self-efficacy has been shown to be an important variable in explaining many types of workplace attitudes and job performance, this study's findings suggest that its importance in explaining the effect of decision aids on cognitive effort may be limited.

With respect to lower-level (factual) learning, only ability (GPA) and cognitive effort showed strong statistical significance. With respect to higher-level (inferential) learning, experience also was statistically significant. In neither case did Type of Return appear to matter much. This finding has implications for tax practitioners who want their staff to not only prepare accurate tax returns, but also gain an understanding of tax law by using computerized decision aids. My results suggest that software use may actually be a hindrance if the facilitation of knowledge transfer is a desired outcome. These implications also may be valid for accounting educators who use software in the classroom. For example, students may exert more cognitive effort when manually recording journal entries and preparing financial statements, than when entering those same journal entries into a computerized accounting system. By working through the accounting cycle on paper, students may gain a better understanding of financial statements.

In addition to the impact of cognitive effort on higher-level learning, an interaction term (Effort × Experience) was found to be significant. This interaction suggests that the more experience a student has in preparing tax returns, the less is the effect of cognitive effort on inferential learning regardless of the type of decision aid utilized.

In previous studies, inexperienced students using a computerized decision aid placed too much reliance on the decision aid, even when informed of the decision aid's inadequacies. This study provides support for this behavior as well. Inexperienced students using tax software exerted a statistically lower mean level of effort than did experienced students that used software. Thus, this study provides additional evidence of the potential behavioral problems associated with the use of computerized decision aids by inexperienced users, a finding which should be of interest to tax practitioners as well.

POTENTIAL LIMITATIONS

The study suffers from an internal validity issue in that subjects completed the tax return outside the laboratory (i.e., in a classroom), and may or may not have collaborated. Since the tax returns were a graded component of the course, this may have provided an incentive for students to collaborate. Students were instructed not to collaborate and, in an effort to prevent such, the students were told that they would be able to correct their first submissions based on instructor feedback. The first time the returns were collected, measures of accuracy were acquired, then the tax assignments were returned with feedback regarding their accuracy. Students then revised the returns and submitted them a second time for a grade. It is hoped that these procedures reduced incentives to collaborate.

Another potential limitation of this study is its failure to control for the problem-solving ability of the student, a factor in the successful completion of a tax return (Rose & Wolfe, 2000, p. 298). Additionally, since this study used students from a single university; the results may not be generalizable to those at other institutions. Finally, since some measures were collected using a written questionnaire; common method bias from self-reported data may have led to overestimates of relationships.

CONCLUSION

Accounting firms use tax software to increase accuracy and preparation speed. Such reasoning may cause one to wonder why the educator would require students to complete paper forms in the classroom. While accounting firms seek a timely and accurate return, the educator seeks the decision aid that best increases student learning. Thus, understanding how learners cognitively process instructional materials becomes an important factor in determining the type of educational technology to be used in a given circumstance.

In the current study, students who prepared paper returns exerted more cognitive effort which, in turn, was associated with higher levels of higher-level learning as measured by a tax issue identification problem. This suggests that the paper form is a better tool for helping students acquire a deeper understanding of the tax law. Instructors may wish to require that the first tax return, or the first set of financial statements, required of students be prepared using a manual decision aid such as 1040 forms or paper journals and ledgers. Conversely, the practitioner will want to continue to benefit from the increased accuracy and speed afforded by software, while recognizing its inherent limitations as a learning device.

ACKNOWLEDGMENTS

I am grateful for the suggestions of participants at the 2003 AIS Educator Association Conference and the 2003 Central States Accounting Research Workshop held at Kansas State University. I am especially grateful to Anthony H. Catanach Jr., Editor, and two anonymous reviewers who added greatly to my understanding of the research process. I am also grateful for the financial support of Pittsburg State University and Emporia State University.

REFERENCES

Bandura, A. (1990). Reflections on nonability determinants of competence. In: J. Kollingran & R. Sternberg (Eds), *Competence Considered: Perceptions of Competence and Incompetence Across the Lifespan*. New Haven: Yale University Press.

Bernardo, A. (1994). Problem-specific information and the development of problem-type schemata. *Journal of Experimental Psychology*, *20*, 379–395.

Bryant, S. M., & Hunton, J. E. (2000). The use of technology in the delivery of instruction: Implications for accounting educators and education researchers. *Issues in Accounting Education*, *15*(1), 129–162.

Clark, R. E. (1982). Antagonism between achievement and enjoyment in ATI studies. *Educational Psychologist*, *17*, 92–101.

Cloyd, C. B. (1997). The influence of decision aids on user behavior: Implications for knowledge acquisition and inappropriate reliance. *Organizational Behavior and Human Decision Processes*, *72*, 232–255.

Glover, S., Prawitt, D., & Spilker, B. (1997). The influence of decision aids on user behavior: Implications for knowledge acquisition and inappropriate reliance. *Organizational Behavior and Human Decision Processes*, *72*, 232–255.

Internal Revenue Service. (2005). IRS efile PSA (cited 8 November 2005). Available at www.irs.gov/newsroom/article/0,,id = 137190,00.html

Jennings, S. E., & Onwuegbuzie, A. J. (2001). Computer attitudes as a function of age, gender, math attitude, and developmental status. *Journal of Educational Computing Research*, *25*(4), 367–384.

Low, R., & Over, R. (1992). Hierarchical ordering of schematic knowledge relating to area-of-rectangle problems. *Journal of Educational Psychology*, *48*(1), 62–69.

Nickell, G. S., & Pinto, J. N. (1986). The computer attitude scale. *Computers in Human Behavior*, *2*, 301–306.

Rose, J., & Wolfe, C. (2000). The effects of system design alternatives on the acquisition of tax knowledge from a computerized tax decision aid. *Accounting, Organizations and Society*, *25*(3), 285–306.

Salomon, G. (1984). Television is "easy" and print is "tough": The differential investment of cognitive effort in learning as a function of perceptions and attributions. *Journal of Educational Psychology*, *76*, 647–658.

Todd, P., & Benbasat, I. (1993). An experimental investigation of the relationship between decision makers, decision aids and decision making effort. *Infor*, *31*(2), 80–99.

Whitecotton, S. M. (1996). The effects of experience and a decision aid on the slope, scatter, and bias of earnings forecasts. *Organizational Behavior and Human Decision Processes*, *66*, 111–121.

REVISITING HIRING DECISIONS BY PUBLIC ACCOUNTING: THE IMPACT OF EDUCATIONAL PATH, AGE AND GENDER

Elizabeth Dreike Almer and Anne L. Christensen

ABSTRACT

Changes in the public accounting labor market and accounting student demographics motivate updating our understanding of the student profile most attractive to CPA firm recruiters. In this exploratory study, public accounting assurance recruiters evaluated hypothetical job candidates with varying educational path, age and gender. We investigated whether accounting courses taken in a non-degree or post-baccalaureate certificate programs are valued differently than the same courses taken through a degree program. We also studied the effect of age and gender on recruiter decision-making. Our results indicate a recruiter preference for Master in Accounting and Management Information System degrees, and the post-baccalaureate certificate was not valued any differently from a bachelor's degree. Although gender appeared to have no effect on the recruiting decision, older students appeared to be assessed less favorably on some dimensions than their younger counterparts. These results are important to both accounting program administrators and students for the insights they provide into program design and counseling.

Advances in Accounting Education: Teaching and Curriculum Innovations, Volume 9, 77–94

ISSN: 1085-4622/doi:10.1016/S1085-4622(08)09004-4

Public accounting is the single largest employer of accounting students (AICPA, 2005, p. 12) and, arguably, the employer of choice for the most sought after students. Accordingly, students are very concerned about the profession's recruiting and selection process. Although prior research has examined public accounting hiring (Kirsch, Leathers, & Snead, 1993, p. 58; Ahadiat & Smith, 1994, p. 59; Almer, Hopper, & Kaplan, 1998, p. 1), the profession's labor market has changed dramatically since these studies were conducted. Consequently, an updated understanding of what public accounting firms look for in students is warranted.

Currently the demand for new accounting graduates exceeds supply (AICPA, 2005, p. 22). The required skill set for new hires also has broadened to include greater systems knowledge (Duffy, 2004, p. 60) and stronger technical accounting skills (Albrecht & Sack, 2000, p. 62). Additionally, recent financial scandals have increased pressure for firms to focus on "softer" qualities like ethical sensitivity and professional skepticism (Wyatt, 2004, p. 52; Toffler & Reingold, 2003, p. 186).

At the same time, the population of prospective new public accounting hires is changing. Whereas in prior years firms primarily hired accounting undergraduates (AICPA, 2005, p. 22), the varied applications of the 150-hour rule have opened up many more academic paths to certification (Hunton, Stone, & Wier, 2005, p. 86). Generally, additional hours are obtained through double major bachelor degrees or master's degrees in accounting (MACC). However, in many states, the 150-hour requirement also may be met by a non-accounting bachelor's degree supplemented with accounting courses taken in a non-degree or post-baccalaureate (post-bac) program. Women now comprise 53 percent of public accounting new hires, compared to 49 percent in 1999 (AICPA, 2005, p. 28). National trends of "older" college students (U.S. Department of Education, 2000, p. 3) also are apparent in accounting where 18 percent of bachelor and 38 percent of master accounting graduates are over 25 years of age (Nelson, Vendrzyk, Quirin, & Allen, 2002, p. 272). Thus, the supply of accounting graduates is likely to be more educated, female and older than in prior years.

This exploratory study asked public accounting firm recruiters to evaluate a series of hypothetical job candidates for assurance positions to examine the relative value that they place on different educational backgrounds, gender, and age. In addition to updating prior research on the hiring decision of accounting recruiters, we extend the literature by including a broader range of dependent measures, which recruiters have indicated impact the final hiring decision.

LITERATURE REVIEW

Over the past two decades, a number of studies have examined attributes that impact the selection of new hires. The earliest wave of research (Dinius & Rogow, 1988, pp. 92–93; Hassell & Hennessey, 1989, p. 217; Lewis, Shimerda, & Graham, 1983, p. 137) focused on the relative importance of academic performance, work experience, references and interpersonal skills. All were considered important by recruiters and partners, though the relative importance varied.

Research in the 1990s began looking at more subtle factors associated with the hiring process. In an examination of personality traits and skills, Kirsch et al. (1993, p. 66) found that "Big Six" recruiters emphasized the ability to aggressively seek responsibility. Similarly, Ahadiat and Smith (1994, p. 67) reported that professional conduct, reliability and communication skills were some of the most highly ranked characteristics in new hires. More recently, Almer et al. (1998, p. 4) examined the impact of potentially sensitive applicant demographics on hiring judgments, particularly when academic performance and interpersonal skills were adequate. They found that race was associated with hiring decisions, but that gender and family structure were not.

This body of research clearly demonstrates the importance of good grades and interpersonal skills to the hiring decision. However, its current usefulness is limited because these studies all were conducted when the supply of accounting graduates was good. Further, these studies all implicitly assumed that a prospective new hire was a traditional aged, undergraduate accounting major. These assumptions simply are not realistic in today's environment of multi-path educational requirements and an aging student population.

RESEARCH QUESTIONS

Effect of Educational Paths in the Hiring Process

The 150-hour requirement allows various educational paths for students pursuing a public accounting career. These include a variety of master's degrees, double undergraduate majors (accounting coupled with another discipline), or in some states, simply sufficient credit hours that include specific accounting courses.

Master's Degree

The career impact of an MACC degree appears uncertain. Public accounting professionals with MACCs pass the certified public accountant (CPA) exam faster and turnover less (Deppe, Smith, & Stice, 1992, p. 34; Spiceland, Siegel, & George, 1992, p. 71). However, they do not receive better performance evaluations (Ferris & Larcker, 1983, p. 8) and faster promotions occur only under certain conditions (Deppe et al., 1992, p. 34; Spiceland et al., 1992, p. 65). While these studies suggest that the MACC may have an impact once hired, none directly assess whether the degree impacts the hiring decision.

Information Systems/Technology

Albrecht and Sack (2000, p. 62) cite the need to link accounting with information systems/technology. They argue that a better understanding of accounting as a part of an organization's information system is critical to the evolving needs of the accounting workplace. However, prior research has yet to examine the relative value of a stronger systems background as compared to other alternative educational paths.

Liberal Arts Background

Albrecht and Sack (2000, p. 62) also discuss the need for accounting graduates with stronger critical thinking and communications skills, and suggest a liberal arts background as a possible solution. In fact, New York University recently fully integrated their business program with the study of liberal arts (Brown, 2002, p. 22) by "layering" technical accounting skills on a foundation of communication and interpersonal skills, creative thinking, global awareness, and professional ethics. While research shows accounting students from liberal arts-based curricula have higher levels of moral development than accounting students from traditional programs (Ponemon & Glazer, 1990, p. 202), it is still unclear as to whether accounting recruiters recognize the benefits of a liberal arts education.

Post-Baccalaureate Certificate in Accounting

We are unaware of any research that has explored whether accounting recruiters differentially value accounting courses taken in a post-bac certificate program versus an actual degree program. Anecdotal reports from some recruiters indicate that students with accounting post-bac certificates are sought because they are more focused on developing their accounting knowledge than students pursuing their first college degrees. Other recruiters indicate that they prefer students with MACC degrees because of the greater technical knowledge these students possess.

Arguments can be made for the benefits of any one of these four academic paths to become "CPA ready". Yet, it is entirely possible that no one particular academic qualification is actually preferred over the others by accounting firm recruiters. Consequently, we pose the following research question:

RQ1. To what extent, if any, are specific educational paths associated with public accounting recruiters' hiring decisions for entry-level assurance positions?

Effect of Age in the Hiring Process

Non-traditional or older accounting students have largely been ignored in the accounting literature even though they increasingly comprise a significant segment of accounting majors, particularly those with master's degrees (Nelson et al., 2002, p. 272). The normal age for those entering public accounting is typically expected to be that of a traditional college graduate, and entry-level public accounting has long had the reputation of being closed to non-traditional age graduates (Brown & Meredith, 1986, p. 180). Dykxhoorn and Sinning (1996, p. 424) confirmed this expectation in a study of MACC graduates, in which "older students", even those under 30, believed that they were subject to age bias in the public accounting interview process. Another study of Canadian public accountants also found evidence of age bias in the performance evaluation process (Saks & Waldman, 1998, p. 417). However, both of these studies were conducted during time periods where evidence existed of other forms of bias, including gender and race (Hammond, 2002, p. 2). Additionally, it is possible that recent patterns of organizational change may have reduced age bias (Johnson, Lowe, & Reckers, 2000, p. 27).

Given the recent shortage of accounting graduates, hiring non-traditional students may make economic sense. Additionally, higher education research has shown that non-traditional students often have better time management skills (Trueman & Hartley, 1996, p. 205), study habits, motivation, and commitment to learning (Delvin, 1996, p. 57; Wynd & Bozman, 1996, p. 234) than their more traditional counterparts. While all of these attributes seem desirable for new public accounting hires, the actual effects on the hiring decision are less clear. Accordingly, we explore the following research question:

RQ2. To what extent, if any, is age associated with public accounting recruiters' hiring decisions for entry-level assurance positions?

Effect of Gender in the Hiring Process

Despite initial evidence of gender bias (Anderson, Johnson, & Reckers, 1994, p. 488; Johnson, Lowe, & Reckers, 1996, p. 187), performance evaluation studies published in the late 1990s and early 2000s found that female accountants are assessed no less favorably (Cohen & Single, 2001, p. 322; Johnson, Kaplan, & Reckers, 1998, p. 64), and in some cases more favorably, than their male counterparts (Lowe, Reckers, & Sanders, 2001, p. 67). Almer et al. (1998, p. 9) also found no gender impact on hiring judgments. Despite these findings, the AICPA (2005, p. 35) noted that only 13 percent of public accounting firm partners are female in accounting firms with over 200 AICPA members, and only 19 percent of partners are female when public accounting firms of all sizes are considered. Given these findings, we investigate the following research question:

> **RQ3.** To what extent, if any, is gender associated with public accounting recruiters' hiring decisions for entry-level assurance positions?

METHODOLOGY AND RESEARCH DESIGN

Participants and Task

Participants in this study were from 16 different offices of public accounting firms across several western states and Florida. Every recruiter in this study was involved in recruiting students from states that require 150 hours for certification. Local and regional recruiters were from firms in Alaska, Florida, Montana, Oregon, and Washington. Big Four recruiters were from offices in Alaska, California, Florida, Montana, Oregon, and Washington. Participating firms included four international, two regional, and six local firms.

All participating firms actively recruit at universities that offer all of the educational paths that are tested, and which enroll both traditional and non-traditional age students. At the end of their recruiting season, the firms distributed a total of 115 experimental instruments to individuals within their firm who were actively involved with campus recruiting. We requested that participants complete the instrument and send it directly back to the researchers. Fifty-two usable instruments were returned,

Table 1. Respondent Demographics ($n = 52$).

Age		Age Started Public Accounting Career	
Mean	38.2	Mean	24.7
Median	36.5	Median	23.0
Range	25–60	Range	20–41
Gender		**Education**	
Male	62.3%	Bachelor's in Accounting	43
Female	37.7%	Bachelor's in other	10
		Master's of accounting	3
		Other master's	3
		Accounting post-baccalaureate	4
Firm Type		**Years Performing Accounting Services**	
Local	50.9%	Mean	13.1
Regional	15.1%	Median	12.0
International	34.0%	Range[a]	0–34
Position in Firm		**Years Recruiting Experience**	
Staff	3.9%	Mean	7.8
Senior	9.6%	Median	5.5
Manager	50.0%	Range	1–33
Partner	36.5%		
Years Employed at Present Firm			
Mean	10.3		
Median	8.0		
Range	2–34		

[a]One respondent from a Big Four Firm worked in the Human Resource department and never worked as an accountant.

a 45 percent response rate. Table 1 provides sample demographic information.

Participants were involved in recruiting on 37 different campuses and reported an average of 7.77 years of recruiting experience. Half of the sample consisted of recruiters from local firms (50.9 percent) with the remainder coming from regional (15.1 percent) and international firms (34.9 percent).

Participants received a series of summary sheets to evaluate 16 hypothetical job candidates. The summary sheets contained short profiles of fictitious accounting students seeking audit positions. Participants assessed the overall likelihood that each applicant would be hired for an entry-level position within their firm. They also evaluated the candidates on five factors likely to affect the overall hiring decision. We presented the summary sheets in four different random orderings to reduce the likelihood of order effects. Subsequent analysis indicated no order effects were present. Fig. 1 illustrates a sample summary sheet.

Scholastic Achievement and Extracurricular Activities

- All-City High School: Graduated 1999
- B.S. Accounting, State University, Expected Graduation Summer 2004
- B.S. Management Information Systems, State University, Expected Graduation Summer 2004

Overall GPA:	3.30	
Accounting GPA:	3.31	Beta Alpha Psi Member
MIS GPA:	3.29	

Summary Assessment of Prior Work Experience: Throughout college career, applicant has worked part time in several clerical and customer service positions.

Summary Assessment of Interview Performance: Applicant had a professional appearance and solid communications skills.

Please respond to the following questions by circling the number that best represents your viewpoint.

1. How likely is Mary to be hired for an entry level position at your firm?

Very Unlikely Very Likely
1 2 3 4 5 6 7

2. How likely is Mary to fit well with the culture of your firm?

Very Unlikely Very Likely
1 2 3 4 5 6 7

3. How likely is Mary to interact effectively with clients?

Very Unlikely Very Likely
1 2 3 4 5 6 7

4. If hired, how likely would you be to recommend Mary for one of your audit teams?

Very Unlikely Very Likely
1 2 3 4 5 6 7

5. If hired, how likely is Mary to need extensive training to participate effectively in an audit engagement?

Very Unlikely Very Likely
1 2 3 4 5 6 7

6. If hired, how likely is Mary to *voluntarily* leave the firm within the first 3 years of employment?

Very Unlikely Very Likely
1 2 3 4 5 6 7

Fig. 1. Mary Robertson Audit New-College Hire Applicant Summary Sheet.

After participants evaluated all 16 candidates, they then selected the three individuals they were most likely to offer entry-level positions. This question was included to evaluate the saliency of our manipulated variables. We then asked participants to list the characteristics they considered most important for individuals working in assurance services and the age at which they believed it was too old to begin a career in public accounting.

Experimental Design

We used a $4 \times 2 \times 2$ design and manipulated educational paths, age, and gender through information provided on the summary sheets. Candidates were identified by gender specific names (e.g., Mary Robertson in Fig. 1), and we manipulated age and educational paths using academic background information provided on the summary sheets. All students had an expected graduation date of 2004. The "traditional students" graduated from high school in 1999 (i.e., degree(s) completed five years after high school graduation), whereas the "non-traditional" students were clearly in their mid-30s, having graduated from high school 13 years earlier in 1986. While the age difference between traditional and non-traditional students may seem large, it would not be unusual for recruiters to interview students in their mid-30s, as they are common in the accounting programs at which the participants recruit.

Academic qualifications were manipulated as follows: (1) an accounting bachelor's degree combined with a management information systems (MIS) bachelor's degree, liberal arts bachelor's degree, or MACC or (2) a liberal arts bachelor's degree in philosophy combined with accounting courses taken as part of a post-bac certificate program. Although a master's degree in business administration (MBA) is another plausible academic path, we excluded this as a manipulation since many MBA programs require significant work experience for admission. This requirement would confound the impact of the broader-based curriculum included in an MBA relative to the other possible academic paths.

To avoid a ceiling effect with candidates being selected primarily on the basis of grades, we described all students as having a GPA of 3.3, plus or minus .01. This value represents the lower end of what is typically considered acceptable by public accounting firms (Almer et al., 1998, p. 7). Information on the applicant's prior work experience and interview performance was held fairly neutral. All candidates worked part-time during their college careers in clerical and customer service positions.

Additionally, each student applicant was a member of Beta Alpha Psi, had a professional appearance, and possessed solid communication skills.

Dependent and Measured Variables

Participants evaluated each potential job candidate on six attributes. The first was an overall assessment of whether the candidate would be hired. Consistent with prior research (Almer et al., 1998, p. 7), we asked participants, "How likely is *applicant name* to be hired for an entry-level position at your firm?" Since this dependent measure is an aggregation of several hiring factors, we also included five criteria drawn from conversations with firm recruiters and prior studies such as Almer et al. (1998, p. 7). We asked participants to assess the applicant's (1) fit with firm culture, (2) ability to interact effectively with clients, (3) desirability for working on an audit team, (4) need for extensive training, and (5) likelihood of voluntarily leaving the firm in the first three years of employment. We adopted this approach to determine which specific hiring criteria were affected by the manipulated variables.

As a post-hoc validation that these criteria are relevant to recruiters, participants were also asked to list the criteria they use in selecting new hires. In addition to a high grade point average (GPA), they most frequently listed fit with firm culture, communication skills, ability to interact with clients, training, and technical skills.

Statistical Analysis

We used Multivariate Analysis of Variance (MANOVA) to assess the relationships among the six dependent measures (i.e., likelihood of hiring, culture fit, client interaction, audit team recommendation, need for training, and voluntarily firm departure) and the three independent variables (i.e., educational paths, age, and gender). As illustrated in Fig. 1, we measured responses to each dependent variable using a Likert scale where one was very unlikely and seven was very likely.

RESULTS AND DISCUSSION

Educational Paths

Research question 1 addresses whether the educational paths of accounting students affect the hiring decisions. The multivariate results presented in

Table 2. MANOVA Results: Variables Related to Hiring Criteria.

Effect Within Subjects	Wilks' Lambda	*F*	*P*-Value
Gender	.918	.698	.653
Age	.626	4.681	.001
Educational paths	.309	4.356	.000
Gender × age	.910	.770	.597
Gender × educational paths	.709	.797	.690
Age × educational paths	.528	1.735	.080
Gender × age × educational paths	.733	.710	.779

Table 3. Univariate Results.

Dependent Variable	Independent Variable	Sum of Squares	Degrees of Freedom	*P*-Value
Hiring judgment	Age	34.887	1	.000
	Educational paths	113.967	3	.000
Fit with firm	Age	21.811	1	.000
	Educational paths	57.651	3	.000
Interact with clients	Age	1.794	1	.288
	Educational paths	19.419	3	.002
Recommend for audit team	Age	5.778	1	.007
	Educational paths	27.929	3	.000
Need extensive training	Age	.058	1	.633
	Educational paths	23.645	3	.024
Voluntarily leave	Age	1.445	1	.307
	Educational paths	14.079	3	.033

Table 2 and univariate results reported in Table 3 indicate that educational paths are consistently associated with all six dependent measures. Tests of within-subjects contrasts (Table 4) reveal that students with MACC degrees are viewed significantly more favorably on nearly every aspect of the hiring decision than those who follow other educational paths.

With respect to hiring likelihood, firm fit, and audit team recommendation, students with accounting and MIS bachelors degrees were viewed significantly more favorably ($p<.05$) than those with accounting and philosophy bachelors degrees or those with post-bac certificates in accounting. Students with accounting and MIS bachelor's degrees also were viewed as significantly less likely to need extensive training than those with a post-bac accounting certificate. We found no significant differences on any of the hiring decision variables between students with the philosophy

Table 4. Tests of Within Subjects Contrasts for Educational Paths.

	MACC[a] vs. BS Accounting & MIS[b]	MACC vs. BA Accounting & Philosophy[c]	MACC vs. BA Philosophy & Post-bac Accounting[d]	BS Acct & MIS vs. BA Accounting & Philosophy	BS Accounting & MIS vs. BA Philosophy & Post-bac	BA Accounting & Philosophy BA Philosophy & Post-bac
Likelihood of hiring	**	**	**	**	**	.174
Fit with firm culture	**	**	**	**	**	.779
Interact well w/clients	**	**	**	.095	.079	.525
Recommend for audit team	.074	**	**	**	**	.942
Need extensive training	*	.076	**	.424	*	.111
Voluntarily leave the firm	*	*	**	.285	.127	.457

*$p < .05$.
**$p < .01$.
[a]Accounting bachelor's degree combined with a masters of accounting degree.
[b]Accounting bachelor's degree combined with a second undergraduate major in management information systems.
[c]Accounting bachelor's degree combined with a second undergraduate major in liberal arts (philosophy).
[d]Liberal arts (philosophy) bachelor's degree combined with accounting courses taken as part of a post-bac certification program.

and accounting degrees, or those with the philosophy degree followed by a post-bac accounting certificate.

Age, Gender, and Applicant Choice

MANOVA results in Table 2 also reveal that age is significantly associated with hiring decisions. The univariate results in Table 3 and cell means in Table 5 suggest that younger students were viewed more favorably with respect to the likelihood of being hired (cell mean 4.4 v. 4.0), firm culture fit (4.5 v. 4.2), and selection for an audit team (5.0 v. 4.9). We found no significant differences with respect to interacting with clients, the need for extensive training, or the likelihood of the individual voluntarily leaving the firm. When asked what age was too old to start a career in public accounting, most recruiters responded with ages of between 40 and 50.

The MANOVA results presented in Table 2 indicate that gender is not significantly associated with any dependent hiring measures.

Finally, we asked respondents to select the three individuals to whom they would most likely offer employment. This question was posed to ensure that the ratings for each individual were consistent with the hiring decision. Preferred candidates were younger students completing MACC degrees regardless of gender. The two individuals selected most frequently were traditional age students, one male (58.5 percent) and one female (64.2 percent), both of whom were pursuing MACC degrees. The third most frequently selected individual was an older female who also was completing a MACC degree.

LIMITATIONS

There are several limitations to this study. First, the sample was small since it is difficult to obtain participants with recruiting experience at campuses with non-traditional students and post-bac programs. Consequently, these professionals may differ from those who recruit in other states, at campuses with traditional populations, in states that specifically require an accounting degree, or do not require 150 hours of education. Also, participants were not randomly selected.

Next, we used summary sheets to provide profiles of 16 hypothetical students seeking auditing positions. While this methodology ensures internal validity, it also reduces external validity since the summary sheets do not

Table 5. Cell Means Related to Hiring Criteria.

	Age			Educational Paths		
	Traditional[a]	Non-traditional[b]	MACC[c]	BS accounting BS MIS[d]	BA accounting BA Phil[e]	Post-bac accounting BA philosophy[f]
Likelihood of hiring	4.403*	3.998	4.726	4.349	3.939	3.788
Fit with firm culture	4.528*	4.208	4.712	4.528	4.104	4.127
Interact well with clients	4.757	4.665	4.939	4.755	4.552	4.599
Recommend for audit team	5.028*	4.863	5.165	5.085	4.764	4.769
Need extensive training	4.835	4.851	4.604	4.797	4.910	5.061
Voluntarily leave firm	3.816	3.899	3.670	3.811	3.943	4.005

Note: Responses are on a seven point scale with 1 = very unlikely and 7 = very likely.
$^{*}p<.01$.
[a]Students completing their education by age 23.
[b]Students completing their education by age 36.
[c]Accounting bachelor's degree combined with a masters of accounting degree.
[d]Accounting bachelor's degree combined with a second undergraduate major in management information systems.
[e]Accounting bachelor's degree combined with a second undergraduate major in liberal arts (philosophy).
[f]Liberal arts (philosophy) bachelor's degree plus accounting courses taken as part of a post-bac certificate program.

provide a level of individual detail that is available in actual resumes and interviews.

Tangentially, we may have introduced demand effects by using a within-subjects experimental design. Our manipulations may have caused subjects to respond in a socially desirable fashion. For example, recruiter attempts to be "politically correct" may have precluded finding a gender effect and muted the "true" age effect. Lastly, our choice of philosophy as a liberal arts major may not be representative of most liberal arts majors also pursing accounting.

SUMMARY AND IMPLICATIONS

Our study focuses on three characteristics of accounting students that may influence recruiter choice: educational paths, age, and gender. We update the accounting recruiting literature by investigating how recruiters evaluate different hypothetical job applicants on these characteristics in terms of the likelihood of being hired, fit with the firm, client interaction, audit team recommendation, need for training, and candidate voluntary firm departure.

Our results yield significant implications for accounting program design and counseling, as well as for students. Despite recent calls for combining accounting with other areas such as MIS or a liberal arts background (Albrecht & Sack, 2000, p. 62), we found that recruiters still prefer students with the greater accounting competencies typically found in MACC programs.

Where a master's degree is not an option, either due to degree availability or student constraints, we find a higher incremental value to coupling an accounting bachelor's degree with a bachelor's degree in MIS, than with a philosophy degree. This preference was evident in the likelihood to be hired, fit with firm culture, and audit team recommendation dimensions. These results are consistent with the Institute of Management Accountants (IMA's) recommendation that accounting students develop greater understanding of technology and information systems (Russell & Smith, 2003, p. 4). They also support the notion that recruiters prefer students who have developed strong technical skills over those with the "softer" skills commonly associated with liberal arts degrees.

Our results indicate that accounting courses obtained through non-degree post-bac programs are viewed no less favorably than courses obtained through a bachelor's degree. This finding provides insight to students who may be weighing the benefits and costs of a bachelor's degree versus a post-bac certificate. From a student advising perspective, it should be noted that post-bac certificates still are not viewed as favorably as MACC.

This study also has implications for students contemplating the best route to meet the 150-hour requirement. Our findings help establish the incremental value of MACC in the job search process, an important consideration when weighing the higher cost of graduate tuition. When a second bachelor's degree is being contemplated to achieve 150 hours, students should consider pairing accounting with a technical second major such as MIS, rather than a liberal arts degree. Finally, for students who already have a non-accounting bachelor's degree, this study suggests that the extra time to obtain an accounting bachelor's degree may not be worthwhile, since completing a post-bac program appears to be viewed just as favorably by recruiters.

Our results on the impact of age on the hiring decision also are quite revealing. They indicate that there is still bias against older students, at least as it relates to recruiters' perceptions of their ability to fit with the public accounting culture and coworkers. Yet on the variables which are costly to firms (i.e., client interaction, need for training, and voluntarily firm departure), older students were rated no less favorably than those of a traditional age. To counteract the bias which is clearly still present, our results suggest that non-traditional age accounting job candidates should focus on their ability to "fit in" to the firm and general employment stability, while emphasizing the benefits that their maturity can bring to client interactions. Our results also call for additional research to examine the subsequent career paths of "older" students to see if the anticipated benefits associated with these students actually do accrue for accounting firms.

The finding that gender was not associated with any of the dimensions of the hiring decision also should encourage students. Although overwhelming evidence exists of a "glass ceiling" for women in accounting (AICPA, 2005, p. 35), gender does not appear to be an issue in the hiring decisions made by public accounting recruiters.

Finally, our results yield some important insights for firms that recruit accounting students. If public accounting firms truly do seek more professionals with the "softer" skills associated with liberal arts degrees, such preferences must be communicated to students, instructors, and administrators. Additionally, as firms continue to recruit the "best and the brightest", they should not ignore the considerable number of accounting majors who are non-traditional age students. Our research suggests that these students may be an answer to current firm staffing shortages.

ACKNOWLEDGMENTS

We are grateful to Montana State University and Portland State University for their financial support for this research. We would like to thank the participants at the Montana State University College of Business Research Workshop and the 2005 AAA Annual Meeting concurrent session for their comments and suggestions. In addition, we would like to thank all the public accounting firms that participated in this study. Finally, we would like to thank our editor, Anthony H. Catanach Jr. and two anonymous reviewers for their helpful suggestions and guidance.

REFERENCES

Ahadiat, N., & Smith, K. J. (1994). A factor-analytic investigation of employee selection factors of significance to recruiters of entry-level accountants. *Issues in Accounting Education, 9*(1), 59–79.

Albrecht, W. S., & Sack, R. J. (2000). *Accounting education: Charting the course through a perilous future*. Sarasota, FL: American Accounting Association.

Almer, E. D., Hopper, J. R., & Kaplan, S. E. (1998). The effect of diversity-related attributes on hiring, advancement and voluntary turnover judgments. *Accounting Horizons, 12*(1), 1–17.

American Institute of Certified Public Accountants (AICPA). (2005). *The supply of accounting graduates and the demand for public accounting recruits – 2003 and 2004*. New York: AICPA.

Anderson, J. C., Johnson, E. N., & Reckers, P. M. J. (1994). Perceived effects of gender, family structure and physical appearance on career progression in public accounting: A research note. *Accounting, Organizations and Society, 1*, 483–491.

Brown, B. C., & Meredith, V. B. (1986). The older entry-level professional. *Journal of Accountancy, 162*(5), 180–184.

Brown, P. R. (2002). CPA journal forum anticipates future. *The CPA Journal, 72*(3), 21–22.

Cohen, J. R., & Single, L. E. (2001). An examination of the perceived impact of flexible work arrangements on professional opportunities in public accounting. *Journal of Business Ethics, 32*(4), 317–328.

Delvin, M. (1996). Older and wiser? A comparison of learning and study strategies of mature age and younger teacher education students. *Higher Education Research and Development, 15*, 51–60.

Deppe, L. A., Smith, J. M., & Stice, J. D. (1992). The debate over post-baccalaureate education: One university's experience. *Issues in Accounting Education, 7*(1), 18–35.

Dinius, S. H., & Rogow, R. B. (1988). Applications of the Delphi method in identifying characteristics Big Eight firms are seeking in entry-level accountants. *Journal of Accounting Education, 6*(1), 83–101.

Duffy, M. N. (2004). Section 404 opens a door. *Journal of Accountancy, 197*(5), 55–64.

Dykxhoorn, H. J., & Sinning, K. E. (1996). Perceptions of master's of accountancy graduates concerning their job search and employment experiences with public accounting firms. *Journal of Accounting Education, 14*(4), 415–434.

Ferris, K. R., & Larcker, D. F. (1983). Explanatory variables of auditor performance in a large public accounting firm. *Accounting, Organizations and Society*, *8*(1), 1–11.

Hammond, T. A. (2002). *A white-collar profession: African American certified public accountants since 1921*. Chapel Hill: The University of North Carolina Press.

Hassell, J. M., & Hennessey, H. W. (1989). An examination of factors important in the CPA recruiting process. *Journal of Accounting Education*, *7*, 217–231.

Hunton, J. E., Stone, D. N., & Wier, B. (2005). Does graduate business education contribute to professional accounting success? *Accounting Horizons*, *19*(2), 85–100.

Johnson, E. N., Kaplan, S., & Reckers, P. M. J. (1998). An examination of potential gender-based differences in audit managers' performance evaluation judgments. *Behavioral Research in Accounting*, *10*, 47–75.

Johnson, E. N., Lowe, D. J., & Reckers, P. M. J. (2000). A new culture? Evidence of support for diversity in public accounting performance evaluation judgments. *Advances in Accounting Behavioral Research*, *3*, 13–35.

Johnson, E. N., Lowe, J. D., & Reckers, P. M. J. (1996). An examination of direct and indirect gender effects in public accounting. *Advances in Accounting*, *14*, 179–192.

Kirsch, R. J., Leathers, P. E., & Snead, K. C. (1993). Student versus recruiter perceptions of the importance of Staff Auditor performance variables. *Accounting Horizons*, *7*(4), 58–69.

Lewis, T. D., Shimerda, T. A., & Graham, G. (1983). What the academic advisor needs to know about job placement. *Journal of Accounting Education*, *1*(Fall), 135–142.

Lowe, D. J., Reckers, P. M. J., & Sanders, D. (2001). The influence of gender, ethnicity, and individual differences on perceptions of career progression in public accounting. *International Journal of Auditing*, *5*, 53–71.

Nelson, I. T., Vendrzyk, V. P., Quirin, J. J., & Allen, R. D. (2002). No, the sky is not falling: Evidence of accounting student characteristics at FSA schools, 1995–2000. *Issues in Accounting Education*, *17*(3), 269–287.

Ponemon, L., & Glazer, A. (1990). Accounting education and ethical development: The influence of liberal learning students and alumni in accounting practice. *Issues in Accounting Education*, *5*(2), 195–208.

Russell, K. A., & Smith, C. S. (2003). Accounting education's role in corporate malfeasance: It's time for a new curriculum! *Strategic Finance*, *85*(6), 1–5.

Saks, A. M., & Waldman, D. A. (1998). The relationship between age and job performance evaluations for entry-level professionals. *Journal of Organizational Behavior*, *19*, 409–419.

Spiceland, J. D., Siegel, P. H., & George, C. R. (1992). Educational preparation of auditors, promotion time, and turnover: A survival analysis. *Advances in Accounting*, *10*, 61–76.

Toffler, B. L., & Reingold, J. (2003). *Final accounting*. New York: Broadway Books.

Trueman, M., & Hartley, J. (1996). A comparison between time management skills and academic performance in mature and traditional entry university students. *Higher Education*, *32*, 199–215.

US Department of Education. (2000). Profile of undergraduates in U.S. postsecondary institutions: 1999–2000. NCES National Center for Education Statistics. Available at http://nces.ed.gov/pubs/web/97578f.asp. Last accessed on 12/20/04.

Wyatt, A. R. (2004). Accounting professionalism: They just don't get it! *Accounting Horizons*, *18*(1), 45–53.

Wynd, W. R., & Bozman, C. S. (1996). Student learning style: A segmentation strategy for higher education. *Journal of Education for Business*, *71*, 232–235.

LEARNING TO INTERPRET AND RECONCILE TAX AUTHORITY

Ernest R. Larkins

ABSTRACT

The ability to correctly interpret legal text and reconcile conflicting authorities is an essential skill for students learning to do tax research. As with other complex tasks, these abilities develop more effectively through instruction that focuses on concepts and strategies; contextually relevant and repeated practice; and tailored, explanatory feedback. This chapter describes an innovative, new instructional web resource that incorporates each of these teaching perspectives to help students interpret and reconcile tax law. Scores on in-class exercises suggest that using this tool improves student evaluative skills.

The American Institute of Certified Public Accountants' (AICPAs) "Core Competency Framework for Entry into the Accounting Profession" (AICPA, 1999a) (Framework) recommends that accounting programs offer curricula based on skills rather than traditional content-based courses. The Framework indicates that entry-level professionals must possess "strong research skills to access relevant guidance or other information, understand it, and apply it." Tax students exhibit this competency when they (1) correctly interpret tax authorities located during research, and (2) reconcile conflicting authorities.

Advances in Accounting Education: Teaching and Curriculum Innovations, Volume 9, 95–113

ISSN: 1085-4622/doi:10.1016/S1085-4622(08)09005-6

However, students misinterpret tax authority for a variety of reasons. Frequently, interpretation errors result from failing to recognize and properly understand the role of: (1) organizational terms (e.g., subsections and paragraphs); (2) general rules, exceptions, and exceptions to exceptions; (3) specially defined terms and their locations; (4) small words and short phrases (e.g., "unless" and "if and only if"); and (5) measuring language dealing with ownership and time periods (e.g., "more than 50 percent").

To assist students in developing these skills, I developed an innovative, web-based instructional resource that encourages students to focus on concepts and strategies. This pedagogical tool also provides practice opportunities together with explanatory feedback to assist students in learning how to interpret and reconcile tax law. Assessment results indicate that graduate students in a tax research course improved their performance by using this resource. Since the AICPA (1999b) recommends that graduate accounting and tax programs require students to take a tax research course, the web-based resource examined in this chapter can assist students in acquiring the evaluative skills necessary to conduct tax research.

The remainder of this chapter consists of six sections: (1) a brief review of the literature affecting the design and implementation of this resource; (2) a description of the institutional context; (3) an introduction to tax research tools; (4) a discussion of the instructional resource itself; (5) a review of assessment and related findings; and (6) a concluding summary.

LITERATURE REVIEW

This teaching tool specifically considers the effects of *instruction*, *practice*, *feedback*, and *context* in its design. When individuals are asked to process information in challenging and unstructured environments, they sometimes fail because they lack internalized strategies to complete complex tasks, the self-confidence to persevere when cognitive demand increases, or both. Academic or professional *instruction* on how to accomplish complex tasks may be helpful, particularly if it facilitates understanding, rather than simply enumerating correct steps (Bonner & Walker, 1994, p.159).

Newell and Simon (1972, p. 462) assert that internalizing strategies also requires recurring *practice*. However, to optimize learning, Ericsson (1996, pp. 20–21) contends that *feedback* should accompany repeated practice. Quality feedback can "fine tune" an activity, purging bad practices while reinforcing good ones. In effect, practice and feedback act together to internalize proper constructs or strategies that one recalls later when accomplishing similar tasks. Bonner and Walker (1994, pp. 169–71) find that "explanatory" feedback that provides details on how students can improve performance, trumps "outcome" feedback that merely comments on the quality of performance. Lou, Dedic, and Rosenfield (2003, p. 251) and Sims (2003, p. 271) also assert that the timeliness of feedback affects performance. For example, feedback that immediately follows practice yields greater student learning than delayed feedback.

The *context* in which practice and feedback occur also may influence learning. Brown, Collins, and Duguid (1989, p. 36) asserts that more realistic contexts lead to more effective learning. Wood, Atkins, and Tabernero (2000, p. 438) indicates that realistic and relevant contexts actually boost self-confidence and motivation.

INSTITUTIONAL CONTEXT

This section describes the educational setting where I teach, as well as my motivation for creating a different pedagogical method for teaching students to read, analyze, interpret, and reconcile tax law.

Educational Environment

Georgia State University offers undergraduate as well as graduate programs in business, including a Master of Taxation (MTx). The MTx program currently enrolls about 60 students, most of whom have professional experience in accounting, tax, or law. As part of the MTx program, students take a required tax research course, usually during their first semester.

Classes meet once a week for two and a half hours during a 15-week semester. The objectives of the course are to help students learn how to identify tax issues, locate and evaluate various sources of tax law, and effectively communicate conclusions and recommendations from their research. During the first few weeks of the semester, I deliver PowerPoint lectures about legislative, administrative, judicial, and secondary sources of the tax law, as well as the role of tax services and electronic subscription services in locating tax authority. After a mid-term exam, students individually submit one written assignment each week. In one week, the assignment focuses specifically on the skill of identifying tax issues. On alternate weeks, students must identify issues in a short fact pattern, find relevant tax authorities, interpret and reconcile such authorities, reach conclusions, and communicate results in a well-documented tax research memo.

Motivation for Change

During my teaching career, I have noticed that students often make fundamental mistakes when interpreting legal text, especially the Internal Revenue Code (IRC). They also struggle with resolving conflicts in tax authorities. To develop student abilities to read and understand legal text, I have tried several pedagogical approaches. Early in my teaching career, I required students to prepare research memos for which I provided written feedback. This approach proved less than satisfactory for several reasons. Not only was grading very time consuming, but significant improvements on later assignments did not manifest themselves. Students appeared to understand my feedback, but their lack of practice in applying this knowledge limited their ability to do so in different contexts.

Next, I decided to assign ungraded end-of-text-chapter discussion questions and exercises before they attempted more substantive graded research assignments. Again, I did not notice any improvement in student abilities to interpret and reconcile legal text. I concluded that the textbook materials did not focus explicitly enough on the target skills I wished to develop. Additionally, several students viewed these assignments simply as "busy work."

My next attempt at skill development required students to bring copies of the IRC to class. Within the lecture on statutory law, I would direct students to a particular area of the law. Then I illustrated various interpretation issues and demonstrated how and when to consult historical footnotes. While this approach proved a little better than assigning end-of-text-chapter materials, it still fell short of my expectations for student learning in subsequent assignments.

More recently, I began thinking about all of the written comments I have made on student tax research memos, particularly their similarity among assignments, and between semesters. It occurred to me that recording all of these comments in some organized and easily accessible form might be useful to students in their tax studies. I also decided to include examples to illustrate important points that would demonstrate the application of interpretation and reconciliation skills. Further, I decided to add self-assessment tests (with feedback) so that students could develop and evaluate their analytical skills before attempting substantial research assignments.

These materials became key elements of the teaching innovation described in detail in a later section.

INTRODUCTION TO TAX RESEARCH TOOLS

Conducting tax research can be viewed as a series of integrated steps: (1) establish facts, (2) identify issues, (3) locate tax authority, (4) evaluate tax authority, (5) draw conclusions and make recommendations, and (6) communicate results (Raabe, Whittenburg, Sanders, & Bost, 2006, p. 47). Thinking about tax research as a series of steps is instructive since it highlights the various skills students must develop to become proficient tax researchers and prepare for entry into the accounting profession. Inattention to any one step lessens the effectiveness of the entire process. Based on these premises, I developed five separate but linked web sites to assist students in acquiring the skills related to steps 2 through 6. Though Larkins (2005, pp. 94–96) first introduced several of these sites, the following paragraphs briefly describe the content of four of these sites to place the instructional resource with which this chapter deals in the broader context of tax research. A description of the "Evaluating Tax Authority" site appears in the next section.

When identifying tax issues (step 2), tax researchers must be able to recognize both questions of fact and law. A question of fact or factual issue requires the researcher to establish the related fact (i.e., returns her/him to step 1) while a question of law or legal issue requires the researcher to locate authority for resolving the issue (i.e., points her/him to step 3). Failing to identify either type of issue can lead to serious error. The "Identifying Tax Issues" site provides five instructive lessons to assist students in acquiring and developing this skill (see www2.gsu.edu/~wwwerl/iid). The first lesson defines questions of fact and law and explains why it is important to distinguish between them. Three lessons give students strategies for identifying questions involving gross income, deductions, and property transactions. A final lesson addresses miscellaneous points not addressed elsewhere such as the impact of experience and training on the ability to identify issues. The importance of clearly wording issues as part of the research process is also discussed. Following the instructive lessons, students take four self-assessment tests. The first two multiple-choice tests help students assess whether they can distinguish between questions of fact and questions of law and whether they can word issues correctly. The other two tests provide short fact scenarios for which students must identify and write questions of law and related questions of fact using an internet template. After writing their issues, students consult a scoring rubric. This evaluative tool is based on average weights assigned by 15 tax professionals and professors. All four self-assessment tests provide explanatory feedback to students for questions they miss or issues they fail to identify.

Step 3 of the tax research process involves finding authority to resolve legal issues. The "Locating Tax Authority" web site (Diaz III & Larkins, 2006, pp. 147–50) contains three lessons for developing this skill and covers: (1) basic search approaches using keywords, topical indices, tables of content, and some combination of these approaches; (2) specific strategies for constructing Boolean searches (e.g., how and when to truncate keywords); and (3) natural language searches and when they might be more effective (see www2.gsu.edu/~wwwerl/lta). The site's 20 self-assessment tests provide practice and explanatory feedback in both constructing and deconstructing Boolean searches. All 20 tests begin with a fact scenario. Half of the tests provide partial search requests that students must complete by typing keywords or connectors in blanks. The other 10 tests list a series of completed Boolean search requests that students must characterize from a pull-down menu of choices (e.g., "pulls too many documents" or "likely misses key authorities"). Students receive a percentage score and detailed, explanatory feedback for wrong choices. Diaz III and Larkins (2006) also provide evidence that students using the tools on this site improve their ability to write Boolean search requests and locate tax authority.

The "Marginal Tax Rates" site assists students in making economic decisions (step 5) based on their interpretation of legal text (step 4) (see www2.gsu.edu/~wwwerl/mtr). Students often have trouble understanding the economic implications of their legal research when it involves complex situations with multidimensional considerations. To develop these abilities, this site presents five lessons that teach students to model decisions and compute marginal tax rates. The first lesson introduces students to the basic concepts of statutory, effective, average, and marginal tax rates, and illustrates these ideas through several examples. The remaining lessons guide students through the calculation of marginal tax rates in situations with multiple years (which integrates present value concepts), multiple jurisdictions (either state and federal taxes or domestic and foreign taxes), multiple persons (corporations and shareholders), and more complex situations (e.g., decisions related to multiple persons over multiple years). Ten self-assessment tests, each containing six multiple-choice questions, allow students to practice computing marginal tax rates in a variety of decision-making contexts. Again, students receive explanatory feedback and percentage scores.

The last step tax professionals must complete is to communicate their research. The "M.Tx. Writing Web Site" provides guidance in structuring sentences and writing research memos, client letters, judicial briefs, and journal articles (see www2.gsu.edu/~accerl). The sentence structure lessons teach students to reduce wordiness and write more concisely, use correct punctuation, and convert passive voice to active. Although these grammatical prescripts may not seem to make much difference for an isolated sentence, when applied to entire documents, good sentence structure can improve readability and clarity. Thirty self-assessment tests provide ample opportunities for students to practice these writing skills and receive explanatory feedback. When testing for wordiness and passive voice, students receive sentences with structural problems followed by the same sentences with blanks where some words formerly appeared. By typing words in the blanks, students restructure the original sentence to reduce wordiness, or convert to active voice. The punctuation tests require students to type correct punctuation into blanks within sentences. Cleaveland and Larkins (2004, pp. 219–23) demonstrate that using these writing tools improves written communication skills. In addition to the lessons and self-assessment tests, this site includes examples of a research memo, client letters, and judicial briefs. A trouble-shooting link provides guidance for improving a tax research memo when a student receives review notes from the professor or fellow students (Newmark, Hutton, & Cruz, 2007, p. 58). The "M.Tx. Writing Web Site" won the American Taxation Association/Deloitte Teaching Innovation Award in 2004.

Table 1 summarizes the content of the aforementioned four "companion" web sites that educators can use to develop tax research skills in their students.

THE EVALUATING TAX AUTHORITY RESOURCE

To enhance students' ability to evaluate legal text (step 4 of the tax research process), I created the "Evaluating Tax Authority" web site, which can be found at www2.gsu.edu/~wwwerl/eta. This innovative research tool introduces students to legal analysis skills in the broader context of tax research. It also provides instructional materials that can help students understand, apply, and reconcile tax authority, abilities that are critical for entry-level tax professionals.

Table 1. Introduction to Tax Research Tools.

Identifying Issues

Five lessons addressing the following topics: fact and legal issues, gross income, deductions, property transfers, and additional pointers.

Four self-assessment tests (two multiple-choice and two short answer issue identification exercises).

Locating Tax Authority

Three lessons addressing basic research approaches, Boolean searches, and natural searches.

Twenty self-assessment tests using either CCH Tax Research, LEXIS, RIA CheckPoint, Tax Analysts, TaxBase, or Westlaw syntax (10 fill-in-the-blank exercises and 10 pull-down-menu selections).

Developing Conclusions and Recommendations

Five lessons addressing the following concepts: Basic tax rates, multiple tax years, multiple jurisdictions, multiple persons, and more complex situations.

Ten multiple-choice self-assessment tests.

Communicating Results

Three basic writing skill lessons addressing wordiness, punctuation, and passive voice.

Thirty fill-in-the-blank self-assessment tests covering sentence structure issues.

Four additional tax-related communication lessons with examples of a research memo, client letters, and judicial briefs

Understanding, Applying, and Reconciling Tax Authority Lessons

Existing tax research materials usually focus more on available tax law resources, rather than on how to read and decipher legal text. Similarly, traditional tax research teaching materials also often provide little to help students understand, apply, or reconcile tax authorities. Consequently, this instructional resource provides six lessons to address the common interpretation errors made by students when researching tax issues. Each lesson includes strategies, cautions, and specific examples. Consistent with the literature cited earlier, this pedagogical tool requires students to internalize more, rather than providing a step-by-step "cookbook" set of procedures. Table 2 describes each lesson, its objectives, and related content.

The first lesson illustrates the use of organizational terms in the IRC (subsection, subtitle, chapter, etc.). It warns students that failing to consider the importance of organizational terms in tax research can be disastrous, since such terms often clarify how a definition or rule should be applied, or where exceptions might be found. The lesson also explains how Treasury Regulations use organizational terms differently than the IRC, why this can be confusing, and how researchers can use this knowledge to their advantage when interpreting legal text.

Table 2. Understanding, Applying, and Reconciling Tax Authority Lessons.

Organizational Terms
Introduces students to the organizational terms needed to interpret the IRC including chapters, subchapters, and code sections. Explains how such terms are represented differently in Treasury Regulation cites.

General Rules and Exceptions
Describes the use of general rules and exceptions in statutory and regulatory provisions. Teaches students to look for exceptions rather than applying the general rule too quickly.

Defined Terms
Explains how tax law uses modifiers such as "qualified," "qualifying," or "eligible" when defining terms. Teaches students to identify words and phrases that may be defined in a particular way and provides guidance about where to look for the definitions.

Small Words and Short Phrases
Illustrates how a "small word focus" can help students deal with difficult to read IRC and Treasury Regulation sections. Helps students to think about complex sentences in abstract but simpler terms.

Measuring Language
Discusses the importance of measurement language in statutory and regulatory provisions. Addresses the need to interpret each passage in its strictest mathematical sense.

Resolving Conflicts with the Code
Explains how inconsistencies between the IRC and other tax authorities arise. Reviews the process for resolving such conflicts using information from historical footnotes.

The second lesson calls attention to a common legal construction: the use of general rules and exceptions. It teaches students to look for this construction rather than jumping to conclusions based on a general rule before making a thorough search for exceptions. Additionally, the lesson explains how to interpret exceptions to an exception.

The role of definitions in legal text is the subject of the third lesson. Students learn to identify words and phrases which the law defines elsewhere. These words and phrases often have the adjective "qualifying" preceding it. Further, they receive instruction on where to look for definitions, and how broadly or narrowly they should apply definitions.

The fourth lesson deals with the seemingly omnipresent small words and short phrases found in the tax law. Students learn to focus on these words and phrases as a means of breaking long sentences into smaller pieces. One example highlights the small words in a familiar IRC section and then encourages students to mentally recast the statutory language in abstract terms as follows:

Rule applies *if* condition 1 exists *and* condition 2 exists.

The lesson also discusses phrases that students sometimes interpret incorrectly such as "substantially all" and "to the extent."

The next lesson explains how to interpret legal text dealing with measurements. Such language often sets conditions that depend on ownership (e.g., more than 50 percent versus 50 percent or more of voting power) or time periods (e.g., 30 days versus one calendar month). The examples illustrate how similar phrases involving measurements often have different meanings.

The final lesson explains how to reconcile legal passages that appear inconsistent. Students learn to examine historical footnotes following IRC sections to determine when statutory changes occurred that created an inconsistency. Confirming that a conflict, in fact, does exist between the IRC and either an administrative ruling or judicial decision allows the researcher to follow the established hierarchical rules more confidently (e.g., the Code trumps conflicting regulations).

Self-Assessment Tests

This innovative web site also provides 10 self-assessment tests so that students can receive recurring practice. Each is contextually relevant to practice and provides timely, explanatory feedback to help students interpret legal authorities and resolve conflicts among tax law sources. To assure their accuracy, I monitor IRC changes and periodically update them. The self-assessment tests address areas familiar to most tax students. Table 3 summarizes specific IRC sections that students must consult when taking the self-assessment tests.

Each test consists of 10 multiple-choice questions for which students must consult the IRC. The questions require students to perform a variety of tasks:

- Determine whether a particular IRC section appears within a portion of the Code (e.g., Chapter 1).

Table 3. Evaluating Tax Authority Self-Assessment Tests.

Income Concepts (§§61–68)
Trade or Business Expenses (§162)
Personal and Dependency Exemptions (§§151–153)
Social Security Benefits (§86)
Compensation for Injuries and Sickness (§104)
Discharge of Indebtedness (§§108, 1017)
Capital Gains and Losses (§§1201–1223)
Basis Rules (§§1012–1016)
Charitable Contributions (§170)
Interest Deductions (§163)

- Identify and count the paragraphs within a specific IRC section.
- Locate definitions of words appearing in the IRC.
- Determine whether cites within a Regulation (e.g., paragraph (c)(5)) refer to the IRC or the Regulation.
- Identify general rules and exceptions within an IRC section.
- Determine to what portion of the IRC a particular definition applies.
- Interpret and apply legal passages with numerous small words and phrases to a fact pattern.
- Count how many conditions must be satisfied before a statutory rule applies.
- Determine when a rule within an existing Regulation disappeared from the IRC.
- Identify the year when Congress added a particular provision to the IRC.

Incorrect responses trigger explanatory feedback tailored to the incorrect answer. Students must repeat a question until they select the correct answer.

Each self-assessment test gives students a cumulative percentage grade. The grade first appears at the top of a self-assessment test after a student correctly answers the initial multiple-choice question, and changes after he/she responds correctly to each subsequent question. The grade depends on the number of incorrect answers not selected. Since multiple-choice questions have five possible answers, there are one correct and four incorrect choices. For the first question of a self-assessment test, one incorrect answer (before picking the correct choice) results in a grade of 75 percent (i.e., three incorrect answers not chosen divided by four incorrect choices in total). If the student then selects two incorrect responses on the second question, before answering it correctly, the cumulative grade drops to 63 percent (i.e., five incorrect answers not chosen divided by eight incorrect choices for the two questions combined). The cumulative score allows students to self-assess their abilities and track their progress.

Resource Implementation

The "Evaluating Tax Authority" web site includes a link to a "Class Assignment" file, which provides instructors with guidance on assigning lessons and self-assessment tests. The document instructs students to read the home page and six lessons and, using a recent copy of the IRC, complete the

10 self-assessment tests contained on the site. The directions also ask students to print the self-assessment tests and attach them to the back of an instruction sheet, which also serves as a cover page for their submission. On this cover page, students record their scores and compute an average for all 10 tests. They also are asked to provide seven-point Likert responses to three statements which evaluate student effort, perceptions on resource feedback, and the self-assessment test's value. Lastly, students record the time spent on completing the assignment.

My students use this research tool about one-third of the way through the semester after receiving class lectures on various tax law sources and completing assignments on the "M.Tx. Writing Web Site" and the "Identifying Tax Issues" web site. The course syllabus provides a hyperlink to the "Evaluating Tax Authority" site and further directs students to the "Class Assignment" directions. Students complete all assignments on their own time, which frees class time for other activities. While I do collect the assignments, I do not discuss them in class since the web site provides sufficient feedback related to any incorrect choices. Although students receive credit for completing the assignment on time, I do not assign grades based on their self-assessment test scores at this point in the semester, as I want students to focus on skill acquisition rather than grades. Additionally, basing grades on self-assessment test scores might encourage students to simply retake the self-assessment tests after determining correct answers on their initial attempts. In short, this approach allows students to acquire research skills without requiring professors to grade assignments or reallocate class time devoted to other activities or topics. Other efforts to enhance research skills, such as that noted by Duffy and Leinicke (2004, p. 145), require professorial time and some classroom activity trade-offs.

INNOVATION ASSESSMENT

Informal Feedback

According to the data provided by students on their assignment cover page, reading all lessons and taking all self-assessment tests requires 5–8 hours. Additionally, they indicate that they try to do their best on self-assessment tests (average 5.9 response on seven-point scale), nearly always find the feedback helpful (average 5.9 response on seven-point scale), and believe that completing the self-assessment tests represents a good investment of time (average 6.2 response on seven-point scale). These responses suggest that students perceive the web site as a valuable learning tool, a result consistent with positive student reactions to other web-based pedagogy, such as Abdolmohammadi, Howe, and Ryack (2003, p. 190).

Users uniformly have reacted positively to the resource. To date, no student in my class has questioned or complained about the assignments' length, difficulty, or relevance. One unsolicited, but representative e-mail from a student *not* in my class stated simply, "Your website is great! I've learned a lot!"

Another tax research instructor at my institution also uses this tool in her course. Though noting that the assignment requires significant student time, she states:

> I can lecture all day on how to read and interpret the IRC, but until the students actually have to analyze and pick apart a Code provision themselves, they don't really grasp the complexity. Students who can read a Code or regulation section and quickly zero in on exceptions, related definitions, and complicated effective dates can cut their research time significantly and achieve more accurate results. By offering a controlled set of practice exercises with feedback, we can now offer students a systematic approach to interpreting statutory language that, with practice, becomes a lifelong professional skill.

Other adopters include tax professors at Baylor University, the University of Missouri at Saint Louis, Montana State University, and the University of Northern Colorado.

Formal Assessment

To determine whether this instructional resource actually enhances learning, I collected data from two graduate tax research classes using a pre- versus post-treatment design. One class received the treatment effect, which consisted of reading the six web site lessons and taking the 10 self-assessment tests. The other class served as a control group, completing a more traditional textbook assignment involving the interpretation of authorities and reconciliation of conflicting provisions.

All students read the same textbook chapters, heard identical PowerPoint lectures from the same instructor, and met class at the same time (but different semesters). The treatment group consisted of 17 students in fall 2004, while the control group included 24 students in fall 2005. Table 4 summarizes the demographic, academic, and professional characteristics of the two groups. A mean difference test finds the control group's mean grade point average (GPA) to be greater than that of the treatment group ($p = 0.043$). To the extent that GPA reflects one's ability or motivation to

Table 4. Student Group Demographic Data.

	Treatment Group	Control Group
Basic Demographics		
Number of students	17	24
Percent females	71%	54%
Percent minority	35%	21%
Percent U.S. citizens	82%	83%
Mean age	31	29
Admission Data and Knowledge		
Mean undergraduate grade point average	3.2	3.5
Professional Experience		
Percent with professional experience	82%	92%
Mean full-time years of professional experience	3.4	3.2
Percent CPAs	12%	17%

Note: The author obtained undergraduate grade point average and minority status from actual student records. Students reported all other information directly to the author. The undergraduate grade point average of the control group exceeds that of the treatment group ($p = 0.043$). The two groups do not differ statistically on any other attributes at a p-value of 0.05.

learn, this difference, if anything, could represent a conservative bias. However, Krausz, Schiff, Schiff, and Hise (2000, p. 174) found that GPA did not significantly affect performance in an initial graduate accounting course, and the same might be expected here. Other than GPA, none of the listed attributes differ between groups at a p-value of 0.05, thus providing evidence of group similarity.

During two consecutive weeks, students used a copy of the IRC to answer 15 multiple-choice questions intended to assess their abilities to interpret and reconcile legal text. Four questions dealt with organizational terms, two involved general rules and exceptions, three contained definitions, three addressed short words and phrases, one involved measuring language, and two dealt with reconciling conflicting tax authorities. Two versions of the instruments (X and Y) contained parallel exercises of similar difficulty. The average pre-treatment scores for versions X and Y equaled 23.3 and 21.7 ($p = 0.648$), respectively, providing no evidence of dissimilarity. To minimize possible learning effects from pre- and post-treatment administrations, version X dealt with tax rules that distinguish between U.S. and foreign source income (i.e., Code §§861–865), while version Y addressed tax rules related to nonresident aliens (i.e., Code §§871–879). Using a specialized area for question content (i.e., international tax) lessened the possibility that students would be familiar with the statutory language.

Within both treatment and control groups, I randomly divided students into subgroups A and B. During the fifth class, subgroup A students completed version X, while subgroup B students completed version Y. Students believed that everyone received identical exercises, since versions X and Y were distributed based on subgroup and the two versions appeared identical. Between the fifth and sixth classes, students in the treatment group were required to use the instructional resources described in Tables 2 and 3 (i.e., received the treatment effect). Students in the control group completed textbook discussion questions and exercises from Raabe et al. (2006) dealing with interpretation and conflict resolution. During the sixth class, students in both subgroups A and B received a different exercise set than in the fifth week. For example, subgroup A students completed version Y exercises, and subgroup B students completed version X exercises.

Results

Students had 1 hour to complete instruments X and Y during the fifth and sixth weeks. The pre- and post-treatment time averaged 53 and 48 minutes, respectively. Instructions to both X and Y exercise sets defined "scores" as four times the number of correct answers minus the number of wrong answers. Omitted questions did not affect scores. Thus, 60 was the maximum possible score (15 questions times four).

To encourage best performance, instructions also informed students that whoever scored in the top (middle) third of the class would receive four (two) bonus points on the course's mid-term exam. Among participants, overall pre-treatment scores average 22.9 and 22.1 for the control and treatment groups, respectively. Overall post-treatment scores within the control and treatment groups average 28.4 and 35.9, respectively. Measuring "improvement" as the difference between post- and pre-treatment scores, the 13.8 average improvement of the treatment group exceeds the 5.5 average improvement of the control group ($p = 0.017$).

Table 5 disaggregates the overall improvement scores into the target six areas addressed by this teaching resource. Results in Panel A suggest at least marginal improvement in treatment group students in five of six areas: organizational terms ($p<0.001$), general rules and exceptions ($p = 0.015$), definitions ($p = 0.055$), measuring language ($p = 0.044$), and reconciling conflicts ($p = 0.036$). Since these pre- versus post-results occurred before students completed any major research assignments in the course, practice received elsewhere in the tax research class did not

Table 5. Standardized Scores for Treatment Results.

	Average Standardized Scores			
	Post-treatment	Pre-treatment	Improvement	*p*-value
PANEL A				
Treatment Group (n = 17)				
Organizational terms	2.85	1.01	1.84	0.000
General rules, exceptions	1.62	0.41	1.21	0.015
Defined terms	2.92	2.47	0.45	0.055
Small words and phrases	1.57	1.84	−0.27	n.s.
Measuring language	1.41	0.00	1.41	0.044
Reconciling conflicts	3.21	2.12	1.09	0.036
Control Group (n = 24)				
Organizational terms	1.79	0.85	0.94	0.003
General rules, exceptions	0.92	1.04	−0.12	n.s.
Defined terms	2.78	2.17	0.61	0.005
Small words and phrases	1.19	2.00	−0.81	n.s.
Measuring language	1.37	0.08	1.29	0.091
Reconciling conflicts	3.06	2.40	0.66	0.012
	Average Post-Treatment Standardized Scores			
	Treatment group	Control group	Difference	*p*-value
PANEL B				
Organizational terms	2.85	1.79	1.06	0.023
General rules, exceptions	1.62	0.92	0.70	n.s.
Defined terms	2.92	2.78	0.14	n.s.
Small words and phrases	1.57	1.19	0.38	0.041
Measuring language	1.41	1.37	0.04	n.s.
Reconciling conflicts	3.21	3.06	0.15	n.s.

n.s., Not statistically significant at the .10 level.
Note: To standardize across areas, I divided post- and pre-treatment measures by the number of questions dealing with that specific area. For example, on the four questions covering "organizational terms," the maximum possible score equaled 16 (i.e., four questions times four points for a correct answer). The treatment group averaged 11.412 and 4.059 on post- and pre-treatment administrations, respectively, each of which I divided by four to obtain the standardized scores of 2.85 and 1.01 above. I derived all other measures similarly. Improvement in each area equals the difference between post- and pre-treatment scores.

contribute to the improvements. While these findings suggest that the web site tools improve students' abilities to interpret and reconcile legal text, they provide no evidence that the teaching tools improve learning better than a more traditional approach. In fact, the control group showed at least marginally improved performance in four areas: organizational terms ($p = 0.003$), definitions ($p = 0.005$), measuring language ($p = 0.091$), and reconciling conflicts ($p = 0.012$). Based on these results, a more traditional approach also improves learning, though the control group showed no significant gains in the category of general rules and exceptions.

Panel A of Table 5 indicates that the directional sign of the difference in post- and pre-treatment scores is consistent with the instructional tools (i.e., the treatment effect) enhancing learning more than a traditional approach (i.e., the control group activity) in five of six areas. Only for the third area involving "defined terms" the sign is inconsistent. The difference in scores for this area is 0.45 for the treatment group, but greater for the control group at 0.61, contrary to expectations.

However, the more appropriate comparisons are those between post-treatment control and treatment groups in Panel B. In two areas, "organizational terms" ($p = 0.023$) and "general rules and exceptions" ($p = 0.041$), the improvement in scores between treatment and control groups is statistically significant. The lessons and self-assessment tests seem to be particularly beneficial in teaching students about organizational terms and the statutory construction involving general rules and exceptions. While a more traditional approach may be just as effective in developing the other four evaluative skills in students, the lack of statistical significance may be due to several limitations.

Limitations

This resource's assessment was limited by four factors: sample size, graduate student subject pool, evaluative method, and the control group task. First, the small sample size reduced the power of testing. Also, given that graduate tax students comprised all of the subject pool, the results might not be applicable to other populations (e.g., law or undergraduate accounting students).

Next, the web site's use of multiple-choice questions in self-assessment tests as part of the treatment effect, differed from the more open-ended textbook questions that the control group received. It is possible that treatment group students performed differently on post-treatment exercises because of their prior exposure to multiple-choice questions on the web site, and the fact that I wrote questions for both the web site and post-treatment exercises. However, it should be noted that control group students also were exposed to multiple-choice questions that I wrote in the pre-treatment phase.

Finally, the control group's task represented one of several that I might have assigned. I could have selected discussion questions and exercises from a different tax research text, or a different set of end-of-chapter problems from the same text. Alternatively, to examine more closely the benefits of computer-assisted learning, the assignment might have included the same questions appearing in the self-assessment tests on the web site even though administered as a "pencil-and-paper" task. Also, students in the control group could have received verbal in-class answers or written solutions through a handout or access to the instructor's manual after completing their assignment. In short, I could have structured the control group's task differently.

CONCLUSION

The ability to interpret and reconcile legal authority is an essential skill for students learning to conduct tax research. Many students struggle to understand legal text and often do not proceed correctly or confidently when confronted with possible conflicts between tax authorities. The "Evaluating Tax Authority" instructional web site provides strategic guidance, repeated contextual practice, and immediate, explanatory feedback to aid students in developing these important skills. Formal assessment results suggest that students using the instructional tool improved more than a traditional textbook group, especially for interpretation issues involving "organizational terms" and "general rules and exceptions." In addition, informal student feedback through an online survey indicates that they perceive the instructional tool to be helpful.

ACKNOWLEDGMENTS

The author gratefully acknowledges a Faculty Development Summer Grant received from the Robinson College of Business at GSU to develop the educational web site used in this study. This teaching tool received the American Accounting Association's Innovation in Accounting Education Award in 2006 for which the author thanks members of the Award Committee for their work and Ernst & Young for its support of accounting education. The author also appreciates the comments and suggestions of two anonymous reviewers and my editor, Anthony H. Catanach Jr.

REFERENCES

Abdolmohammadi, M., Howe, M., & Ryack, K. (2003). Students' perceptions of learning in a web-assisted financial statement analysis course. *Advances in Accounting Education: Teaching and Curriculum Innovations*, *5*, 181–197.

American Institute of Certified Public Accountants (AICPA). (1999a). *AICPA core competency framework for entry into the accounting profession* (http://www.aicpa.org/edu/corecomp.htm). New York, NY: AICPA.

American Institute of Certified Public Accountants (AICPA). (1999b). *Model Tax Curriculum* (http://ceae.aicpa.org/Resources/Education+and+Curriculum+Development/Model+Tax+Curriculum/). New York, NY: AICPA.

Bonner, S. E., & Walker, P. L. (1994). The effects of instruction and experience on the acquisition of auditing knowledge. *Accounting Review*, *69*(1), 157–178.

Brown, J. S., Collins, A., & Duguid, P. (1989). Situated cognition and the culture of learning. *Educational Researcher*, *18*(1), 32–42.

Cleaveland, M. C., & Larkins, E. R. (2004). Web-based practice and feedback improve tax students' written communication skills. *Journal of Accounting Education*, *22*, 211–228.

Diaz III, J., & Larkins, E. R. (2006). Improving the effectiveness and efficiency of Boolean searches for relevant tax authority. *Journal of Legal Tax Research*, *4*, 135–150.

Duffy, W. A., & Leinicke, L. M. (2004). Using the financial accounting research system to develop a professional research competency in intermediate financial accounting. *Advances in Accounting Education: Teaching and Curriculum Innovations*, *6*, 133–154.

Ericsson, K. A. (1996). The acquisition of expert performance: An introduction to some of the issues. In: K. A. Ericsson (Ed.), *The road to excellence: The acquisition of expert performance in the arts and sciences, sports, and games* (pp. 1–50). Mahwah, NJ: Lawrence Erlbaum Associates.

Krausz, J., Schiff, A., Schiff, J., & Hise, J. V. (2000). The impact of GMAT scores and undergraduate GPAs on placement and performance in graduate accounting classes: A replication and extension. *Advances in Accounting Education: Teaching and Curriculum Innovations*, *3*, 169–178.

Larkins, E. R. (2005). Developing legal tax research skills. *Journal of Legal Tax Research*, *3*, 94–96.

Lou, Y., Dedic, H., & Rosenfield, S. (2003). A feedback model and successful e-learning. In: S. Naidu (Ed.), *Learning & teaching with technology: Principles and practices* (pp. 249–259). London: Kogan Page.

Newell, A., & Simon, H. H. (1972). *Human problem solving*. Englewood Cliffs, NJ: Prentice Hall.

Newmark, R. I., Hutton, M. R., & Cruz, C. A. (2007). Using a researcher–reviewer pedagogy to teach tax research. *Advances in Accounting Education: Teaching and Curriculum Innovations*, *8*, 53–77.

Raabe, W. A., Whittenburg, G. E., Sanders, D. L., & Bost, J. C. (2006). *Federal tax research* (7th ed). Mason, OH: Thomson South-Western.

Sims, R. (2003). Interactivity and feedback as determinants of engagement and meaning in e-learning environments. In: S. Naidu (Ed.), *Learning & teaching with technology: Principles and practices* (pp. 261–275). London: Kogan Page.

Wood, R. E., Atkins, P., & Tabernero, C. (2000). Self-efficacy and strategy on complex tasks. *Applied Psychology: An International Review*, *49*(3), 430–446.

A NEW APPROACH TO IMPROVING AND EVALUATING STUDENT WORKPLACE WRITING SKILLS

Susan A. Lynn and Thomas E. Vermeer

ABSTRACT

Over the last twenty years, many studies have examined the impact of structured writing programs on improving accounting students' writing skills. In this chapter, we extend this research by using writing assignments that are representative of the workplace writing experiences that students encounter in their professional careers, by developing an evaluation instrument to assess the effectiveness of structured writing programs, and by using business advisory board members to evaluate improvement in students' writing. Our results suggest that our new approach to designing writing assignments representative of workplace writing helps students improve their writing skills. Our business advisory board members' ratings indicate that the overall quality of the students' writing improved over two semesters of completing a series of workplace writing assignments. Specifically, our structured writing program improved students' business writing skills in the areas of organization (paragraph unity, layout, and conclusion) and style and tone (conciseness and word choice). Students also improved in their ability to explain technical aspects of accounting work and in certain aspects of spelling, punctuation, and grammar. The results and tools provided in this study should assist other programs in either implementing or improving a structured writing program.

Advances in Accounting Education: Teaching and Curriculum Innovations, Volume 9, 115–150

ISSN: 1085-4622/doi:10.1016/S1085-4622(08)09006-8

Over the past two decades, beginning with the recommendations of the Bedford Commission (American Accounting Association, 1986) and the recommendations of the then Big 8 accounting firms (*Perspectives on Education*, 1989), there has been considerable discussion about the importance of written communication skills for accounting professionals and about the weaknesses of recent accounting graduates in this area. These discussions have involved not only faculty but stakeholder groups such as recent graduates, employers, and accrediting agencies. Surveys of accounting professionals indicate that accounting professionals write frequently in their jobs, that they believe writing skills are very important for success in their current positions, and that new accounting hires believe their level of writing skills is deficient (Christensen & Rees, 2002, pp. 4–6; Stowers & White, 1999, pp. 28, 32; Ulrich, Michenzi, & Blouch, 2003, pp. 131–132). AACSB International – The Association to Advance Collegiate Schools of Business (AACSB, 2006, p. 15) also continues to emphasize communication abilities as part of the learning experience in an undergraduate business degree program. As a result, many business schools have competency in written communication skills as a learning goal of their undergraduate business programs.

Employers consistently rank written communication skills among the most important skills required of new hires. Employers consider writing to be a "threshold skill" for hiring and promotion (National Commission on Writing, 2004, pp. 3, 8) and "an essential skill for the many" rather than "a frill for the few" (National Commission on Writing, 2006, p. 49). A recent survey of mid-career professionals found that over 90% consider the "need to write effectively" to be "of great importance" in their daily work (National Commission on Writing, 2006, p. 49).

Nevertheless, employers repeatedly complain about the weak writing skills of college graduates (National Commission on Writing, 2004, pp. 13–14; Stowers & White, 1999, pp. 28–29) – a deficiency that Chase (1991, p. 31) termed "corporate illiteracy." A Conference Board study of workforce readiness (Conference Board, 2006, pp. 20, 38) found that 93% of the employers surveyed considered written communication skills to be "very important" for four-year college graduates but that over a quarter of employers (28%) found written communication skills to be a "deficiency" among four-year college graduates. In a survey of members of several professional accounting organizations about the communication abilities of entry-level accountants, Christensen and Rees (2002, p. 6) found that employers were least satisfied with the writing skills of recent college graduates.

Although educators have recognized the importance of written communication skills, Watson, Apostolou, Hassell, and Webber (2003, pp. 287–288) discuss the lack of recent empirical evidence about the development of students' core competencies such as written communication skills. Rebele (2002, p. 22) notes that accounting educators need new approaches for improving students' writing skills. In this chapter, we develop a structured writing program for undergraduate accounting students that extends prior research. Specifically, we: (1) create writing assignments that are representative of the workplace, (2) provide an evaluation instrument to measure workplace writing skills, (3) illustrate how business advisory board professionals can evaluate the success of a structured writing program, and (4) assess whether our program improves students' workplace writing skills.

The next sections: (1) review prior research about incorporating writing into accounting curricula and (2) discuss our research questions. The remaining sections explain the design of our writing improvement program, present the research results, and discuss the conclusions and limitations of the study.

PRIOR RESEARCH-STRUCTURED WRITING PROGRAMS IN ACCOUNTING CLASSES

DeLespinasse (1985) examined the effectiveness of a letter writing assignment in the accounting program at Adrian College. Students prepared formal business letters in a variety of situations to communicate answers to technical questions. The assignments were modifications of problems in the students' Intermediate Accounting textbook. The instructor graded the letters for technical correctness of accounting as well as the ability to communicate without using technical jargon. DeLespinasse (1985, p. 197) did not objectively measure writing improvement but believed that preparing formal business letters improved students' writing skills.

Stout, Sumutka, and Wygal (1991) examined the impact of using both formal (term paper) and informal ("freewrites") writing assignments on student examination scores and student evaluations of the course and the instructor. Students in Principles of Auditing and Fundamentals of Federal Taxation at Rider College and Villanova University answered theoretical questions on key concepts covered in class (Stout et al., 1991, pp. 128–130). The authors examined the relationship between writing activities and exam performance to assess writing improvement. They found some beneficial impact of writing on course knowledge and instructor evaluation scores for the evening classes (Stout et al., 1991, p. 135).

Mohrweis (1991) examined improvement in student writing skills in two upper-level accounting courses. Students in Intermediate Accounting and Auditing, assuming roles such as audit partner and financial vice-president, wrote three memos about technical accounting and auditing topics addressed to a variety of audiences (e.g., controller, board of directors) (pp. 312–313). Students in sections of each course that did not use the writing assignments served as the control groups. The author measured improvement in student writing using a sample of multiple-choice questions from the GMAT skills exam in Intermediate Accounting and a holistically scored in-class writing quiz in Auditing (pp. 313–314, 319–320). Mohrweis (1991, pp. 316–317, 320–321) found the writing program improved student writing in both Intermediate Accounting and Auditing based on administering the respective instruments at the beginning and end of the semester.

McIsaac and Sepe (1996) discuss the development of a writing program at Santa Clara University. The program began with a transition workshop in Intermediate Accounting I in which the accounting instructor, an English Department consultant, and accounting practitioners collaborated to help students become familiar with differences between classroom writing and workplace writing and the importance of writing for success in the accounting profession. The accounting instructor introduced students to a variety of workplace writing samples as well as to an example of a poorly written workplace document. The students completed a memo assignment related to a financial accounting topic. Students peer-graded the assignments using a grading guide that emphasized technical accounting correctness as well as organization and grammatical correctness. The authors did not provide any empirical evidence related to the success of their program.

Riordan, Riordan, and Sullivan (2000) examined whether a writing program in three junior-level accounting courses improved the written communication skills of accounting students at James Madison University. Students completed a variety of writing assignments including a business letter and a memorandum that were graded by both an accounting instructor and a writing consultant (pp. 53–54). The authors evaluated the success of their program by having students correct a business letter containing twenty-six errors in grammar, syntax, and organization. The authors found that their structured writing program significantly improved the students' ability to recognize weaknesses in grammar, syntax, and organization (pp. 54–55).

Christ (2002, p. 41) discusses the use of an unstructured Annual Report Project "to develop students' analytical, problem solving, and communication skills" in an Intermediate Accounting course at Valparaiso University. The author (2002, pp. 50–51) assigned "a large portion of the students' grade" to how students presented and explained their annual report analysis. She (2002, p. 52) does not present any objective measure of student writing skills other than student comments that "it was a good learning experience."

Ashbaugh, Johnstone, and Warfield (2002) compared the writing skills of accounting students who participated in a writing improvement program at the University of Wisconsin-Madison with the writing skills of other accounting students who did not participate. Students in the writing improvement program completed eight writing assignments over a two-year period involving accounting research and the preparation of a report or memorandum (pp. 125–126). A Ph.D. student in the English or Journalism Department and the course instructor or an Accounting Department teaching assistant graded the assignments. The Ph.D. student directly assessed students' written responses to the question "What does it mean to be a business professional?" The evaluation instrument also included an indirect multiple-choice question assessment of grammar and punctuation (pp. 129–130). The authors found that accounting students who participated in the writing improvement program experienced a greater improvement in their writing skills than accounting students who did not participate (pp. 138–139).

Cleaveland and Larkins (2004) used web-based lessons and self-tests to help students improve three sentence structure issues (passive voice, punctuation, and wordiness) in graduate tax research classes at Georgia State University. The authors used a pre–post design with both control and treatment groups and measured improvement in student writing using quizzes requiring students to identify and correct errors related to each of the above sentence structure issues. They concluded that their approach improved students' writing skills (pp. 220–222).

Reinstein and Houston (2004) measured improvement in the readability of student writing in three accounting courses at Wayne State University. Students completed three term paper assignments and received instruction in the Securities and Exchange Commission (SEC)'s "Plain English" guidelines. Using a computerized Readability Calculation, the authors concluded that instruction in the SEC guidelines improved students' writing skills (p. 55).

Stout and DaCrema (2004) discuss the use of a "writing intervention" to help students deal with the grammatical problem of faulty modifiers.

Instructors of upper-level accounting classes and MBA managerial accounting classes at Villanova University and Youngstown State University used a handout and an in-class discussion of the problem of faulty modifiers. Using both direct (three diagnostic tests) and indirect (students' questionnaire) measures in a pre-test/post-test design, Stout and DaCrema (2004, p. 310) concluded that their approach had a positive effect on the writing skills of students with respect to the problem of faulty modifiers.

Stout and DaCrema (2005) also developed a one-class writing improvement module for an MBA managerial accounting class addressing various grammatical and punctuation errors. Using student perceptions of the quality, value, and planned use of the resource, Stout and DaCrema (2005, p. 314) concluded that the results support "the use of the resource by other accounting faculties."

As discussed earlier, many researchers have examined the impact of writing programs on improving accounting students' writing. In these studies, students have primarily completed structured assignments that accounting faculty have evaluated. Rebele (2002) calls for new approaches to improve students' writing skills. In this study, we respond to this call by developing writing assignments that are representative of workplace writing experiences and by using business advisory board members to evaluate the improvement in students' writing. These extensions should provide faculty additional options to use in developing a new writing program or in revising a current program.

DEVELOPMENT OF RESEARCH QUESTIONS

In order to be effective in helping students develop workplace writing skills, writing experts suggest that assignments should be "relevant to real world situations" (Business-Higher Education Forum, 1999, p. 7) and allow students "to communicate to a real audience" (National Writing Project and Nagin, 2006, p. 48). Catanach and Golen (1997, p. 53) emphasize that accounting educators should design assignments so that students are "writing as professionals within a specific accounting context" and learn to consider the written communication needs of users of accounting information. Many writing improvement programs emphasize academic rather than workplace writing and do not incorporate a real-world perspective. Singh-Gupta and Troutt-Ervin (1997, pp. 6–8) noted that these programs should present students with writing assignments that are more representative of what newly recruited graduates will do in their first jobs. Beaufort (1998, p. 180) noted that most workplace writing involves "greater complexity" in issues of audience and purpose than academic writing where students write to a "single audience," the teacher, for the purpose of demonstrating knowledge. Students normally address academic writing to "professors who know more about the subject matter than the writer." However, after college, students will have to write to "audiences less informed on the topic than the writer" (Boyer Commission, 1998, p. 24).

Although entry-level employees predominately write business memos in their jobs (National Commission on Writing, 2004, pp. 11–12; Northy, 1990, p. 481; Singh-Gupta & Troutt-Ervin, 1997, p. 5), May and May (1989, p. 242) found that the term paper was the type of written communication assignment used in 82% of undergraduate courses and 92% of graduate courses. Many "workplace" writing assignments included in academic writing programs focus on tasks not usually performed by entry-level employees and ask students to make decisions as Chief Executive Officers and Chief Financial Officers (Thomas, 1994, p. 13). In addition, many academic writing assignments are far too simplistic and fail to address the power relationships between the parties and the politics inherent in all writing situations (Thomas, 1994, p. 12). In order to enhance the development of student workplace writing skills, students should complete assignments that require them to "consider their audience" and "the complexities of their writing context" (Schneider & Andre, 2005, p. 211). Rebele (2002, p. 21) indicates that more "effort" needs to be put into designing writing assignments "in such a way that they *logically could* develop the identified competency." The present study extends prior research and addresses the following research question.

> **Research Question 1.** Can accounting faculty design writing assignments in upper division accounting classes with a role, audience, and purpose that are representative of the types of writing students will experience in their first professional positions after graduation?

In order to be effective in developing workplace writing skills, assessment of these skills needs to be "authentic" (National Commission on Writing, 2006, p. 42) and representative of the types of writing skills considered important in the workplace. Prior studies usually have measured writing improvement using exam grades or multiple-choice assessments of student perceptions of writing quality. Some prior studies have used evaluation instruments that measure improvement in specific skills. However, these studies have measured improvement in skills such as content, technical correctness, organization, grammar, and punctuation, rather than workplace writing skills such as issues of style and appropriateness for a specific audience.

Another reason for developing an assessment instrument (rubric) to measure workplace writing skills is that many business school faculty believe they do not have enough time to teach both professional writing skills and field-specific course content (Epstein, 1999, p. 37). Business school faculty consider themselves ineffective teachers of writing (Plutsky & Wilson, 2001, pp. 35–37). Faculty are not comfortable in teaching students the writing process, do not feel competent in grading writing, and base their evaluation of student writing on limited criteria that often do not include "students' mastery of a business writing style" (Plutsky & Wilson, 2001, p. 39). Development of a workplace writing skills rubric could assist faculty in evaluating student writing using criteria that are important in the workplace. Business school faculty can use the results of this course-embedded assessment to meet the assessment needs of an individual course as well as assurance of a written communication learning goal for AACSB reaccredidation (AACSB, 2006, pp. 63–64). The present study extends prior research and addresses the following research question.

> **Research Question 2.** Which factors should faculty include in an evaluation instrument to measure students' workplace writing skills?

Another aspect related to authentic assessment of student workplace writing skills is that in prior research, accounting academics, either alone or in collaboration with academic writing faculty, have evaluated the improvement in student writing. However, studies that have used both faculty and business professionals to evaluate student writing have found that business professionals use different criteria to evaluate writing than academics (Amare & Brammer, 2005, p. 188; Campbell, Brammer, & Ervin, 1999, pp. 82–83; Seshadri & Theye, 2000, p. 20). Also, as Catanach and Golen (1996, pp. 112–113) note, users of accounting information are an important party in the communication process and should evaluate the writing skills of accountants. AACSB also suggests that schools should use "external constituencies" such as employers and business advisory boards to evaluate the learning goals of the school "from the perspective of persons who must put knowledge into practice on a daily basis." These evaluations can give "perspectives ... that will be unavailable if the faculty operates alone" (AACSB, 2006, p. 62). The present study extends prior research and addresses the following research question.

Research Question 3. How can accounting faculty include business advisory board professionals in evaluating the success of a structured workplace writing program?

It is imperative that we test our new approach to improving and evaluating students' workplace writing skills. These findings can validate the approach as well as provide justification for future use of this new approach. The present study uses an evaluation instrument to determine whether workplace writing assignments improved students' writing skills. The present study extends prior research and addresses the following research question.

Research Question 4. In which areas will students' writing skills improve after the use of a year-long structured workplace writing program?

The next section explains the design of our writing improvement program, which includes workplace writing assignments, an evaluation instrument that measures workplace writing skills, and assessment of improvement in writing skills by business advisory board members. The remaining sections present the results and the conclusions and limitations of the study.

THE DESIGN OF THE WRITING IMPROVEMENT PROGRAM

The workplace writing improvement program was adopted at the University of Baltimore, an urban public university on the East Coast. The university has a primarily non-traditional student population, many of whom have some professional business experience. Many are first-generation college students.

At our university, students study Intermediate Accounting in a three-semester format, using the Spiceland, Sepe, and Tomassini (2004) Intermediate Accounting textbook. The instructor included the program as part of the course requirements in Intermediate Accounting I and II over a two-year academic period. Students completed six business memos on a variety of financial accounting topics during each two-semester academic year. The writing assignments represented 15% of the students' course grade. Appendices A and B present the topics covered in Intermediate Accounting I and II and the topics covered in the writing assignments. Students completed writing assignments after the instructor had covered the topics in the class.

The instructor designed the assignments so that they had a role, audience, and purpose representative of workplace writing rather than academic writing. Academic writing assignments typically place students in the role of a student writing to an instructor who is more knowledgeable than the student about the subject being discussed. In contrast, our assignments placed the student in the role of an entry-level staff accountant at a CPA firm, writing to a non-accountant client who was not knowledgeable about the accounting issue being discussed. Students answered the client's question and provided a solution to the client's problem. This perspective allowed students to adopt a role they are likely to experience in their first professional positions. The instructor presented the role, audience, and purpose of the assignment to the student in the body of the actual assignment rather than listing them as requirements at the end of the assignment. The instructor used this design in order to increase the realism of the assignments and to distinguish them from the academic writing assignments with which the students were familiar.

In Intermediate I, the topic of the first memo was adjustments made to convert a client's records from cash-basis to accrual-basis accounting. The topic of the second memo was revenue realization issues for the client in the first memo. The third memo addressed methods of accounting for bad debt expense. In this assignment, students had to create a spreadsheet illustration which they discussed in their memos.

In Intermediate II, the topic of the first memo was classifying expenditures as capital or revenue for operational assets. The topic of the second memo was the effective interest method for long-term debt. In this assignment, students also created a spreadsheet illustrating the difference between accounting for debt using the stated rate and the effective rate and discussed the spreadsheet in their memos. The topic of the third memo in Intermediate II was the same as the topic as the first memo in Intermediate I – adjustments made to convert a client's records from cash-basis to accrual-basis accounting.

We used the first memo assignment in Intermediate I and the third memo assignment in Intermediate II to evaluate the success of our writing program. These assignments asked students to explain adjustments made to convert a client's financial records from cash-basis accounting to accrual-basis accounting. This task is representative of the type of assignment students are likely to complete early in their professional careers. Students not only had to provide the correct technical accounting information (as they would in a typical academic writing assignment) but also had to address the memo to a small business owner who may not understand accounting jargon. The client was a non-accountant frustrated with understanding the differences between cash-basis and accrual-basis accounting. Students had to provide correct information to the client while ensuring that they did not alienate the client. Thus, they had to consider the effect of writing to a non-accounting audience (rather than to a professor). Students needed to consider issues of tone and appropriateness for the reader, issues important in workplace writing, but not the academic writing with which they were familiar.

At the beginning of each semester, the instructor distributed an example of a poorly written workplace memo. Students critiqued the memo and learned to recognize pitfalls they should avoid in their own writing. The instructor graded the writing assignments. When the instructor returned the assignments, she distributed examples from the students' memos that represented "good" workplace writing and discussed areas in which the students needed to improve their writing.

At the end of the second year, we asked members of the university's business advisory board to evaluate the students' writing to determine whether we were successful in meeting our objective of improving our students' workplace writing skills. We wanted to use the results of the advisory board's evaluation in the spirit of continuous improvement of our writing program. We assessed the effectiveness of our writing program by comparing the writing quality of the first memo students completed in Intermediate Accounting I with the writing quality of a memo students completed on a similar topic at the end of Intermediate Accounting II. (See Appendices C and D for assignments.) In the pre-test analysis, thirty-five students completed the memo in Appendix C in Intermediate Accounting I. This was the first business memo that students completed over two semesters of Intermediate Accounting. In the post-test analysis, twenty-five students completed the memo in Appendix D in Intermediate Accounting II. This was the last business memo that students completed in the second semester of Intermediate Accounting.

Thirty-seven members of the business school advisory board evaluated the students' memos. Twenty-two advisory board members evaluated pre-test memos and fifteen advisory board members evaluated post-test memos. Because the pre-test and post-test assignments used different scenarios, each business advisory board member either reviewed three pre-test memos or three post-test memos. The advisory board members saw only the memo assignment that they reviewed and were not aware of the student's grade on the assignment. Advisory board members were not involved in grading the memos during the semester. Their ratings were not used as part of the students' grades. Since each business school advisory board member evaluated three memos, we received 111 evaluation instruments. We received 66 evaluations of pre-test memos and 45 evaluations of post-test memos.

The instructions asked the business advisory board members to first read the assignment (Appendix C or D) to become familiar with its requirements. The business advisory board members then read each student's memo individually and completed an evaluation instrument after reading each memo. The instructions did not indicate whether the memos assigned for review were pre-test memos or post-test memos.

We developed the evaluation instrument that the advisory board members used to assess improvement in our students' writing. The evaluation instrument included scales evaluating the memo's organization, style and tone, and spelling, punctuation, and grammar (see Appendix E for the evaluation instrument). It also included scales evaluating how well the memo met the requirements of the assignment. Within each section, there were several measures. We adapted the individual scales from *Revising Professional Writing in Science and Technology, Business, and the Social Sciences* (Riley, Campbell, Manning, & Parker, 1999) to meet the goals of our structured writing improvement program. Scales in the organization and style and tone sections included definitions of the item being measured in order to improve the reliability of the evaluation instrument. We also included an overall holistic evaluation question adapted from Campbell et al. (1999, p. 81). Varner and Pomerenke (1998, pp. 83–85) note that an evaluation instrument should be adapted to ensure that the assessment fits local conditions.

Business advisory board members also completed background questionnaires. The questionnaire included questions regarding their academic and professional experience, their experience in writing business memos and letters, their familiarity with the financial accounting issues included in the memo, their opinion of how well the assignment reflected workplace writing, and their opinion of the appropriateness of the memo and of the evaluation instrument.

We pilot tested the instrument with business school faculty members. Originally, we intended that each business advisory board member would review four memos. Pilot study faculty members suggested that reviewing four memos was too time consuming and would reduce our response rate. Based on their recommendations, we reduced the number of memos reviewed by advisory board members to three. Besides this issue, the faculty members provided positive feedback regarding our rubric and some indicated that they planned to use our instrument in their courses.

Table 1 presents background information about the business advisory board members who participated in the evaluation process for years of total work experience, years of accounting-related work experience, education, frequency of writing business memos and letters, and number of credit and non-credit classes taken to improve general writing skills. Advisory board members had a mean of 27.7 years of total work experience (range from 7.5 to 43 years) and 16.1 years of accounting-related work experience (range of 2 to 42 years for those advisory board members with accounting-related work experience). Eighteen (49%) had masters or doctoral degrees. Thirty-five advisory board members (95%) indicated that they wrote a business memo on a daily or weekly basis.

Since the pre-test and post-test assignments were different, we asked each business advisory board member to review either three pre-test memos or three post-test memos. We randomly assigned individual student memos to

Table 1. Background of Advisory Board Members ($N = 37$).

Work experience	Mean =	27.7 years
Accounting-related work experience	Mean =	16.1 years
Highest degree earned (number of board members)	High school/associates-	3
	Bachelor's	16
	Master's	12
	Doctoral	6
Frequency of writing business memo or email (number of board members)	Daily	25
	Weekly	10
	Monthly	2
Frequency of writing business letter (number of board members)	Daily	9
	Weekly	24
	Monthly	2
	Yearly/Infrequently	2
Number of credit classes to improve writing skills (number of board members)	No classes	17
	One class	5
	Two classes	4
	Three classes	5
	Four classes	4
	Five to seven classes	2
Number of non-credit classes to improve writing skills (number of board members)	No classes	30
	One class	3
	Two classes	2
	Three classes	2

each business advisory board member. To further ensure that there were no systematic differences between the business advisory board members who reviewed the pre-test and post-test memos, we analyzed the demographic information obtained from the background questionnaires to determine if any statistically significant differences existed between the two groups of reviewers. We performed parametric independent sample t-tests for variables with normal distributions and non-parametric χ^2 tests for variables with non-normal distributions (Kennedy, 1994, p. 71). These tests indicated that there was no difference, at a p-value of 0.10 or less, between the business advisory board members who reviewed the pre-test and post-test memos for any of the demographic variables in Table 1 and, thus, no apparent systematic differences between the two groups of reviewers.

Although we designed the pre-test and post-test assignments to be comparable (in terms of topic, role, audience, and purpose), we evaluated possible differences in the difficulty of the two assignments using responses from two additional items on the background questionnaires. As part of the review process, the business advisory board members rated how representative the assignments were of workplace writing and indicated the average length of time they spent in reviewing each memo. There was no statistically significant difference, at a p-value of 0.10 or less, between the ratings of how representative the assignments were of workplace writing for pre-test and post-test memos (mean of 7.2 and 7.6, respectively, on a ten-point scale where 10 = Very Representative and 1 = Not Representative at All). Consistent with these findings, there was also no statistically significant difference, at a p-value of 0.10 or less, between the average lengths of time spent in reviewing the pre-test and post-test memos (mean of 11.89 min and 11.11 min, respectively).

Results

This section presents our results and discusses the four research questions presented earlier.

> **Research Question 1.** Can accounting faculty design writing assignments in upper division accounting classes with a role, audience, and purpose that are representative of the types of writing students will experience in their first professional positions after graduation?

The business advisory board members who evaluated our students' writing had "real world" experience averaging over 27 years, with over

16 years of accounting experience. Most of them regularly wrote memos to clients and were familiar with the financial accounting issues included in the memo. On a ten-point scale (10 = Very Familiar; 1 = Not Familiar at All), 86% of the business advisory board members rated their familiarity with the financial accounting issues included in the memos as six or above. The board also believed that the assignment was representative of workplace writing. On a ten-point scale (10 = Very Representative; 1 = Not Representative at All), 72% rated how representative the assignment was of workplace writing as six or above. We also included an open-ended question asking advisory board members how the assignment could be changed to better represent workplace writing. There were no major suggestions for changing the assignment and many respondents indicated that they believed that the assignment was a "reasonable attempt at workplace correspondence." These results suggest that we were successful in developing assignments that were representative of the types of workplace writing performed by recent accounting graduates.

> **Research Question 2.** Which factors should faculty include in an evaluation instrument to measure students' workplace writing skills?

Our evaluation instrument included both individual scales measuring various aspects of workplace writing skills as well as an overall holistic evaluation of the memo's quality. We adapted our instrument from Riley et al. (1999) and Campbell et al. (1999). We pilot-tested it with business faculty. We also asked business advisory board members to evaluate how our evaluation instrument could be changed to improve its effectiveness in evaluating a student's workplace writing skills. There were no major suggestions for changing the instrument. Several respondents indicated that they believed that the evaluation instrument was "very effective." These results suggest that we were successful in developing an evaluation instrument to measure students' workplace writing skills.

> **Research Question 3.** How can accounting faculty include business advisory board professionals in evaluating the success of a structured workplace writing program?

Our results indicate that business advisory board members can help in evaluating whether students are meeting a university's learning goals. Ninety percent of the advisory board members whom we contacted returned evaluations of our students' writing. Their extensive "real world" experience was valuable in helping us evaluate whether our year-long program was successful in improving our students' workplace writing skills and in meeting AACSB's (2006, pp. 62–63) suggestion that external stakeholders provide information about critical skills and knowledge required of business school graduates. The business advisory board's evaluation assisted us in answering our last research question.

Research Question 4. In which areas will students' writing skills improve after the use of a year-long structured workplace writing program?

As mentioned earlier, the business advisory board members used the evaluation instrument in Appendix E to evaluate each student's memo. To test whether our structured writing program improved students' writing skills, we used parametric independent sample *t*-tests to compare the ratings of the pre-test memos by advisory board members with their ratings of the post-test memos. We also used non-parametric Mann–Whitney U tests to test these differences. The non-parametric results were consistent with those of the parametric *t*-tests. We discuss the parametric *t*-test results below.

Organization

Table 2 (Panel A) presents the mean ratings by advisory board members for pre-test and post-test memos for the six scales evaluating the memos' organization. Post-test ratings were higher than pre-test ratings for all six items evaluating the memos' organization, indicating that the overall organization of the students' memos had improved between the pre-test and post-test memos. All post-test organization scale ratings were above average (i.e., above 3, the mid-point of the scales). *T*-tests indicated that there was a statistically significant difference at a *p*-value of 0.10 or less between the scores for pre-test memos and post-test memos for three scales evaluating the memos' organization – paragraph unity, layout, and conclusion.

Style and Tone

Table 2 (Panel B) presents the mean ratings by advisory board members for pre-test and post-test memos for the three scales evaluating the memos' style and tone. Post-test ratings were higher than pre-test ratings for all three items evaluating the memos' style and tone. All post-test style and tone scale ratings were above average (i.e., above 3, the mid-point of the scale). *T*-tests indicated that the differences in conciseness and word choice were statistically significant at a *p*-value of 0.10 or less. The difference between

Table 2. Comparison of Pre-Test Memos and Post-Test Memos.

Panel A – Organization Scales

	Pre-Test Memos ($N = 66$)		Post-Test Memos ($N = 45$)	
	Mean	Standard deviation	Mean	Standard deviation
Introduction	2.99	1.12	3.29	1.27
Paragraph unity	3.05**	1.05	3.53**	1.10
Paragraph length	3.05	0.94	3.31	1.04
Building transitions	2.86	1.07	3.09	1.14
Layout of text	3.11**	0.93	3.58**	1.06
Conclusion	2.65***	1.23	3.16***	1.21

Panel B – Style and Tone Scales

	Pre-Test Memos ($N = 66$)		Post-Test Memos ($N = 45$)	
	Mean	Standard deviation	Mean	Standard deviation
Conciseness	2.80***	1.11	3.24***	1.23
Word choice	2.77***	1.08	3.18***	1.28
Tone	3.08	1.07	3.40	1.23

Panel C – Requirements of the Assignment Scales

	Pre-Test Memos ($N = 66$)		Post-Test Memos ($N = 45$)	
	Mean	Standard deviation	Mean	Standard deviation
Technical correctness of discussion	3.02*	1.11	3.63*	1.09
Appropriateness of examples	3.05	1.17	3.42	1.16
Technical correctness of reasons provided	2.89***	1.13	3.33***	1.13
Addressing concerns of clients	2.66***	1.29	3.16***	1.19

*A t-test rejects the hypothesis of no difference in the means at a p-value of <0.01.
**A t-test rejects the hypothesis of no difference in the means at a p-value of <0.05.
***A t-test rejects the hypothesis of no difference in the means at a p-value of <0.10.

the ratings of tone for pre-test and post-test memos was not statistically significant. The mean of 3.08 for tone in the pre-test memos was the highest rating among the style and tone measures during the pre-test phase. It is possible that students did not significantly improve the tone of their memos from the pre-test to the post-test phase because of their initial high ratings in this area. The instructor also emphasized the importance of tone in discussing the pre-test memo assignment with the students because of the emphasis of the writing program on developing workplace writing skills and writing to an audience besides the teacher.

Meeting the Requirements of the Assignment

Table 2 (Panel C) presents the mean ratings by advisory board members for pre-test and post-test memos for the four scales evaluating whether memos met the requirements of the assignment. Post-test ratings were higher than pre-test ratings for all four scales, indicating that students had improved in all areas. All post-test requirements of the assignment scale ratings were above average (i.e., above 3, the mid-point of the scale). Students improved in the areas of technical correctness of discussion of differences between cash and accrual-basis accounting, using appropriate examples, technical correctness of reasons provided, and addressing the concerns of the client. Except for using appropriate examples, *t*-tests indicated that these differences were significant at a *p*-value of 0.10 or less. This improvement could have resulted from the students' increased familiarity with the business memo writing process through the various assignments completed over two semesters. It also could have resulted from the students' increased familiarity with the difference between cash-basis and accrual-basis accounting that the students had by taking additional accounting courses. The cause of the improvement could also be a combination of both reasons.

Spelling, Punctuation, and Grammar

Table 3 (Panels A–E) presents the results of the analysis of the five scales evaluating the students' use of spelling, punctuation, and grammar. In contrast to the interval response scale used to evaluate the memos' organization, style and tone, and meeting the requirements of the assignment, the response scales in punctuation and grammar allowed the business advisory board members to indicate whether they believed the student had used correct spelling, punctuation, and grammar, made one or two errors, or made more than two errors. For this reason, we used χ^2 tests to determine whether there was any statistically significant difference in the students' use of spelling, punctuation, and grammar between the pre-test and post-test memos. Advisory board members believed that in comparison with pre-test

Table 3. Comparison of Pre-Test Memos and Post-Test Memos.

Panel A – Uses Correct Spelling

		Pre-Test Memos	Post-Test Memos	Total
Yes	*N*	49	35	84
	%	74.20%	77.78%	75.68%
No, makes one or two spelling errors	*N*	13	8	21
	%	19.70%	17.78%	18.92%
No, makes more than two spelling errors	*N*	4	2	6
	%	6.10%	4.44%	5.40%
Total	*N*	66	45	111
	%	100.00%	100.00%	100.00%

Panel B – Uses Correct Punctuation

		Pre-Test Memos*	Post-Test Memos*	Total
Yes	*N*	23	26	49
	%	34.80%	56.50%	44.15%
No, makes one or two punctuation errors	*N*	24	12	36
	%	36.40%	28.30%	32.43%
No, makes more than two punctuation errors	*N*	19	7	26
	%	28.80%	15.20%	23.42%
Total	*N*	66	45	111
	%	100%	100%	100%

Panel C – Uses Complete Sentences

		Pre-Test Memos	Post-Test Memos	Total
Yes	*N*	44	30	74
	%	67.70%	68.18%	67.89%
No, uses one or two incomplete sentences	*N*	16	12	28
	%	24.60%	27.27%	25.69%
No, uses more than two incomplete sentences	*N*	5	2	7
	%	7.70%	4.55%	6.42%
Total	*N*	65	44	109[a]
	%	100%	100%	100%

Table 3. *(Continued).*

Panel D – Uses Run-on Sentences

		Pre-Test Memos	Post-Test Memos	Total
No	*N*	40	27	67
	%	60.60%	60.00%	60.36%
Yes, uses one or two run-on sentences	*N*	19	11	30
	%	28.80%	24.44%	27.03%
Yes, uses more than two run-on sentences	*N*	7	7	14
	%	10.60%	15.56%	12.61%
Total	*N*	66	45	111
	%	100%	100%	100%

Panel E – Achieves Subject–Verb Agreement

		Pre-Test Memos*	Post-Test Memos*	Total
Yes	*N*	39	35	74
	%	59.10%	77.78%	66.67%
No, makes one or two subject/verb or verb tense errors	*N*	17	8	25
	%	25.80%	17.78%	22.52%
No, makes more than two subject/verb or verb tense errors	*N*	10	2	12
	%	15.20%	4.44%	10.81%
Total	*N*	66	45	111
	%	100%	100%	100%

*A χ^2 goodness of fit test indicates that there is a significant difference in business advisory members' evaluations of the pre-test memos and the post-test memos at a p-value of <0.10.
[a]Business advisory board members did not complete the evaluation of "Uses Complete Sentences" for two memos.

memos, more students used correct punctuation, and had correct subject/verb agreement in post-test memos. The differences in punctuation and subject/verb agreement were significant at a p-value of 0.10 or less. The results indicate no improvement in the students' use of spelling and sentence structure (use of complete sentences and no use of run-on sentences). The response choices in the spelling, punctuation, and grammar scales did not use a Likert scale and included scales with a limited number of choices. It is possible that there was an improvement between the pre-test and post-test memos but that the scales in the instrument did not capture it.

In addition, although the instructor corrected the students' use of spelling, punctuation, and grammar, these corrections were not emphasized in class because of the focus of our program on developing skills unique to workplace writing.

OVERALL EVALUATION OF THE MEMO

Table 4 presents the results of the analysis of the overall holistic evaluation of the memos. The holistic response scale asked the business advisory board members to indicate whether they believed the memo should be sent to the client in its present form, sent with minor revision, sent with major revision, or not sent to the client. For this reason, χ^2 tests were used to determine whether there was any statistically significant difference in the advisory board members' overall evaluation of the pre-test and post-test memos. Advisory board members believed that 33.3% of the pre-test memos should be sent to the client in their present form or with minor revision. In contrast, they believed that 60% of the post-test memos should be sent to the client in their present form or with minor revision. χ^2 tests indicated that these differences were statistically significant at a p-value less than 0.01, indicating that advisory board members believed that students' overall memo writing skills had improved between the pre-test and post-test assignments.

Table 4. Overall Evaluation of Memos.

		Pre-Test Memos*	Post-Test Memos*	Total
The memo should be sent to the client in its present form	*N*	3	11	14
	%	4.50%	24.44%	12.61%
The memo should be sent to the client with minor revision	*N*	19	16	35
	%	28.80%	35.56%	31.53%
The memo should be sent to the client with major revision	*N*	26	11	37
	%	39.40%	24.44%	33.33%
The memo should not be sent to the client	*N*	18	7	25
	%	27.30%	15.56%	22.53%
Total	*N*	66	45	111
	%	100%	100%	100%

*A χ^2 goodness of fit test indicates that there is a significant difference in business advisory members' evaluations of the pre-test memos and the post-test memos at a p-value of <0.01.

CONCLUSIONS AND LIMITATIONS

Over the last twenty years, many studies have examined the impact of structured writing programs on improving the writing skills of accounting students. In this chapter, we extend this research by using writing assignments that are representative of the workplace writing experiences that students encounter in their professional careers, by developing an evaluation instrument to assess the effectiveness of structured writing programs, and by using business advisory board members to evaluate improvement in students' writing. Our research addresses Rebele's (2002, p. 22) concern that "accounting educators need new approaches for improving students' writing skills." Our results suggest that our new approach to designing writing assignments representative of workplace writing helps our students improve their writing skills. The feedback from our business advisory board members suggests that our writing assignments were representative of the types of workplace writing performed by recent accounting graduates.

Our business advisory board members' ratings indicate that the overall quality of our students' memos improved over two semesters of completing a series of workplace writing assignments. Our structured writing program improved our students' business writing skills in the areas of organization (paragraph unity, layout, and conclusion) and style and tone (conciseness and word choice). The students also improved in the area of meeting the requirements of the assignment, meaning that their ability to explain technical aspects of accounting work improved. All of our students' post-test ratings in the areas of organization, style and tone, and meeting the requirements of the assignment were above average. Finally, the students also improved in certain aspects of spelling, punctuation, and grammar. However, we were unable to specifically identify all the factors that influenced the students' improvement in writing business memos because there was not a statistically significant improvement between the pre-test and post-test memos for all the scales we used in our evaluation instrument.

Faculty can use our individual scales instrument to become more effective graders of writing and to provide specific feedback to students on their workplace writing skills. Business schools can adopt our holistic overall assessment instrument as a course-embedded direct assessment measure of the program learning goal of written communication competency for AACSB accreditation (AACSB, 2006, pp. 63–64). For use in program assessment, the rating categories in our evaluation instrument in Appendix E can be modified and collapsed into three categories – does not meet standards, meets standards, and exceeds standards. Using business advisory board members to evaluate student writing also meets AACSB's (2006, p. 69) emphasis on the importance of using feedback from stakeholder groups such as employers, alumni, or advisory boards to evaluate a school's success in meeting the learning goals of its programs.

We also have used the results of the assessment of our writing program to make changes and additions to our accounting curriculum. All of the courses in our accounting curriculum now include both writing and spreadsheet assignments. We are now using workplace writing assignments similar to those used in Intermediate I and II in Intermediate III and Advanced Auditing. We use business cases in our managerial and cost classes. We have begun to develop grading rubrics that are returned to the students and plan to do another assessment of our writing program in the future.

The nature of our writing improvement program required that we use a within-subject design. To minimize the impact of multiple exposures to a writing assignment, we developed a different instrument for the pre-test and post-test assignments. Both assignments covered the same topic but we presented them in a different context. The results of our sensitivity analysis suggest that we were able to develop similar assignments that could measure improvement in our students' writing skills. Future research should attempt to replicate our results with different assignments. Also, because we did not use a control group, we could not determine whether improvement in our students' writing resulted from the workplace writing approach we used in our program or simply from the students' completing six writing assignments over the course of two semesters. However, we conclude, as did Reinstein and Houston (2004, pp. 62–63) in their study that lacked a control group, that at the end of our program, "students were writing at a level appropriate to their audience and subject matter."

Our results assume that the advisory board members who reviewed our assignments were qualified to perform this task. Although our board members did have significant business experience, we did not provide training to them in the use of our evaluation instrument. Although it is unlikely that we could ask advisory board members to attend a training session, we could have used a third reader to evaluate scores where the scoring by two board members was more than one number apart. For example, if one reader ranked the introduction as a 2 and another ranked it a 5, the third reader could provide feedback regarding which score was more appropriate. Future research should consider this design issue and plan for a third person review when scores by original reviewers are not consistent.

We evaluated the success of our program in improving student workplace writing using a macro approach, suggested by the Federation of Schools of Accountancy (1999) "to measure changes in performance ... as educational changes are implemented." Future research should examine the impact of writing improvement programs on individual students. This type of design would allow researchers to examine whether individual characteristics, such as GPA, age, and employment or internship experience, affect the success of a writing improvement program. This micro approach may assist in determining the specific factors that lead to a successful writing improvement program.

ACKNOWLEDGMENT

We would like to thank Anne McCarthy, former Dean of the Robert G. Merrick School of Business at the University of Baltimore, and members of the Merrick School of Business Advisory Board for their assistance with this project. Without their assistance, this project would not have been possible.

REFERENCES

AACSB International – The Association to Advance Collegiate Schools of Business. (2006). *Eligibility procedures and accreditation standards for business accreditation*. Tampa, FL: AACSB.

Amare, N., & Brammer, C. (2005). Perceptions of memo quality: A case study of engineering practitioners, professors, and students. *Journal of Technical Writing and Communication*, *35*(2), 179–190.

American Accounting Association (AAA). (1986). Committee on the future structure, content, and scope of accounting education (The Bedford Committee). Future accounting education: Preparing for the expanding profession. *Issues in Accounting Education*, *1*(1), 168–195.

Ashbaugh, H., Johnstone, K. M., & Warfield, T. D. (2002). Outcome assessment of a writing-skill improvement initiative: Results and methodological implications. *Issues in Accounting Education*, *17*(2), 123–148.

Beaufort, A. (1998). Transferring writing knowledge to the workplace: Are we on track? In: M. Garay & S. Benhardt (Eds), *Expanding literacies – English teaching and the new workplace* (pp. 179–199). Albany, NY: State University of New York Press.

Boyer Commission on Educating Undergraduates in the Research University. (1998). *Reinventing undergraduate education: A blueprint for America's research universities*. Retrieved on November 20, 2006. Available at http://naples.cc.sunysb.edu/Pres/boyer.nsf/ (from the State University of New York at Stoney Brook website).

Business-Higher Education Forum. (1999). *Spanning the chasm: A blueprint for action.* Retrieved on November 20, 2006. Available at http://www.bhef.com/publications/spanningthechasmablueprintforaction.pdf (from the Business-Higher Education Forum website).

Campbell, K. S., Brammer, C., & Ervin, N. (1999). Exploring how instruction in style affects writing quality. *Business Communication Quarterly*, *62*(3), 71–86.

Catanach, A. H., & Golen, S. (1996). A user-orientated focus to evaluating accountants' writing skills. *Business Communication Quarterly*, *59*(3), 111–121.

Catanach, A. H., & Golen, S. (1997). Developing a writing model for accountants. *Accounting Education: A Journal of Theory, Practice, and Research*, *2*(1), 41–57.

Chase, S. (1991). The corporate illiterates: The hidden illiterates of Silicon Valley. *The Bulletin*, *54*(4), 31–35.

Christ, M. Y. (2002). Developing intermediate accounting students' analytical and communication skills through the annual report project. *Advances in Accounting Education*, *4*, 41–47.

Christensen, D. S. & Rees, D. (2002). An analysis of the business communications skills needed by entry-level accountants. *Mountain Plains Journal of Business and Economics*, *3*. Retrieved on November 20, 2006. Available at http://www.mountainplains.org/articles/2002%20Articles/Commun ication%20Skills4_MPJ_.pdf

Cleaveland, M. C., & Larkins, E. R. (2004). Web-based practice and feedback improve tax students' written communication skills. *Journal of Accounting Education*, *22*, 211–228.

Conference Board. (2006). *Are they really ready to work? Employers' perspectives on the basic knowledge and applied skills of new entrants to the 21st Century U.S. workforce*. Retrieved on November 20, 2006. Available at http://www.conference-board.org/publications/describe.cfm?id = 1218 (from the Conference Board, Inc website).

DeLespinasse, D. (1985). Writing letters to clients: Connecting textbook problems and the real world. *Journal of Accounting Education*, *3*, 97–200.

Epstein, M. H. (1999). Teaching field-specific writing: Results of a WAC survey. *Business Communication Quarterly*, *62*(1), 29–41.

Federation of Schools of Accountancy. Education Research Committee. (1999). *Recommendations for the design of empirical studies examining curricular efforts to develop student critical thinking skills.* Retrieved on November 20, 2006. Available at http://www.thefsa.org/publications/studies.htm (from the Federation of Schools of Accountancy website).

Kennedy, P. (1994). *A guide to econometrics* (3rd ed.). Cambridge, MA: The MIT Press.

May, G. S., & May, C. B. (1989). Communication instruction: What is being done to develop the communication skills of accounting students? *Journal of Accounting Education*, *7*, 233–244.

McIsaac, C. M., & Sepe, J. F. (1996). Improving the writing of accounting students: A cooperative venture. *Journal of Accounting Education*, *14*(4), 515–533.

Mohrweis, L. C. (1991). The impact of writing assignments on accounting students' writing skills. *Journal of Accounting Education*, *9*, 309–325.

National Writing Project and C. Nagin. (2006). *Because writing matters: Improving student writing in our schools*. San Francisco: Jossey-Bass.

Northy, M. (1990). The need for writing skills in accounting firms. *Management Communication Quarterly*, *3*(4), 474–495.

Perspectives on education: Capabilities for success in the accounting profession. (1989). New York: Arthur Andersen & Co., Arthur Young, Coopers & Lybrand, Deloitte, Haskins & Sells, Ernst & Whinney, Peat Marwick Main & Co., Price Waterhouse, and Touche Ross.

Plutsky, S., & Wilson, B. A. (2001). Writing across the curriculum in a college of business and economics. *Business Communication Quarterly*, *64*(4), 26–41.

Rebele, J. R. (2002). Accounting education's uncertain environments: Descriptions and implications for accounting programmes and accounting education research. *Accounting Education: An International Journal*, *11*(1), 3–25.

Reinstein, A., & Houston, M. (2004). Using the securities and exchange commission's "plain English" guidelines to improve accounting students' writing skills. *Journal of Accounting Education*, *22*, 53–67.

Riley, K., Campbell, K. S., Manning, A., & Parker, F. (1999). *Revising professional writing in science and technology, business, and the social sciences* (1st ed.). Superior, Wisconsin: Parlay Press.

Riordan, D. A., Riordan, M. P., & Sullivan, M. C. (2000). Writing across the accounting curriculum: An experiment. *Business Communication Quarterly*, *63*(3), 49–59.

Schneider, B., & Andre, J. (2005). University preparation for workplace writing: An exploratory study of the perceptions of students in three disciplines. *Journal of Business Communication*, *42*(2), 195–218.

Seshadri, S., & Theye, L. D. (2000). Professionals and professors: Substance or style? *Business Communication Quarterly*, *63*(3), 9–23.

Singh-Gupta, V., & Troutt-Ervin, E. (1997). Assessment of workplace writing and incorporation into curriculum. *Journal of Vocational and Technical Education*, *13*(2), 44–53.

Spiceland, D., Sepe, J., & Tomassini, L. (2000). *Intermediate accounting* (3rd ed.). New York: McGraw-Hill.

Stout, D. E., & DaCrema, J. J. (2004). A writing intervention for the accounting classroom: Dealing with the problem of faulty modifiers. *Journal of Accounting Education*, *22*, 289–323.

Stout, D. E., & DaCrema, J. J. (2005). A writing improvement module for accounting education. *Advances in Accounting Education: Teaching and Curriculum Innovations*, *7*, 313–334.

Stout, D. E., Sumutka, A. R., & Wygal, D. E. (1991). Experimental evidence on the use of writing assignments in upper-level accounting courses. *Advances in Accounting*, *9*, 125–141.

Stowers, R. H., & White, G. T. (1999). Connecting accounting and communication: A survey of public accounting firms. *Business Communication Quarterly*, *62*(2), 23–40.

The National Commission on Writing. (2004). *Writing: A ticket to work … Or a ticket out – a survey of business leaders*. Retrieved on November 20, 2006. Available at http://www.writingcommission.org/prod_downloads/writingcom/writing-ticket-to-work.pdf (from the National Commission on Writing website).

The National Commission on Writing. (2006). *Writing and school reform*. Retrieved on November 20, 2006. Available at http://www.writingcommission.org/prod_downloads/writingcom/writing-school-reform-natl-comm-writing.pdf (from the National Commission on Writing website).

Thomas, S. G. (1994). Preparing business students for real-world writing. *Education and Training*, *36*(6), 11–15.

Ulrich, T. A., Michenzi, A. R., & Blouch, W. E. (2003). CPAs assess the development of professional skills of recent accounting graduates. *Journal of the Academy of Business Education*, *4*, 126–137.

Varner, I. I., & Pomerenke, P. J. (1998). Assessing competency in business writing. *Business Communication Quarterly*, *61*(4), 83–91.

Watson, S. F., Apostolou, B., Hassell, J. M., & Webber, S. A. (2003). Accounting education literature review (2000–2002). *Journal of Accounting Education*, *21*(4), 267–325.

APPENDIX A. SCHEDULE OF ASSIGNMENTS INTERMEDIATE ACCOUNTING I

Week	Chapter in Spiceland, Sepe, and Tomassini, *Intermediate Accounting*, Third Edition	Topic
1	2	Review of the accounting process
2	2 (cont.)	
	1	Environment and theoretical structure of financial accounting
3	1 (cont.)	
4	4	Income statement and statement of cash flows
5	4 (cont.)	Pre-test memo-writing assignment #1 due (converting cash-basis accounting to accrual-basis accounting)
	3	Balance sheet and financial disclosures
6		Exam I
7	7	Cash and receivables
8	7 (cont.)	
9		Writing assignment #2 due (revenue realization)
	5	Income measurement and profitability analysis
10	5 (cont.)	
11	13	Current liabilities and contingencies
12		Exam II
13		Computer project/writing assignment #3 due (accounting for uncollectible accounts including a spreadsheet illustration)
	8	Inventories: measurement

APPENDIX A. (*Continued*)

Week	Chapter in Spiceland, Sepe, and Tomassini, *Intermediate Accounting*, Third Edition	Topic
14	8 (cont.)	
	9	Inventories: Additional issues
15	9 (cont.)	
16		Final exam

APPENDIX B. SCHEDULE OF ASSIGNMENTS INTERMEDIATE ACCOUNTING II

Week	Chapter in Spiceland, Sepe, and Tomassini, *Intermediate Accounting*, Third Edition	Topic
1	10	Operational assets – acquisition and disposition
2	10 (cont.)	
3	10 (cont.)	
	11	Operational assets – utilization and impairment
4	10 & 11 (cont.)	
5		Writing assignment #1 due (capital versus revenue expenditures)
	6	Time value of money concepts
6		Exam I
7	14	Bonds and long-term notes
8	14 (cont.)	
9		Writing assignment #2 due (recording debt using the effective, rather than the stated rate, including a spreadsheet illustration)

APPENDIX B. (*Continued*)

Week	Chapter in Spiceland, Sepe, and Tomassini, *Intermediate Accounting*, Third Edition	Topic
	14 (cont.)	
	12	Investments
10	12 (cont.)	
11		Exam II
12	19	Shareholders' equity
13	19 (cont.)	
14	20	Earnings per share
15	20 (cont.)	Post-test memo – writing assignment # 3 due-cash versus accrual-basis accounting
16		Final exam

APPENDIX C. PRE-TEST ASSIGNMENT

While Sharyn Stone had been doing the craft show circuit, her activities typically followed a monthly cycle. She would spend three weeks fabricating shimmering silver into earrings, bracelets, and necklaces accented with bright stones. She spent the last two weekends of the month on the road, selling at craft shows. She paid cash for the materials needed to craft her jewelry and for booths at the shows. Her customers paid by cash, check, or credit card. She generally sold out her production each month. There were no significant receivables, payables, or inventory carried over from one month to the next. The books virtually cleared themselves each month.

When Sharyn tired of being on the road constantly, she decided to open a retail business in Rivers Edge, a community with many artists and craft people. Her jewelry production was different now that she opened the store. First, she needed to create an inventory to meet demands of her own customers as well as those of dealers. In order to accomplish this, she bought her jewelry supplies in far larger quantities than she had before and set up accounts with her suppliers. She found that both her wholesale and retail customers wanted to set up accounts with her as well. She also needed to make other cash outlays – for property and liability insurance, utilities, and salaries for clerks in the store.

She had considerable savings she could invest to set up the store, but she needed a small bank loan to make it go. She also needed some working capital to expand production. Her preliminary talks with the bank did not go well. The loan officer asked her many questions that she could not understand or answer. After she left the bank, she called Emory's office.

Sharyn had preliminary discussions with Emory and Jerri at Emory's office. Afterwards, Jerri made several visits to Sharyn's Silverworks to examine the store's books and records. On the day Emory had been called away because of his mother's illness, Emory and Jerri had planned to meet with Sharyn at her office. They planned to discuss why the bank needed Sharyn's financial statements prepared on an accrual basis. This was the meeting with Sharyn that Jerri had conducted on her own.

When Emory returned to the office after his mother's death, he and Jerri scheduled another meeting with Sharyn. Jerri reminded Emory how defensive Sharyn had become when Jerri tried to explain the advantages of the accrual method. Jerri told Emory, "Sharyn thinks on a cash basis and she has no idea what the bank is talking about when they ask for statements on an accrual basis. She thinks they are being obstructive and bureaucratic in their demands."

At the meeting, Emory explained to Sharyn what the bank needed to see on her accrual-basis financial statements. Emory explained why accruals and deferrals appear on financial statements under GAAP and give information that isn't available on cash-basis statements. He gave Sharyn several examples from her business. He concluded the meeting by promising that he would send her a summary of their discussion. They scheduled a meeting to follow-up. After Sharyn left, Emory asked Jerri to draft in memo format a summary of the discussion for his review. He asked her to include examples of the differences between cash-basis and accrual-basis statements in terms that Sharyn could understand.

APPENDIX D. POST-TEST ASSIGNMENT

Karen Corcoran's next assignment was with a new client of Coleman and Associates, Eric's Exercise Emporium. Eric Martin, the owner of Eric's Exercise Emporium, contacted Coleman and Associates for help in preparing his company's financial statements on an accrual basis. Eric has been in business for almost two years and has always prepared his financial statements on the cash basis. He has applied for a bank loan in order to open a second location. The bank has asked Eric to submit a balance sheet and an income statement for FY 2000 and 2001 prepared using the accrual basis of accounting as part of his loan application.

Karen had a brief meeting with Eric before she began her review of Eric's financial records. Eric told Karen that he always recorded any cash he paid out as an "expense" and any cash received as "revenue."

Karen noted several items which would have to be adjusted to convert Eric's books to the accrual basis.

- Eric opened his exercise business on July 1, 2000. On that date, he signed a five-year lease on his building. He paid the first and last months' rent as well as his security deposit.
- Eric bought various types of exercise equipment for his facility, including treadmills, rowing machines, and weight-lifting equipment. Eric told Karen that because of heavy use, he expected to have to replace the equipment in 2003.
- Although customers can pay to use the facilities of Eric's Exercise Emporium on a daily basis, most customers take out two-year memberships. Eric sold two-year memberships in both July 2000 and July 2001.
- Eric hired several personal trainers to work at Eric's Exercise Emporium. Trainers were paid on the 15th of the month for their services during the previous month.

When Karen returned to the office, she discussed her meeting with George Coleman, the partner on the engagement. George tells Karen, "Please write a memo to Eric explaining in layman's terms why we are making each of the adjustments to convert his financial statements to the accrual basis. Be sure to explain how we will be recording his revenues, expenses, assets, and liabilities under accrual accounting. Let's get the letter to Eric by May 7."

APPENDIX E. EVALUATION INSTRUMENT PROVIDED TO BUSINESS ADVISORY BOARD MEMBERS

After reading the assignment, read each student's memo individually and complete an evaluation instrument for each student after reading EACH memo. We ask that you do NOT read all three memos and then complete the evaluation instruments.

PART I

Background

Intermediate Accounting students wrote memos to inform a client about the differences between the cash basis and accrual basis methods of accounting. We would like you to evaluate each memo on the four dimensions below.

Organization

When informing a reader about a specific financial accounting topic, it is important that a memo is well organized. The following items measure the memo's organization:

(1) *Introduction* – a memo should include an appropriate introductory paragraph that establishes the purpose of the memo. It should identify what the memo is about and why it was written. How would you rate the student's introductory paragraph? (*circle the appropriate response*)

1	2	3	4	5
Poor	Below average	Average	Above average	Excellent

(2) *Paragraph unity* – the information in each paragraph of a memo should relate to a central idea. The paragraph should also contain a topic sentence explaining the main idea of the paragraph. How would you rate the student's paragraph unity? (*circle the appropriate response*)

1	2	3	4	5
Poor	Below average	Average	Above average	Excellent

(3) *Paragraph length* – a well-designed paragraph is an appropriate length. How would you rate the length of the student's paragraphs? (*circle the appropriate response*)

1	2	3	4	5
Poor	Below average	Average	Above average	Excellent

(4) *Building transitions* – a transition is a word or phrase that signals the relation between two pieces of information (i.e., two clauses, two sentences, two paragraphs, or even two sections). How would you rate the student's use of transitions? (*circle the appropriate response*)

1	2	3	4	5
Poor	Below average	Average	Above average	Excellent

(5) *Layout of text* – a well-designed layout is internally consistent, attractive, and consistent with standard practice of the field. The layout should be easy to read, easy to follow, and attractive to the reader. How would you rate the student's layout of text? (*circle the appropriate response*)

1	2	3	4	5
Poor	Below average	Average	Above average	Excellent

(6) *Conclusion* – A memo should also include an appropriate concluding paragraph that brings the memo to a reasonable close. How would you rate the student's conclusion? (*circle the appropriate response*)

1	2	3	4	5
Poor	Below average	Average	Above average	Excellent

Style and Tone

When informing a reader about a specific financial accounting topic, it is important that the writer uses the appropriate style and tone. The following items measure the memo's style and tone:

(1) *Conciseness* – conciseness involves stating a message in fewer words without sacrificing important information, detracting from readability, or creating an undesirable tone. How would you rate the conciseness of the student's memo? (*circle the appropriate response*)

1	2	3	4	5
Poor	Below average	Average	Above average	Excellent

(2) *Word choice* – the writing in a business memo should be accurate, clear, and consistent with professional and standard word usage. The writer should avoid the use of jargon when ordinary language will convey the same meaning. How would you rate the student's choice of words for this memo written to a *non-accountant*? (*circle the appropriate response*)

1	2	3	4	5
Poor	Below average	Average	Above average	Excellent

(3) *Tone* – tone refers to the impression that a memo conveys about the writer's attitude toward the reader and the topic being discussed. Tone includes the appropriateness of the writing for a specific audience. How would you rate the tone of the student's memo written to a *non-accountant*? (*circle the appropriate response*)

1	2	3	4	5
Poor	Below average	Average	Above average	Excellent

Punctuation and Grammar

An effective memo should include appropriate punctuation and grammar. The following items are used to evaluate the punctuation and grammar of the memo:

(1) Does the student use correct spelling? (*circle the appropriate response*)

Yes	No, makes one or two spelling errors	No, makes more than two spelling errors

(2) Does the student use correct punctuation? (*circle the appropriate response*)

Yes	No, makes one or two punctuation errors	No, makes more than two punctuation errors

(3) Does the student use complete sentences? (*circle the appropriate response*)

Yes	No, uses one or two incomplete sentences	No, uses more than two incomplete sentences

(4) Does the student use run-on sentences? (*circle the appropriate response*)

No	Yes, uses one or two run-on sentences	Yes, uses more than two run-on sentences

(5) Does the student achieve subject/verb agreement and use the correct verb tense? (*circle the appropriate response*)

Yes	No, makes one or two subject/verb or verb tense errors	No, makes more than two subject/verb or verb tense errors

Requirements of the Assignment

An effective memo should also meet the requirements of the assignment. The following items are used to evaluate whether the memo met the requirements of the assignment:

(1) *Not considering the student's writing skills*, how would you rate the technical correctness of the student's discussion of the differences between the cash basis and accrual basis of accounting? (*circle the appropriate response*)

1	2	3	4	5
Poor	Below average	Average	Above average	Excellent

(2) *Not considering the student's writing skills*, how would you rate the appropriateness of the student's examples of the differences between the cash basis and accrual basis of accounting? (*circle the appropriate response*)

1	2	3	4	5
Poor	Below average	Average	Above average	Excellent

(3) *Not considering the student's writing skills*, how would you rate the technical correctness of the reasons provided by the student for the benefits of using the accrual basis over the cash basis of accounting? (*circle the appropriate response*)

1	2	3	4	5
Poor	Below average	Average	Above average	Excellent

(4) *Not considering the student's writing skills*, how would you rate how well the student addressed the client's concerns about adopting accrual basis accounting? (*circle the appropriate response*)

1	2	3	4	5
Poor	Below average	Average	Above average	Excellent

PART II

In your opinion (*check the appropriate response*)

☐ The memo should be sent to the client in its present form.
☐ The memo should be sent to the client with minor revision.
☐ The memo should be sent to the client with major revision.
☐ The memo should not be sent to the client.

INTEGRATING TAX AND FINANCIAL ACCOUNTING: THREE EXERCISES FOR USE IN TAX AND FINANCIAL ACCOUNTING CLASSES

Sharon Bruns, Diana Falsetta and Timothy J. Rupert

ABSTRACT

In this chapter, we present a series of exercises designed to help students integrate their understanding of tax and financial accounting. The exercises describe a small business, Nuñez Security Services, Inc., that has chosen to operate as a corporation. These exercises can be used separately or together, and require identification of items that will result in either permanent or temporary differences in financial and tax reporting. The exercises also help students develop an understanding of the implications of these differences on the calculation of tax expense for financial reporting purposes and the calculation of taxable income for tax reporting.

In recent years, the AICPA and other professional organizations have stressed the importance of the ability of professionals to integrate

Advances in Accounting Education: Teaching and Curriculum Innovations, Volume 9, 151–187

ISSN: 1085-4622/doi:10.1016/S1085-4622(08)09007-X

knowledge across the various accounting disciplines and have called for accounting educators to further develop these skills among their students. Despite these calls for better integration, few resources are available for instructors who wish to facilitate this integration in their classes.

In response to these calls, we developed a series of exercises entitled Nuñez Security Services, Inc. These three related exercises, which are designed to complement each other, tell the story of the first two years of a small family business which incorporates, thereby facing both tax and financial accounting issues. The exercises provide students with an opportunity to integrate their understanding of the relationship between tax and financial accounting by requiring students to identify issues that lead to permanent and temporary differences between financial and tax reporting. Students then incorporate the impact of these differences in the calculation of financial accounting journal entries, the book/tax reconciliation, and taxable income. We have also included a series of follow-up exercises to introduce more advanced topics such as the balance sheet approach to deferred taxes, valuation accounts, and the basic workings of FIN 48 for uncertain tax positions. These follow-up exercises can be handed out to the students after Exercise B in a financial accounting class or after Exercise C in a taxation class.

In the following sections of this chapter, we discuss the purpose of the exercises, educational objectives, implementation guidance, and student feedback.

PURPOSE

For the past several decades, various evaluations of the state of accounting education have noted an increased need for the ability to integrate knowledge from various disciplines in order for accounting students to successfully enter the accounting profession.[1] For example, Albrecht and Sack (2000, p. 52) note that practitioners are increasingly concerned that as accounting programs expand to 150 hours, the focus of expanded programs may be on additional courses rather than on how the topics relate to each other. They demonstrate this concern by quoting one practitioner who participated in their focus groups as suggesting that "the 150-hour rule is about not only what we are going to add on, but about how we should approach students' entire education so that we can make it integrated and stop teaching those things that are no longer relevant."

Recently, the AICPA has reiterated a concern about the ability of students to integrate financial reporting and tax through the Model Tax Curriculum. In a recent revision of the Model Tax Curriculum, the AICPA indicated that students should have the ability to "analyze how taxes affect financial reporting" (AICPA, 2007, p. 3). In particular, they focused on the following three abilities: "comparing and contrasting book and tax differences and how they impact tax-based and financial reporting-based income statements and balance sheets; detecting FAS 109 issues including applying the accounting standards for determining deferred tax assets and liabilities; developing an awareness of internal control issues related to tax reporting" (AICPA, 2007, p. 3).

Recent developments in both the tax and financial accounting settings have further underscored the importance of the integration of these two bodies of knowledge. For example, the first round of Sarbanes–Oxley Section 404 filings uncovered that tax-related material weaknesses were the most common form of material weakness (Frieswick, 2005, p. 101). Many companies are responding to this situation by either integrating tax professionals into business units or using tax professionals "to serve as 'interpreters' between tax and financial functions" (Frieswick, 2005, p. 103). This suggests that students who are beginning their professional careers may need to integrate their knowledge of both tax and financial accounting to a greater extent than their predecessors.

Additionally, the introduction of the Schedule M-3[2] by the Internal Revenue Service has renewed the focus on the reconciliation of book and tax income. Following a great deal of discussion about the difficulty of interpreting book/tax differences, the Schedule M-3 was introduced in an effort to provide greater transparency between the two reporting systems (Boynton, DeFillipes, & Legel, 2005, p. 1580). To aid in the preparation and analysis of the information included on this new schedule, students entering the accounting profession will need an increased understanding of how the tax and financial accounting reporting systems relate to each other. In recognizing the importance of these skills, the AICPA had included the reconciliation of book and tax income as part of its content specifications for the CPA exam and has designed the exam to test the candidate's skill in analyzing, understanding, and applying appropriate judgments to these issues.

In response to the previous calls for greater integration, several accounting educators have published ideas for integrating various aspects of accounting. In some cases, these have taken the form of broad frameworks for comparing treatment of items (see, e.g., Baldwin & Chesser, 2003).

Others (e.g., Bloom & Weinstein, 2004; Torres & Albin, 1997) have provided guidance for incorporating tax implications into journal entries or charts that compare specific items for tax and financial accounting. However, none have provided a comprehensive approach to the integration of financial and tax in a series of exercises. As a result of the increasing importance of an ability to integrate tax and financial accounting, we believe that additional teaching tools for helping students achieve this integration are necessary. Therefore, we developed these exercises for use in both tax and intermediate accounting classes.

EDUCATIONAL OBJECTIVES

As noted in the previous section, each exercise was developed with a specific educational objective. The exercises address the importance of understanding and identifying book/tax differences, financial reporting and tax reporting implications. These objectives are consistent with requirements set forth in SFAS 109. SFAS 109 (paragraph 17 a–e) provides five specific procedures for the determination of the annual computation of deferred tax assets and liabilities. The first step includes identification of the types and amounts of existing temporary differences. We begin our exercises with this first step of identification, and then provide a transition to financial reporting and then to tax reporting.

The first exercise is appropriate for both tax and intermediate accounting classes and is designed to provide an introduction to book/tax differences by requiring students to identify potential situations that could create differences in the way an item is treated for tax and financial accounting.[3] To provide a setting for identifying these potential differences, we present a description of owners who recently have decided to start a new security devices business. Appendix A contains a copy of the exercise along with a list of potential book/tax differences that could result from the transactions planned by the business.

The second exercise, designed for use in intermediate accounting classes, helps students understand the financial accounting implications of these book/tax differences. For this exercise, five book/tax differences are identified and students must complete the journal entry to account for any deferred tax assets or liabilities that might result from these differences. The students also use the information to complete the Schedule M-1. A copy of this exercise and its suggested solution are included in Appendix B.

The third exercise is designed for use in tax classes and helps students understand the tax reporting implications of book/tax differences. This exercise requires students to utilize the company's income statement and additional supplementary information to calculate the company's federal tax expense in the second year of the company's existence. The students then are required to use this information to calculate the taxable income of the company and create the Schedule M-1 reconciliation. Appendix C contains a copy of the exercise along with its suggested solution.

In developing the three exercises, we purposefully avoided some complexities. For example, throughout the exercises, we assume a federal income tax rate of 35% and ignore state income taxes. In addition, SFAS No. 109 uses a balance sheet approach for deferred taxes. In the exercises, we only provide income statements, eliminating the requirement to prepare balance sheets with related deferred tax asset and deferred tax liability accounts. Follow-Up Exercise 1 in Appendix D provides a short exercise that introduces this approach. SFAS No. 109 also addresses the need to revalue deferred tax assets if they have a less than 50% probability of being realized. Follow-Up Exercise 2 in Appendix D introduces the use of valuation accounts. Finally, FIN 48 refines the treatment of uncertain tax positions. Follow-Up Exercise 3 in Appendix D offers an introduction to the role this interpretation plays. These exercises can be handed out to students after either Exercise B or Exercise C has been covered.

IMPLEMENTATION GUIDANCE

The three main exercises are designed such that each can be used independently or concurrently in both financial and tax accounting courses. We used the exercises in three different classes: a graduate level intermediate accounting class, two undergraduate level intermediate accounting classes, and an undergraduate tax accounting class. Exercises A and B were first used in the graduate class as an individual homework assignment that was then discussed in class. In effect, we used this administration of these two exercises as a pilot test that allowed us to test the feasibility of the exercises and their difficulty level.

For the undergraduate tax and intermediate accounting classes, we coordinated their syllabi at the beginning of the semester. The students enrolled in these classes were juniors and seniors, who already had some experience working in accounting firms or in accounting positions as part of an internship program before taking these classes. We scheduled the exercises in both courses to appear sequentially in a brief period of time for those students who were taking tax and intermediate accounting concurrently. We believed the exercises would work best after students were instructed in the related topics, such as the theory and circumstances under which permanent and temporary differences occur; deferred tax assets and liabilities; and tax methods of reporting income and deducting expenses, including tax depreciation.

Students in the undergraduate courses were placed into groups to read Exercise A; then we asked the groups to designate a group leader to write a list of possible circumstances where differences might occur on the board. Discussion of the results followed. The group work took approximately 30 min, with another 20 min devoted to discussion.

In the intermediate accounting class, Exercise A was followed by instruction in identifying numerical differences and determining the financial accounting entry to recognize tax expense. Exercise B was then used in the next class, again with about 30 min of group work followed by discussion. In the tax class, students again worked in groups on Exercise C for about 30 min, with another 30 min devoted to discussion of results. More comprehensive instructions pertaining to each exercise are provided in the Appendices, along with their suggested uses.

STUDENT FEEDBACK

To provide more formal validation of the usefulness of the exercises, students were asked to evaluate the exercises by completing a short survey. For the issue identification exercise (Exercise A), the students considered the exercise to be of medium difficulty as the mean difficulty rating was 3.05 on a five-point scale (1 = very easy, 5 = very hard). The student ratings also indicate that the exercise was successful in helping students learn how to identify those items that result in different treatment for tax and financial accounting purposes. The average student rating on this dimension was 3.95 on a five-point scale (1 = not useful, 5 = very useful), with 77% of the students rating the exercise as a 4 or better. Similarly, the students also indicated that the exercise helped them understand how tax and financial accounting relate (mean = 3.87 on a five-point scale), with 72% of the students rating the exercise as a 4 or better. A complete summary of responses is included in Table 1.

We also examined the ratings for the subset of students who were currently in the tax class, but either had previously taken intermediate

Table 1. Overall Evaluation of the Exercise A: Issue Identification Exercise.

	Relative Frequency of Responses ($n = 77$)				
	(1)	(2)	(3)	(4)	(5)
Difficulty level (1 = very easy, 5 = very hard)	0%	20%	55%	25%	0%
Usefulness in learning to identify tax and financial differences (1 = not useful, 5 = very useful)	0%	3%	20%	57%	20%
Usefulness in understanding how tax and financial relate (1 = not useful, 5 = very useful)	0%	4%	24%	53%	19%

	Comparison of Means for Student Groups			
	Mean for all students ($n = 77$)	Mean for Tax/ Intermediate[a] ($n = 29$)	Mean for Intermediate only ($n = 38$)	Mean for Tax only ($n = 10$)
Difficulty level	3.05	3.07	3.05	3.00
Usefulness in learning to identify tax and financial differences[b]	3.95	4.00	3.87	4.10
Usefulness in understanding how tax and financial relate[b]	3.87	4.07	3.74	3.80

[a]This subset of students was either taking both classes concurrently or had completed either Intermediate Accounting or Tax in a previous semester and was taking the other course during the period of the study.
[b]These ratings are significantly higher than the midpoint of the scale of 3.0 ($p < .05$) based on the one-sample t-test.

accounting or was taking it concurrently. We hoped that these students would particularly benefit from this series of exercises given that they should have a greater understanding of both tax and financial accounting and should thus be able to better integrate the two areas. These students rated the usefulness of the exercise in helping them identify tax and financial differences and in helping them understand how tax and financial accounting relate above 4.0.

The financial reporting exercise (Exercise B) was administered in intermediate accounting classes and was designed to help students understand the financial accounting implications of book/tax differences. The students rated the exercise as useful both in learning how to account for deferred tax differences (mean = 4.02 on a five-point scale) and in understanding how tax and financial accounting relate (mean = 3.85 on a five-point scale). A more complete summary of responses for this exercise is contained in Table 2.

Finally, as indicated previously, the tax reporting exercise (Exercise C) was administered in the tax class and was designed to help students to better understand the tax reporting implications of book/tax differences. The students found this exercise to be of moderate difficulty, as indicated by the mean rating of 3.28 (five-point scale). In addition, they found it to be useful in both furthering their understanding of how income is defined for tax purposes and in understanding how tax and financial accounting relate

Table 2. Overall Evaluation of the Exercise B: Financial Reporting Exercise.

	Relative Frequency of Responses (n = 66)				
	(1)	(2)	(3)	(4)	(5)
Difficulty level (1 = very easy, 5 = very hard)	2%	11%	46%	36%	5%
Usefulness in learning to identify tax and financial differences (1 = not useful, 5 = very useful)	0%	0%	18%	62%	20%
Usefulness in understanding how tax and financial relate (1 = not useful, 5 = very useful)	0%	2%	28%	53%	17%

	Comparison of Means for Student Groups		
	Mean for all students (n = 66)	Mean for Tax/ Intermediate[a] (n = 20)	Mean for Intermediate only (n = 46)
Difficulty level[b]	3.32	3.35	3.30
Usefulness in learning to identify tax and financial differences[b]	4.02	3.90	4.07
Usefulness in understanding how tax and financial relate[b]	3.85	3.75	3.89

[a]This subset of students either was taking both classes concurrently or had completed Tax in a previous semester and was taking Intermediate Accounting during the period of the study.
[b]These ratings are significantly higher than the midpoint of the scale of 3.0 ($p < .05$) based on the one-sample t-test.

Table 3. Overall Evaluation of the Exercise C: Tax Reporting Exercise.

	Relative Frequency of Responses ($n = 66$)				
	(1)	(2)	(3)	(4)	(5)
Difficulty level (1 = very easy, 5 = very hard)	0%	9%	53%	38%	0%
Usefulness in learning to identify tax and financial differences (1 = not useful, 5 = very useful)	0%	0%	19%	53%	28%
Usefulness in understanding how tax and financial relate (1 = not useful, 5 = very useful)	0%	0%	19%	47%	34%

	Comparison of Means for Student Groups		
	Mean for all students ($n = 32$)	Mean for Tax/ Intermediate[a] ($n = 24$)	Mean for Tax only ($n = 8$)
Difficulty level[b]	3.28	3.33	3.13
Usefulness in learning to identify tax and financial differences[b]	4.09	4.04	4.25
Usefulness in understanding how tax and financial relate[b]	4.16	4.17	4.13

[a]This subset of students were either taking both classes concurrently or had completed Intermediate Accounting in a previous semester and was taking Tax during the period of the study.

[b]With the exception of the difficulty rating for those students who had taken tax only, these ratings are significantly higher than the midpoint of the scale of 3.0 ($p<.05$) based on the one-sample t-test.

(means of 4.09 and 4.16, respectively), with 81% of the students rating the exercise as a 4 or better on both dimensions. A more complete summary of responses is included in Table 3.

ALTERNATIVE USES

In the preceding sections, we described the ways in which we have used the three exercises in both tax and financial accounting classes to enhance the ability of students to integrate these two areas of accounting. However, the exercises are versatile in that they can be modified to meet other classroom objectives.

We incorporated the exercises in our classes as a classroom exercise in which the students worked in groups. However, instructors could choose to use the exercises as a graded component of the courses and could assign the exercises to be worked on independently. For those instructors who wish to use the exercises as part of a graded component, they can vary Exercises B and C each year by choosing different book/tax differences from the potential list developed in Exercise A.

In addition to issue identification and the mechanics of the book/tax reconciliation, the exercises can also be part of a larger module on book/tax differences that includes classroom discussion about policy issues. For example, tax instructors can accompany the exercises with a discussion of the justification for differences in the tax definition of income and the financial accounting definition of income. Instructors might also assign some of the recent articles written on the Schedule M-3 and ask students to discuss whether its implementation will achieve its intended goals of increased transparency.

For a more comprehensive approach to financial reporting, the exercises can be expanded to include balance sheet information, adding the requirement to adjust and report the deferred tax asset and liability accounts on the first and second year balance sheets, as well as preparation of the footnote disclosures.

CONCLUSIONS

Regardless of which means instructors choose for incorporating these exercises, the series of exercises presented in this chapter provides instructors with an additional tool for enhancing the ability of their students to integrate their understanding of tax and financial accounting. Hopefully, this ability will help them meet the increasing demand for this skill that the profession expects from those entering its ranks.

NOTES

1. See, for example, AAA Committee on the Future Structure, Content and Scope of Accounting Education (The Bedford Committee) (1986). Future Accounting Education: Preparing for the Expanding Profession, *Issues in Accounting Education*, pp.168–195; Accounting Education Change Commission (1990). Objectives of Education for Accountants: Position Statement Number One, *Issues in Accounting Education*, pp. 307–312; AICPA (1999). *AICPA Core Competency Framework for Entry into the Accounting Profession.*

2. The new Schedule M-3, Net Income (Loss) Reconciliation for Corporations with Totals Assets of \$10 Million or More, replaces the Schedule M-1 for Corporations with total assets of at least \$10 Million. It requires a reconciliation between the financial income statement and the tax return for various items, including whether such differences are temporary or permanent.

3. Depending on the sequencing of prerequisites, implementation may be adjusted to coincide with the specific course content. Both financial and tax must be covered before the existing exercise can be used; however, instructors may modify the exercise and select those particular items which are covered in their course.

ACKNOWLEDGMENTS

The authors wish to thank the editor (Bill Schwartz), two anonymous reviewers, Julie Hertenstein, Jennifer Kahle, Jim Maroney, and Marty Wartick as well as the participants at the 2006 AAA Northeast regional meeting and the 2007 ATA mid-year meeting for their helpful comments on earlier drafts of the chapter.

REFERENCES

AAA Committee on the Future Structure, Content and Scope of Accounting Education (The Bedford Committee). (1986). Future accounting education: Preparing for the expanding profession. *Issues in Accounting Education*, *1*, 168–195.

Accounting Education Change Commission. (1990). Objectives of education for accountants: Position statement number one. *Issues in Accounting Education*, *5*, 307–312.

AICPA. (1999). AICPA Core Competency Framework for Entry into the Accounting Profession.

AICPA. (2007). Model Tax Curriculum.

Albrecht, W., & Sack, R. (2000). *Accounting education: Charting the course through a perilous future*. AAA Monograph, Sarasota, FL: American Accounting Association.

Baldwin, J., & Chesser, D. (2003). An approach to integrating accounting courses. *Journal of Accounting Education*, *21*, 101–126.

Bloom, R., & Weinstein, G. (2004). Income tax aspects of accounting changes and error corrections: An instructional approach. *Advances in Accounting Education*, *6*, 87–115.

Boynton, C., DeFillipes, P., & Legel, E. (2005). Prelude to Schedule M-3: Schedule M-1 corporate book-tax difference data 1990–2003. *Tax Notes*, *109*(December 19), 1579–1599.

Frieswick, K. (2005). Too taxing. *CFO Magazine*, November, pp. 101–103.

Torres, P., & Albin, M. (1997). Integrating the curriculum: A resource for including tax. *Issues in Accounting Education*, *12*(Fall), 561–572.

APPENDIX A. EXERCISE A – IDENTIFYING DIFFERENCES BETWEEN TAX AND FINANCIAL ACCOUNTING

Exercise Description

Exercise A describes events in a general manner in the first year of a small business start-up. The objective of the exercise is to help students learn to analyze and identify circumstances that may lead to differences between book and tax accounting.

Use

This exercise can be used in either financial accounting classes (usually at the intermediate level) or principles of taxation classes. The exercise can stand alone if the subject of differences between book and tax accounting will not be covered in any numerical detail. However, it is generally intended to be used as the prelude to Exercise B or Exercise C or both.

Suggested Instructions

Nuñez Security Services, Inc. (Exercise A) works well as a group exercise, administered after the instructor has covered the theory and circumstances under which permanent and temporary differences occur. Divide the class into a workable number of groups. In a class of 30 students, 5 groups of 6 students work well. Although it is easy to let students group themselves, it generally works better for the instructor to distribute students to groups such that each group will have students of different abilities. (A group of the smartest students, or a group of the least academically gifted will change the dynamics of the discussion in a generally negative manner.)

Distribute the exercise to the students with the following directions:

1. Choose a group name and a group leader. This student should work to encourage all members of the group to participate and will be responsible for writing the group's results on the board. He or she should make a list with the following columns:

   A. *Possible Difference* B. *Type of Difference (Permanent or Temporary)*

2. Identify all the possible differences between book and tax accounting that you see in the exercise first. After you have found all you can, go back and discuss whether you think the difference is permanent or temporary. It is more important that you finish Column A than Column B.
3. When the instructor calls time, each group leader should go to the board and, under the group name, list the differences in their Column A.

At this point, it works well for the instructor to treat the exercise as a contest between groups. The instructor works through the master list of possible differences, keeping score as to which groups found the difference, while at the same time explaining each difference as reinforcement. The winning group or groups are congratulated for their prowess. Do not give in to prizes such as extra points on the exam!

Column B can be used in several ways. As the instructor goes through the list, he or she can discuss the nature of the difference. Alternatively, Column B can be used to break ties for best group.

NUÑEZ SECURITY SERVICES, INC. (EXERCISE A) – IDENTIFYING DIFFERENCES BETWEEN TAX AND FINANCIAL ACCOUNTING

Introduction

As José and Christine Nuñez waited to meet their accountant, they were excited to learn just how well their business had done over the last year. It had long been their dream to start their own business, and they had finally decided they were ready to give it a try last year. Unlike many other new business owners who struggle to show a profit in the early years, they knew that their security services business had made a considerable profit during the last year, but they wondered just how much.

As the couple greeted Bob Wilson (the CPA they had hired) and entered his office, José could not wait any longer. "What's the bottom line? How much profit did we make last year?" he asked. "According to your tax return or according to your financial statements?" Bob asked in return. He could tell from the puzzled looks on the couple's faces that they needed more explanation. "You see," he continued, "for a business that uses accrual accounting, like yours, financial accounting follows Generally Accepted Accounting Principles (GAAP) and attempts to allocate expenses, including tax expense, to the time period in which the major earnings activity occurred in an effort to accurately measure income. Tax accounting follows Internal Revenue Code rules and regulations, which have been passed to ensure that taxpayers do not understate their income, and to accomplish a wide range of social and economic objectives." He further explained that because of these different goals, it was not unusual for differences to arise in identifying the financial accounting and tax effects of transactions, both in terms of nature and timing.

To identify some of the potential differences that arise between financial reporting and tax reporting, Bob suggested that they review some of the basic facts that the couple had shared about their business, Nuñez Security Services, Inc. (hereafter, NUÑEZ), during its first year of operations.

The Facts

José and Christina Nuñez were interested in starting a business of their own. They conducted a market study and investigated the local demand for security devices. The results were promising; therefore, José and Christina started a small retail business specializing in providing security devices to other small businesses. NUÑEZ sold video cameras, door alarms, and other devices. Other revenues came from selling warranty contracts for its devices. NUÑEZ also provided continuous monitoring services to customers who generally paid in advance for quarterly contracts.

The year was very profitable for a start-up year. The only negative mark on an otherwise successful year was the fine NUÑEZ paid to the Environmental Protection Agency for illegally disposing of some of the materials left behind from the previous building owner, who operated a paint store on the premises. NUÑEZ purchased the building in early January. The previous owner had divided the building into two retail spaces. Therefore, José and Christina decided to operate their business in one of the retail spaces and rent the other. They were able to find a tenant by the end of the year and received the first and last month's rent, as well as a security deposit of one month's rent. Although the retail space was a good size for their small business, José and Christina spent a considerable amount outfitting the space with counters, shelves, computers, and other depreciable property.

Their accountant advised them to form the business entity as a C corporation, using an accrual basis and calendar year-end. Their attorney filed the Articles of Incorporation with the state, and issued certificates of stock ownership to José and Christina. As a former security consultant to the Mall of America, José's experience was very valuable for the business. To protect themselves from losing José's expertise, they decided to have the corporation purchase a life insurance policy on José. NUÑEZ also purchased a property insurance policy on the building. The entire 24-month premium was required to be paid on July 1st of the current year.

Cash flow for the year was better than expected due to the company policy of requiring customers to pay in advance for quarterly contracts for monitoring services. Given the healthy cash flow, NUÑEZ invested a portion of its cash in municipal bonds that paid a small amount of interest income. NUÑEZ also made a contribution to the re-election campaign of the state representative, whom José and Christina strongly supported, and a contribution to the local chapter of Habitat for Humanity.

José and Christina worked hard to promote their business and create additional customer contacts. They spent considerable time and money inviting business owners to dinner to discuss opportunities to provide security devices. The accountant for NUÑEZ carefully considered any expected future expenses on the warranty contracts sold during the year. He recorded an estimate of this future liability, which was reflected in the financial statements. He also determined that a portion of accounts receivable would be uncollectible and recorded an estimate of this uncollectible amount.

Instructions

Study the preceding description of the first year's operations. Identify the areas where there might be differences in the way financial accounting and tax accounting deal with the effects of various activities. Use the worksheet in Exhibit A1 to organize your response. Note whether you think the difference might be permanent or temporary.

Exhibit A1. Worksheet for Identifying Tax Differences.

Column A: Item	Column B: Temporary or Permanent
1.	
2.	
3.	
4.	

Exhibit A1. (*Continued*).

Column A: Item	Column B: Temporary or Permanent
5.	
6.	
7.	
8.	
9.	
10.	
11.	
12.	
13.	
14.	
15.	
16.	
17.	
18.	

Note: There are not necessarily 18 differences.

SUGGESTED SOLUTION

Column A: Item	Column B: Temporary or Permanent	Explanation of the Difference
1. Business investigation expenses	Temporary	First $5,000 immediately expensed[a]; remainder amortized over 15 years for tax
2. EPA fine	Permanent	Not deductible for tax
3. Depreciation	Temporary	Accelerated rate of depreciation for tax

(*Continued*)

Column A: Item	Column B: Temporary or Permanent	Explanation of the Difference
4. Improvements	Temporary	Accelerated rate of depreciation for tax
5. Prepaid rental income	Temporary	Taxable in year received for tax
6. Security deposit	N/A	No difference
7. Organizational expenditures	Temporary	First $5,000 immediately expensed[b]; remainder amortized over 15 years for tax
8. Stock issuance costs	N/A	No difference
9. Life insurance policy	Permanent	Premiums are not deductible for tax
10. Prepaid property insurance policy	N/A	No difference
11. Prepaid monitoring service income	Temporary	No difference in current year[c]
12. Municipal bond interest	Permanent	Not taxable
13. Political contribution	Permanent	Not deductible for tax
14. Charitable contribution	Temporary/ permanent	Limited to 10% of taxable income[d], five-year carryover
15. Meals and entertainment expense	Permanent	50% not deductible for tax
16. Estimated warranty expense	Temporary	Not deductible for tax until paid
17. Estimated bad debt expense	Temporary	Not deductible for tax until written off

[a]An exception, however, phases out the immediate expensing on a dollar-for-dollar basis when total expenses exceed $50,000.

[b]An exception, however, phases out the immediate expensing on a dollar-for-dollar basis when total expenses exceed $50,000.

[c]Generally, prepaid income is taxed in the year of receipt. However, Revenue Procedure 2004–34 permits an accrual basis taxpayer to defer recognition of service income for the portion of the prepaid service income that relates to services to be performed after the tax year of receipt to the following tax year. Therefore, in the current year, there is no financial/tax difference; however, in the following year, a financial/tax difference may exist.

[d]Taxable income is computed without regard to the charitable contribution deduction, net operating loss or capital loss carryback, and dividends received deduction.

APPENDIX B. EXERCISE B – FINANCIAL REPORTING IMPLICATIONS OF BOOK/TAX DIFFERENCES

Exercise Description

Exercise B introduces numbers into the situation described in Exercise A. The book/tax differences are identified for the students and they are asked to fill out a schedule which calculates tax expense and taxes payable. They then are asked to use this information to fill out a Schedule M-1 on a business tax return. (A Schedule M-1 reconciles financial pre-tax income to taxable income.)

Use

Exercise B is designed to reinforce the intermediate accounting student's knowledge of how to analyze tax differences and calculate tax expense and taxes payable, while at the same time determining deferred tax assets and deferred tax liabilities in a realistic situation. The students then use the information they have gathered to construct Schedule M-1, which is quite different in format from the way that this information is presented in financial accounting texts.

Suggested Instructions

Exercise B also works well with classroom groups. The exercise is much easier for students if they have been given lessons in advance on dealing with identifying deferred tax assets and liabilities, particularly if the same format is used as that in the exercise. The major sticking point for most students is determining net income for the first line in the Schedule M-1. They have been working with income before taxes and frequently forget to subtract the tax expense as determined in the chart. Reminding them of this early in their deliberations helps more of them to figure out the Schedule M-1.

Instructors may also wish to require the students to break out the current and deferred portions of the income tax expense, either as part of the formal journal entry or by illustrating the disclosure of current and deferred taxes in the tax footnote. The exercises can be expanded to include balance sheet information, adding the requirement to adjust and report the related deferred tax asset and deferred tax liability accounts on the balance sheet.

NUÑEZ SECURITY SERVICES, INC. (EXERCISE B) – FINANCIAL REPORTING IMPLICATIONS OF BOOK/TAX DIFFERENCES

Introduction

In January of 2005, José and Christina Nuñez started a retail business specializing in providing security devices and services to other small businesses. NUÑEZ sold video cameras, door alarms, and other devices from a small building which it acquired and outfitted with counters, shelves, computers, and other depreciable property. NUÑEZ also provided continuous monitoring services to customers, who generally paid in advance. During 2005, NUÑEZ rented part of its space to another company.

The first year was very profitable for a start-up company. The only negative mark on an otherwise successful year was the fine that NUÑEZ paid to the Environmental Protection Agency for illegally disposing of some of the materials left behind from the previous tenant, a paint store. NUÑEZ hired Bob Wilson, CPA, to restate its cash receipts and expenditures to the accrual basis and to prepare the tax return. Bob determined that accrual accounting pre-tax income was $187,000. He explained that he had used straight-line depreciation to arrive at this number, but that NUÑEZ would be able to deduct extra depreciation of $45,000 for tax purposes. There were four other differences between financial income and tax income. They were:

a) The fine of $15,000 was a legitimate business expense for financial statement purposes, but the IRS would never accept it as a deduction on the tax return.
b) Financial income included estimated warranty expenses of $6,000 which cannot be deducted for tax purposes until they are actually incurred.
c) At the end of 2005, NUÑEZ received the first month's rent of $2,000 for January, 2006 from a new tenant, plus another $2,000 for the last month's rent. All $4,000 was taxable for tax year 2005.
d) Financial statement income included $1,200 in tax-exempt interest on municipal bonds.

Instructions

1. Exhibit B1 is a schedule that shows how to recognize tax expense for financial statements. Analyze the facts to fill in the schedule and make the journal entry recognizing tax expense. Assume the relevant federal tax rate for all calculations is 35% and ignore any potential state income tax effects.
2. Exhibit B2 is the Schedule M-1 that small businesses must complete to reconcile book financial statement income to taxable income. Use your previous analysis and your completed Exhibit B1 to fill out Schedule M-1.

Exhibit B1. Schedule for Determining Tax Expense Journal Entry.

		This Column Adds Down	**Tax Rate: Same for All Rows**	**This Column Contains the Journal Entry Pieces**
Pre-tax income (loss) per books $________	+/− Permanent differences = $________ =	Book income subject to tax $________	× Tax rate × ______	= Tax expense (debit) $________
−Differences leading to future taxable income being *more* than future pre-tax financial income (depreciation, installment sales, etc.)		$________	× ______	= Deferred tax liability (credit) $________
+Differences leading to future taxable income being *less* than future pre-tax financial income (unearned revenue, estimated expenses, etc.)		$________	× ______	= Deferred tax asset (debit) $________
Taxable income		$________	× ______	= Taxes payable (credit) $________

Exhibit B2. Schedule M-1 – Reconciliation of Income (Loss) per Books with Income per Return.

1	Net income (loss) per books	
2	Federal income tax per books	
3	Excess of capital losses over capital gains	
4	Income subject to tax not recorded on books this year (itemize):	
5	Expenses recorded on books this year not deducted on this return (itemize):	
	a. Depreciation	
	b. Charitable contributions	
	c. Travel and entertainment	
6	Add lines 1 through 5	
7	Income recorded on books this year not included on this return (itemize):	
	Tax-exempt interest	
8	Deductions on this return not charged against book income this year (itemize):	
	a. Depreciation	
	b. Charitable contributions	
9	Add lines 7 and 8	
10	Income (page 1' line 28) – line 6 less line 9	

SUGGESTED SOLUTION

Schedule for Determining Tax Expense Journal Entry

		This Column Adds Down	Tax Rate: Same for All Rows	This Column Contains the Journal Entry Pieces
Pre-tax income (loss) per books $187,000	+/− Permanent differences = (1,200)+15,000 =	Book income subject to tax $200,800	× Tax rate × .35	= Tax expense (debit) $70,280
−Differences leading to future taxable income being *more* than future pre-tax financial income (depreciation, installment sales, etc.)		$(45,000)	× .35	= Deferred tax liability (credit) $15,750
+ Differences leading to future taxable income being *less* than future pre-tax financial income (unearned revenue, estimated expenses, etc.)		$4,000 + $6,000	× .35	= Deferred tax asset (debit) $3,500
Taxable income		$165,800	× .35	= Taxes payable (credit) $58,030

Tax expense	70,280	
Deferred tax asset	3,500	
Deferred tax liability		15,750
Taxes payable		58,030

Schedule M-1 – Reconciliation of Income (Loss) per Books with Income per Return.

Line	Item		Amount
1	Net income (loss) per books		116,720
2	Federal income tax per books		70,280
3	Excess of capital losses over capital gains		
4	Income subject to tax not recorded on books this year (itemize):		
	Unearned revenue		4,000
5	Expenses recorded on books this year not deducted on this return (itemize):		
	a. Depreciation		
	b. Charitable contributions		
	c. Travel and entertainment		
	Warranty expense	6,000	
	Pollution fine	15,000	
			21,000
6	Add lines 1 through 5		212,000
7	Income recorded on books this year not included on this return (itemize):		
	Tax-exempt interest	1,200	
			1,200
8	Deductions on this return not charged against book income this year (itemize):		
	a. Depreciation	45,000	
	b. Charitable contributions		
			45,000
9	Add lines 7 and 8		46,200
10	Income (page 1, line 28) – line 6 less line 9		165,800

APPENDIX C. EXERCISE C – TAX REPORTING IMPLICATIONS OF BOOK/TAX DIFFERENCES

Exercise Description

Exercise C reflects the second year operations of the situations described in Exercises A and B. However, Exercise C is designed such that it is independent of Exercises A and B and may be completed without having finished Exercise A and/or B. Exercise C is a more comprehensive exercise, providing students with company facts and an income statement, and the ability to integrate both financial and tax applications. Using this information, students are asked to identify and calculate book/tax differences, including calculation of tax depreciation, which reinforces cost recovery concepts learned in their tax course. With these differences, they are also asked to calculate taxable income using the financial income statement. Finally, they are asked to prepare the journal entry recording the federal tax expense and federal tax liability, as well as a Schedule M-1, reconciling net income per books and taxable income.

Use

Exercise C is designed for use in tax classes to demonstrate how the differences in financial and tax accounting impact both financial statements and income tax returns. Exercise C fully integrates financial and tax accounting, such that students are able to obtain the full picture of a company's situation. The exercise starts with the financial income statement, continues with calculation of deferred tax assets and deferred tax liabilities, and ends with compilation of the Schedule M-1. This comprehensive approach provides a nice reinforcement of concepts learned in both classes. The exercise can stand alone if instructors do not wish to use Exercise A.

Suggested Instructions

Exercise C also works well with classroom groups, administered after the instructor has covered theory and circumstances under which permanent and temporary differences occur. This would include concepts such as tax methods of reporting income and deducting expenses, as well as specific concepts such as tax depreciation. Given the comprehensive nature of the exercise, the instructor may find it helpful to provide a few key figures (e.g., total tax depreciation, taxable income, etc.) or stopping points for discussion of each exercise, such that students are able to progress through the exercise in an efficient manner. For example, it may be helpful to have students first complete and discuss the tax adjustments (i.e., book/tax differences) and taxable income before continuing on to recording of the journal entry and preparation of Schedule M-1. Most often, students did not adjust for the permanent differences in calculating the federal tax expense. Reminding them of this important detail upfront helps them to progress more easily.

For a more comprehensive approach to financial reporting, the exercise can be expanded to include balance sheet information, adding the requirement to adjust and report the deferred tax asset and deferred tax liability accounts on the second year balance sheet, as well as preparation of the footnote disclosures.

NUÑEZ SECURITY SERVICES, INC. (EXERCISE C) – TAX REPORTING IMPLICATIONS OF BOOK/TAX DIFFERENCES

Introduction

The second year of operations was another profitable year. NUÑEZ continued to specialize in providing security devices to small businesses by selling video cameras, door alarms, and other devices, as well as by selling warranty contracts for its devices. The couple expanded their business and customer base by hosting dinners and other special events. With its healthy cash flow, NUÑEZ continued to invest a portion of its cash in municipal bonds that paid $12,000 interest income annually. In addition, NUÑEZ continued to carefully estimate future warranty expenses on the warranty contracts sold, as well as to estimate the portion of its accounts receivable that might be uncollectible.

Bob Wilson, the NUÑEZ CPA, determined that the accrual accounting pre-tax income for the second year of operations was $364,700. The income statement prepared by Bob is provided in Exhibit C1.

Instructions

1. Use the income statement in Exhibit C1 to calculate the federal tax expense and complete the income statement. Assume the relevant federal tax rate is 35% and ignore any potential state tax effects. Also assume for

this assignment that the second year of operations is independent of the prior year's operations.

2. Use the income statement and the additional information provided below to identify and calculate the financial/tax differences. Include these differences on the worksheet in Exhibit C2 in the column titled "Adjustments." Add/subtract the items in the "Adjustments" column to/from the "Financial" column to total the "Tax" column.

   Additional Information

   a. Actual warranty expenses paid during the second year were $17,000.
   b. Actual bad debts written off during the second year were $3,000.
   c. Depreciation for financial accounting was calculated using the straight-line method with no salvage value for all assets which were placed in service on January 1st of the prior year. Property, Plant and Equipment consisted of the following at the end of year two:

Asset	Cost	Accumulated Depreciation	Recovery Period
Building	$400,000	$20,000	40 years
Land	100,000		
Computers	75,000	30,000	5 years
Total	$575,000	$50,000	

   All assets were acquired in the first year. No additions or deletions were made in the second year of operations. For tax purposes, NUÑEZ did not make any special elections (e.g., §179 immediate expensing election) either last year or this year.

3. Use the Taxable Income calculated in Exhibit C2 to calculate the federal tax liability. Using the schedule in Exhibit C3, prepare the journal entry to record the federal tax expense and federal tax liability.
4. Use the "Tax" and "Adjustments" columns from Exhibit C2 to complete Schedule M-1 in Exhibit C4.

Exhibit C1. NUÑEZ SECURITY SERVICES – Income Statement for the Year Ended December 31, 2006.

Revenue		
Merchandise revenue	$600,000	
Warranty contract revenue	$200,000	
Interest income	12,000	
Total revenues		$ 812,000

Exhibit C1. *(Continued).*

Expenses		
Cost of goods sold	$225,000	
Salaries and wages	100,000	
Warranty expense	20,000	
Bad debt expense	4,000	
Interest	50,000	
Depreciation	25,000	
Advertising	1,800	
Insurance	11,500	
Meals and entertainment	10,000	
Total expenses		447,300
Income before taxes	☐	364,700
Permanent tax differences	☐	
Financial income subject to tax		☐
Federal tax expense (35%)		☐
Net income		

Exhibit C2. NUÑEZ SECURITY SERVICES – Financial to Tax Reconciliation for the Year Ended December 31, 2006.

	Financial	Adjustments	Tax
Revenue			
Merchandise revenue	$600,000		
Warranty revenue	200,000		
Interest income	12,000		
Total revenues	$812,000		$
Expenses			
Cost of goods sold	$225,000		
Salaries and wages	100,000		
Warranty expense	20,000		
Bad debt expense	4,000		
Interest expense	50,000		
Depreciation	25,000		
Advertising	1,800		
Insurance	11,500		
Meals/Entertainment	10,000		
Total expenses	$447,300		$
Income before taxes	$364,700	Taxable income	$
Federal tax expense (35%)	$______	Federal tax	
Net income	$______	liability (35%)	$

Exhibit C3. Schedule For Determining Tax Expense Journal Entry.

		This Column Adds Down	Tax Rate: Same for All Rows	This Column Contains the Journal Entry Pieces
Pre-tax income (loss) per books $______	+/− Permanent differences = $______ =	Book income subject to tax $______	× Tax rate × ______	= Tax expense (debit) $______
−Differences leading to future taxable income being *more* than future pre-tax financial income (depreciation, installment sales, etc.)		$______	× ______	= Deferred tax liability (credit) $______
+Differences leading to future taxable income being *less* than future pre-tax financial income (unearned revenue, estimated expenses, etc.)		$______	× ______	= Deferred tax asset (debit) $______
Taxable income		$______	× ______	= Taxes payable (credit) $______

Exhibit C4. Schedule M-1 – Reconciliation of Income (Loss) per Books with Income per Return.

Line	Item	Amount
1	Net income (loss) per books	
2	Federal income tax per books	
3	Excess of capital losses over capital gains	
4	Income subject to tax not recorded on books this year (itemize):	
5	Expenses recorded on books this year not deducted on this return (itemize):	
	a. Depreciation	
	b. Charitable contributions	
	c. Travel and entertainment	
6	Add lines 1 through 5	
7	Income recorded on books this year not included on this return (itemize):	
	Tax-exempt interest	
8	Deductions on this return not charged against book income this year (itemize):	
	a. Depreciation	
	b. Charitable contributions	
9	Add lines 7 and 8	
10	Income (page 1' line 28) – line 6 less line 9	

SUGGESTED SOLUTION

NUNEZ SECURITY SERVICES, INC. – Financial to Tax Reconciliation for the Year Ended December 31, 2006

	Financial	Adjustments	Tax
Revenue			
Merchandise revenue	**$600,000**		**$600,000**
Warranty contract revenue	**200,000**		**200,000**
Interest income	**12,000**	**(12,000)**	
Total revenues	**$812,000**		**$800,000**
Expenses			
Cost of goods sold	$225,000		$225,000
Salaries and wages	**100,000**		100,000
Warranty expense	20,000	**(3,000)**	17,000
Bad debt expense	4,000	**(1,000)**	3,000
Interest expense	50,000		50,000
Depreciation	25,000	**9,256**	34,256
Advertising	1,800		1,800
Insurance	**11,500**		11,500
Meals and entertainment	10,000	**(5,000)**	5,000
Total expenses	$447,300		$447,556
Income before taxes	$364,700	Taxable income	$352,444
Federal tax expense (35%)	$125,195	Federal tax liability (35%)	$123,355
Net income	$239,505		

Schedule for Determining Tax Expense Journal Entry.

		This Column Adds Down	Tax Rate: Same for All Rows	This Column Contains the Journal Entry Pieces
Pre-tax income (loss) per books $364,700	+/− Permanent differences = (12,000)+5,000 =	Book income subject to tax $357,700	× Tax rate × .35	= Tax expense (debit) $125,195
−Differences leading to future taxable income being *more* than future pre-tax financial income (depreciation, installment sales, etc.)		$(9,256)	× .35	= Deferred tax liability (credit) $3,240
+ Differences leading to future taxable income being *less* than future pre-tax financial income (unearned revenue, estimated expenses, etc.)		$4,000	× .35	= Deferred tax asset (debit) $1,400
Taxable income		$352,444	× .35	= Taxes payable (credit) $123,355

Tax expense	125,195	
Deferred tax asset	1,400	
Deferred tax liability		3,240
Taxes payable		123,355

Schedule M-1 – Reconciliation of Income (Loss) per Books with Income per Return.

1	Net income (loss) per books		239,505
2	Federal income tax per books		125,195
3	Excess of capital losses over capital gains		
4	Income subject to tax not recorded on books this year (itemize):		
5	Expenses recorded on books this year not deducted on this return (itemize):		
	a. Depreciation		
	b. Charitable contributions		
	c. Travel and entertainment	5,000	
	Warranty and bad debt	4,000	
			9,000
6	Add lines 1 through 5		373,700
7	Income recorded on books this year not included on this return (itemize):		
	Tax-exempt interest	12,000	
			12,000
8	Deductions on this return not charged against book income this year (itemize):		
	a. Depreciation	9,256	
	b. Charitable contributions		9,256
9	Add lines 7 and 8		21,256
10	Income (page 1, line 28) – line 6 less line 9		352,444

APPENDIX D. THREE FOLLOW-UP EXERCISES

The three main exercises illustrate major tax and financial integration issues. However, they do not address some of the more complex issues that an instructor may wish to include in his or her class. In this section, we present additional exercises that could be used to illustrate using a balance sheet approach to determine tax expense, using a valuation allowance when uncertainties exist about the future value of an existing tax asset, and accounting for uncertain tax positions. The three exercises are independent of each other, such that one, two, or all of them could be used after the main exercises.

FOLLOW-UP EXERCISE 1 – USING A BALANCE SHEET APPROACH

CPA Bob Wilson had been using an income statement approach to help the Nuñez family account for their tax expense, tax payments, and resulting tax assets and liabilities. This approach examined the financial statement and tax timing differences of revenues and expenses, booking deferred tax assets and deferred tax liabilities based on estimates of which tax effects would be realized in the future. When a company is just starting operations, this method does an accurate job of calculating the value of both the income statement and balance sheet components of tax issues.

After several years, Bob decided that it was important to look at the existing deferred tax assets and liabilities to make sure they remained realistic. Some of the factors to be considered were whether there had been a change in tax rates, or if some of the estimates used in the original transactions (such as warranty or bad debts expectations) were still valid. He found a few issues and decided to explain the situation to José and Christina using T-accounts for illustration. As of the beginning of the year, there was a balance in the deferred tax asset account of $10,500 and in the deferred tax liability account of $15,680. These reflect the tax effects from cumulative underlying differences between tax revenues/expenses and book revenues/expenses of $30,000 and $44,800 using a tax rate of 35%.

Deferred Tax Asset	
10,500	

Deferred Tax Liability	
	15,680

Bob explained that he had analyzed these beginning balances at the same time that he calculated this year's taxable income to be $315,000, with an effective tax rate of 35%. He had also looked at new differences from this year, and along with his analysis of the balances in the deferred accounts, believes that the end of year cumulative underlying differences leading to future deductible amounts to be $38,700 and that end of year cumulative underlying differences leading to future taxable amounts to be $42,000.

Required

1. What should be the ending balances in the deferred tax asset and deferred tax liability accounts?
2. What is the journal entry necessary to recognize tax expense on the financial statements?

Solutions

1. The ending balance in the deferred tax asset should be $13,545 ($38,700 × 35%) and the ending balance in the deferred tax liability should be $14,700 ($42,000 × 35%).
2. Taxes payable is taxable income times the tax rate. The debits and credits to the deferred accounts are determined as the difference between the beginning and ending balances, leaving tax expense as a plug figure.

Tax expense	106,225	
Deferred tax asset	3,045	
Deferred tax liability	980	
Taxes payable		110,250

FOLLOW-UP EXERCISE 2 – USE OF A VALUATION ALLOWANCE

The first few years were quite profitable for Nuñez Security Services, but the company's fortunes declined several years later when a large national security firm opened a branch office in town. Gradually their profits turned into losses. These losses were mitigated somewhat, because Nuñez was able to receive refunds for taxes paid in the past through tax loss carryback provisions. Last year, the carryback benefits were exhausted, and a tax benefit in anticipation of a carryforward was recognized.

The composition of their deferred tax asset at this time was as follows:

1. Attributable to expected tax benefits from a loss carryforward recognized at the end of last year	$14,000
2. Future deductible warranty expenses	5,250
Total deferred tax asset	$19,250

Bob Wilson, the CPA of Nuñez, was concerned about the $14,000 component in the deferred tax asset account. This year's financial results had not provided the turnaround that they had hoped from the new products they introduced. Bob believed that there was a less than 50% probability that the company would ever be able to realize the $14,000 in tax benefits.

Required

1. What criteria should be used in deciding whether or not to establish a valuation allowance for a questionable deferred tax asset account? Based on these criteria should an allowance be determined in this case?
2. Assuming that an allowance is necessary, what is the journal entry and how does it affect the financial statements? By using this allowance this year, how has the matching principle been affected?

Solutions

1. SFAS No. 109 and FIN No. 48 set up a process for analyzing the value of expected tax benefits. Specifically, you need to reduce the value of the deferred tax asset if, based on the weight of evidence, it is more likely than not (a likelihood of more than 50%) that some portion will not be realized. Last year, Bob may have been encouraged by plans for new products. This year he feels that there is less than a 50% probability of value, so the asset should be written down with a valuation allowance.

Tax benefit from carryforward	14,000	
Allowance to reduce		
Deferred tax asset		14,000

The credit in this entry is a contra account to the deferred tax asset account and reduces it to the $5,520 associated with the warranty. The debit in this entry will go to this year's income statement as a negative amount, probably with a more descriptive account title explaining that it reverses a tax benefit taken previously. Unfortunately, matching has suffered from the delay in setting up an allowance. The $14,000 anticipated tax benefit reduced last year's operating loss. Its reversal in the present year results in this year's loss being too overstated by $14,000.

FOLLOW-UP EXERCISE 3 – FIN 48: ACCOUNTING FOR UNCERTAIN TAX POSITIONS

Several years after starting their business, José and Christina began efforts to expand their market into a neighboring state. The couple met with Bob, their CPA, to share information about their business so that he could prepare the couple's financial statements and tax returns for the year. When Bob heard about the additional efforts to move into the neighboring state, he was glad to hear that the couple was looking at ways to expand their business, but he was not entirely sure what the tax implications would be. Recently, the neighboring state had introduced a credit to attract new businesses, and he was not sure whether the couple's business would qualify for the credit. After his meeting with the couple, Bob met with Suzanne, a colleague in his firm who specializes in state tax issues.

After describing the situation to Suzanne, she explained that the statute for the neighboring state was not entirely clear as to whether the business would qualify for the credit or not. Suzanne further explained that currently, there were taxpayers in similar situations to the couple's business and that some of these businesses had been allowed to take the full credit while others had been challenged by the Revenue Department of the state and only allowed the credit on a portion of their sales or no credit at all. After reviewing all of the facts, Suzanne and Bob came to the recommendation that the company should take a credit for $1,000 on the return for the neighboring state.

Bob is now considering how he should account for this tax situation on the financial statements of the company.

Required

Answer the following questions regarding the situation of the couple:

1. What threshold has to be met for the company to be required to book a tax benefit for this situation?

2. Assume that the company expects that the range of possible outcomes on this tax issue is as follows:

Amount of Tax Benefit ($) – Expected to be Sustained	Percentage Likelihood – The Position will be Sustained
1,000	25
800	20
550	15
300	30
0	10

What amount should the company book as the tax benefit related to this credit?

Solutions

1. The standard that must be met to book the transaction is the "More likely than not" standard (i.e., greater likelihood than 50% that there will be some tax benefit).
2. Based on the probability that is given, the amount of tax benefit that should be booked is $550. Instructors can use this example to initiate a discussion of the considerable judgment that is involved in these reporting situations by asking students to consider how they think the probability and dollar amounts used in the questions are determined.

GROUPTHINK IN ACCOUNTING EDUCATION

Michael P. Riordan, Diane A. Riordan and E. Kent St. Pierre

ABSTRACT

Professional organizations are encouraging accounting educators to better prepare their students for their professional careers by improving students' interpersonal skills. Although accounting instructors are responding by including group activities in their courses, they may not be considering the negative impact of the phenomenon known as "groupthink" on the outcome of group problem solving. Our search of the Social Science Citation Index *(2007) provides evidence that groupthink continues to be an area of research interest in academic disciplines other than accounting. Our search provides* no *evidence that accounting educators are acknowledging or addressing the potential influences the groupthink dynamic may have on students working in groups. The dynamics involved with groupthink have the potential to affect the quality of decisions made by accounting students in their classroom assignments as well as in their future professional lives. We describe the dynamics leading to groupthink, provide examples from our own experience, and offer accounting educators guidelines to discourage the impact of groupthink on the process of student work groups.*

Advances in Accounting Education: Teaching and Curriculum Innovations, Volume 9, 189–204

ISSN: 1085-4622/doi:10.1016/S1085-4622(08)09008-1

Accounting educators are encouraged by a multitude of professional bodies, including both the Institute of Management Accountants (IMA) and the American Institute of Certified Public Accountants (AICPA), to prepare students for team-based work (Bryant & Albring, 2006, p. 241). Many of us are responding to this challenge. Albrecht and Sack (2000, pp. 45–54) report that 68% of department heads respond that they have added "group-work components" to most accounting classes and 75% of faculty report using "Team (group)" activities in their teaching.

Although Rebele et al. (1998, p. 12) provide a review of this pedagogical "enhancement," instructors often assign group work with a minimal amount of critical analysis. Hopper (2003, p. 24) posits that, as exciting as such strategies may appear for instructors, new pedagogies "warrant critical inspection no less than the archaic pedagogies they are intended to best."

Because the majority of accounting instructors now assign group work, academics should consider the negative impact of the phenomenon known as "groupthink" on the outcome of group problem solving. Understanding the dynamics of groupthink is important because the phenomenon has the potential to affect not only the quality of decisions made by accounting students in their classroom assignments, but also the quality of their judgments as professionals working in a team-based environment (Moorhead, Neck, & West, 1998, p. 328) – the very reason we have incorporated groups in the accounting curriculum.

In her public address to a college graduating class in 2003, Marcia Angell, senior lecturer at the Harvard Medical School and former editor of the *New England Journal of Medicine*, stated:

> ...beware of groupthink, the passive absorption of the dominant ideas, values and tastes of your group. Groupthink leads inexorably to the dumbing down of the group. Groupthink leads not only to an intellectual dumbing down but also to an ethical dumbing down. Group think diffuses responsibility, sometimes in disastrous ways; group think leaves an important part of your mind idle, the part that wants to think.

Our chapter describes the dynamic process underlying the development of groupthink and offers suggestions to accounting educators to counteract its impact. First we provide readers with a brief overview of the phenomenon known as groupthink. Then we describe how the publication history in current databases provides evidence that accounting educators are not considering the impact of groupthink on the dynamics encountered by students in their group work. In the last section we share our own experiences with student groups and suggest strategies to thwart the development of groupthink.

OVERVIEW OF THE CONCEPT OF GROUPTHINK

Janis (1972, p. 8) introduced a theory commonly referred to as "groupthink." Members in the group strive for unanimity and, as a result, come to premature decisions without realistically appraising alternative courses of action. The term "groupthink" is catchy, and its proposition is intuitively appealing. As a result, most people recognize the concept without formal study, and the term appears frequently in the popular press. For example, in a discussion of the space shuttle Columbia disaster, Schwartz and Wald (2003, p. 5) comment: "The shuttle investigation may conclude that NASA did nothing wrong. But if part of the problem turns out to be the culture of decision making at NASA, it could lead to more group dynamics and words like *groupthink* ...". As another example, in their discussion of Enron's demise, Stephens and Behr (2002, p. A01) report "Some former Enron employees said they embraced the competition. Others, however, said loyalty required a sort of groupthink. You had to ... 'drink the Kool-Aid' ...". The formal theory proposes that the presence of a number of specific antecedent conditions increases the probability that a group will demonstrate characteristics or symptoms representative of groupthink. These characteristics may lead to defects in the group's decision-making process and result in a poor decision.

According to T'Hart (1991, pp. 249–251) at the time he developed his theory, Janis was rare in his broad interdisciplinary approach to theory development and, as a result of the range of appeal, the theory became one of the best-known attempts to explain political decisions. One now can find discussions of the issue in management, political science, and psychology textbooks. The theory has been very prominent in the social sciences. All of the 55 social psychology textbooks published between 1982 and 1997 and examined by Paulus (1998, p. 364) include a discussion of groupthink. In the following paragraphs we provide a brief overview of the theory construction as background information for accounting educators.

Antecedents to Groupthink

Janis (1982, p. 9) noted that the central antecedent is group cohesion, which is considered necessary but not sufficient for groupthink to occur. Additional antecedents are insulation of the group, homogeneity of membership, lack of methodical procedure for search and appraisal of alternatives, and "directive leadership, and high stress with a low degree of hope for finding a better solution than the one favored by the leader or other influential persons" (Janis & Mann, 1977, p. 132). Thus, the leader's behaviors and the members' beliefs are significant antecedents of groupthink. According to Esser and Lindoerfer (1989, p. 176), the theory does not require all antecedents to be present for groupthink to occur. These attitudes and behaviors lead to the symptoms of groupthink which in turn result in the increased probability of the group's reaching a poor decision.

Symptoms of Groupthink

The symptoms of groupthink include:

- Illusions of invulnerability and belief in inherent group morality,
- Collective rationalization and stereotyping of other groups, and
- Self-censorship, direct pressure, mind guards, and the illusion of being in agreement (Janis & Mann, 1977, p. 132).

Three of the antecedents proposed by Janis – directive leadership, insulation of the group, and lack of methodical procedures for search and appraisal – result in encouraging early adoption of a particular decision and may have a joint impact with cohesiveness on the probability of the dynamic emerging in a group's processing (Longley & Pruitt, 1980, p. 91).

The illusion of invulnerability creates excessive optimism and encourages taking extreme risks, and an unquestioned belief in the group's morality inclines the members to ignore ethical consequences of their decisions (Montanari & Moorhead, 1989, p. 210). T'Hart (1991, p. 265) describes the relationship between the categories of symptoms and the group's assumption of risk. Overestimation (illusions of invulnerability and beliefs in group morality) sets the stage for over-optimism. The sense of optimism is reinforced by closed-mindedness while cautionary forces are restrained by the uniformity pressures. The group neglects to consider risk because they neglect to consider the future and are insensitive to contemplating that they are even taking any risks (p. 266). The symptoms of groupthink result in premature consensus-seeking behaviors by group members, and these behaviors produce poor decisions.

LACK OF CONSIDERATION OF "GROUPTHINK" IN ACCOUNTING EDUCATION LITERATURE

Montanari and Moorhead (1989, p. 209) state that, since the publication of Janis' theory, few studies report an examination of the groupthink hypothesis. In an issue dedicated to the concept of groupthink a decade later, Turner and Pratkanis (1998, p. 107) continue to report fewer than two dozen empirical investigations. They propose that the sheer number of variables inflates the power requirements of controlled experimental research and complicates archival research.

Esser (1998, p. 117) reports that the hundreds of publications citing groupthink continue to far outnumber the publications reporting empirical studies on the concept. Only a few of the existing case studies at that time involve tests of the theory, and many of the studies focus on a retrospective analysis of the same international incidents. The incidents analyzed for evidence of groupthink include the Bay of Pigs crisis, Watergate, and Vietnam (see, for example, Kramer, 1998; Raven, 1998). Park (2000, p. 873) also reports about two dozen empirical studies providing only partial support of the model with most evidence in support of the model being supplied by the results of case studies and content analyses rather than experimental design.

Turner and Pratkanis (1998, p. 107) report a rate for empirical publications on groupthink at "roughly one per year." We searched the *Social Science Citation Index* (2007) for articles with the term "Groupthink" or "groupthink" in their titles during the period of 1/1/1998 to 6/11/2007. We find a similar rate of publication during this latter period with a total of 31 articles for this nine and one-half year period, twelve of which are empirical studies. Researchers continue to use the framework to analyze current events for evidence of groupthink, including Enron and the Gulf crisis (see, for example, O'Connor, 2003; Yetiv, 2003, respectively). Authors also continue to debate the model's overall merit and explore the relationships among the variables.

The journal *Organizational Behavior and Human Decision Processes* published a special issue in February/March 1998 to commemorate the theory's 25th anniversary. Paulus (1998, p. 362) comments on the collection summarizing that, despite little consensus among the papers in the issue, it is evident that groupthink is an influential and highly cited construct. Of the 55 textbooks he examined published during the 1990s, all devoted from three to five pages to the construction (p. 364).

Our purpose in writing this chapter is not to provide a comprehensive review of the general theory of groupthink. Rather we are motivated to ask why accounting educators are ignoring the implications of such a popular theory in psychology and other disciplines. A search of the ERIC (accessed through EBSCO) education database for this time period (1/1/1998–6/11/2007) produces not a single journal article with a focus on groupthink in higher education in accounting.

Hopper (2003, p. 26) cautions that the decision to assign group work in the classroom should consider the learners' interests. According to Hopper, a course in a physical therapy program that prepares the student to be a member of a medical team is a better fit for team-based work than a course teaching medical terminology. In other words, as instructors we should be able to identify a purpose to the team-building exercise itself. As *accounting* educators, we may be able to justify our team-based assignments because we are following the recommendations of professional bodies, such as the AICPA and IMA, to prepare our students for their careers. However, as *educators*, we have the additional responsibility to consider the impact of the environment, such as group work, on student learning, and to improve the quality of students' individual decision-making.

Johnson and Weaver (1992, p. 99) relate certain groupthink antecedents directly to the classroom environment in higher education "[w]ith a plausible, though unproven, link between the classroom and group think decision making…" Traditional classrooms discourage independent thought and action in students. Educators may strive for cohesiveness in their classroom because cohesiveness suggests a sense of sharing, comfort, and acceptance. Lectures, especially in large classes, may promote insulation with students rarely questioning the professor. As instructors, time pressures often prevent us from presenting many alternative views. Lastly, teachers are authoritative in our culture and are influential leaders. Therefore, it is likely that many of our accounting classrooms in higher education present an environment with the antecedents for groupthink even without our considering the impact in smaller groups of students.

Auer-Rizzi and Berry (2000, pp. 264–282) have documented the impact of groupthink on college-age groups of international business students. The groupthink dynamic described the processes undertaken by all the groups. Video recorded and written reflective data provide evidence of the overconfidence of the groups in their decision-making. In the other exercise, one group came to a premature decision before discussing alternatives and then proceeded to confirm each other's views without adequate discussion. Whatever the label one attaches to these group behaviors (groupthink or something else) given the pressure on accounting educators to include student group work and the extent we adopt group work into the curriculum, we are drawn to share our own observations and the strategies we use to improve student group dynamics.

In the next section of this chapter we draw upon the theory of groupthink to interpret our own experiences with student groups. We cite the results of specific studies along with our observations to support our interpretation. Lastly, we offer suggestions to mitigate the impact of these influences on student group work in the accounting education environment. Whether or not the problem is accepted as a symptom attributable to "groupthink theory" by our readers, our strategies are helpful in the practice of managing certain problems in student groups that emerge when students fail to adequately contemplate a problem and arrive at premature decisions – the ultimate result of the groupthink phenomenon.

OUR OBSERVATIONS AND SUGGESTIONS

Based upon our extensive experience in the classroom, we believe that our traditional students are probably more susceptible to the symptoms of groupthink than the general public because of their maturity level. Young adults may feel more invulnerable, and their beliefs sometimes can lead them to engage in high risk personal behaviors such as speeding or experimentation with illegal substances. We also believe that college-aged students working in groups may be predisposed to the groupthink syndrome due to the structures for learning encountered in higher education.

The traditional college student is often subject to peer pressure, and self-censorship and direct pressure by other group members are major symptoms of groupthink. Groups exhibiting symptoms of groupthink apply subtle pressure to censor expressions of personal concerns in order to achieve group unanimity. The illusion of unanimity arises when the group thinks it is in agreement when it has simply reached concurrence in order not to disagree.

Flippen (1999, p. 146) has explored the motivation underlying the behavior of group members and describes how for some members currying favor with the leader may be more important than reaching a good decision. Some members may fail to criticize a proposal because they lack confidence in their knowledge of the subject matter (Flippen, 1999, p. 149). We propose that our students are prone to conformity because they want to please the other members of their group, and, as novices, they are unsure of their solutions. During our own interactions with students, we have observed repeatedly in different contexts that they follow the lead of who they believe are the most competent students.

If the symptoms or characteristics of groupthink are present, the theory predicts that defective decision-making may occur because of one or more of the following actions taken by the group (Janis, 1972, p. 10, 1982, pp. 9–10). The group may conduct a weak information search and an incomplete survey of objectives and alternatives. The group may be biased or simply fail to reappraise initially rejected alternatives. The members may fail to critically examine the drawbacks and risks of the preferred choice, may not consider the values implied by the decision, and may fail to have contingency plans if the decision is not acceptable. Under these conditions, the decision process suffers from the lack of critical analysis.

In the following paragraphs we present examples of these symptomatic behaviors from our own experiences and offer strategies to help groups improve critical analysis and avoid premature decisions. The first two observations described in the following paragraphs derive primarily from the antecedent of directive leadership. The third experience is consistent with the antecedents of homogeneity of group membership and insulation of the group during its decision-making.

Observation No. 1 – The Undergraduate Solution Set Challenge

One of the authors assigned a problem set to 36 sophomore accounting students who worked in 12 groups outside of the classroom. She informed them that she would call randomly on the groups to present the various solutions to the problem set in front of the class. On the day of the presentations the instructor made the additional announcement to students that, after hearing the presentation of another group's answer, each student would have the opportunity to ask questions, challenge, and ultimately develop a solution to each question on an individual basis. The purpose in delaying the announcement of this last-minute option was to offer students incentives to do their best on the original assignment and then to follow the classroom presentations.

During the presentation and challenge exercise, one of the brightest students in the sophomore class supported an incorrect challenge of another group to a correct algebraic response on the board. She made the challenge in a loud, confident manner and simply assured the class, "I have checked this out." Of the 36 individual student responses, only one student did not follow the challenger. Even students who originally submitted the correct answer in the group solution substituted the incorrect solution provided by the challenger. Completing the same exercise in a subsequent semester, all of the students ($n = 30$) followed the lead of a non-traditional student who had led the curve on examinations. As a result, after a similar presentation and challenge session, the entire class earned a perfect score on the group project. In these "unplanned" experiments the author found that her students ultimately were engaged in an exercise of "following the leader."

Ahlfinger and Esser (2001, p. 31) provide evidence from a laboratory experiment with student groups that promotional leadership does impact group dynamics. They did not rely on observation alone, but also made assessments using the Groupthink Index, a questionnaire developed by Glaser (1993), and a questionnaire reporting on the group leader's behavior. Their study provides evidence that "groups with promotional leaders produced more symptoms of groupthink, discussed fewer facts and reached a decision more quickly than did groups with nonpromotional leadership" (p. 39) and that empirical research of the groupthink model is hampered by measurement problems.

What strategies can instructors adopt to counteract promotional leadership in student groups? In the case of an in-class discussion, we suggest appointing a "devil's advocate." Appointing a devil's advocate in the group provides a structure for conflict and debate, a process that strengthens the decision-making process. In addition to providing a ready source of disagreement, the devil's advocate role informs students that the professor feels it is important to challenge the group's process and decisions. At first it is necessary to explain this role and assist the students in understanding the function of a devil's advocate. The instructor involved in our first observation now assigns this role to the extra students when the class does not divide evenly into groups in class. For groups making classroom presentations, the instructor assigns the devil's advocate role to one of the non-presenting groups prior to class and before the presentations are made.

Observation No. 2 – The Annual Student Case Competition

One of the authors is an academic advisor to groups of students in the annual IMA case competition. Students in the video case competition are hand-selected by the advisor into a competing group based on their successful academic achievements in undergraduate accounting classes. In some of the debriefing sessions with groups in the earlier years of the competition, the traditional students expressed a hesitancy to disagree with the older, non-traditional student. As a result of their comments, this author subsequently made changes to the composition of the groups.

What strategies are effective in this situation? Whenever possible, he adds a second non-traditional student as a counter balance. If the groups include only one non-traditional student, the instructor appoints a traditional student as the team leader with veto power in cases where the group is divided in terms of a particular decision.

We also have observed groupthink at the graduate level when groups have a dominant personality who drives the group agenda. If the class has students who are at the management level in their firm and are involved in daily decision-making where they work, they may have difficulty sharing the decision-making function with group members. This desire to control the group results in the same issues that occur with undergraduates dealing with a non-traditional student in their groups.

Some additional strategies are useful in diffusing directive leadership. Consider dividing student groups into subgroups and requiring separate meeting times for the smaller groups prior to the larger group meeting in order to prevent one strong personality from dominating the entire process. This strategy works for larger work groups. Another alternative is to assign leadership roles in the group and rotate these roles so that everyone in the group has an opportunity to be in charge of the discussion. The devil's advocate previously mentioned also is effective in both large and small groups. You may find that some students enjoy this role and will volunteer for the position.

Observation No. 3 – Graduate Student Groups that Lack Heterogeneity

Another antecedent for groupthink is homogeneity of group membership. The group is insulated from outside influences. Homogeneous groups are more predisposed to groupthink. When offered the opportunity to self-select, undergraduate students often form groups with their friends. Obviously, the solution to this problem is for instructors to assign students to working groups and separate students with an existing alliance, such as the same sports team, former high school, or club.

At the graduate level, student preference for group composition expresses itself with students grouping with members from the same company or working in the same industry. One of the authors encountered such biases in two different situations with part-time graduate financial accounting students. When graduate students self-selected, the resulting groups produced a bias by company or industry. The groups presented their solutions to the instructor with an air of "having all the answers." This dynamic is symptomatic of groupthink's illusions of invulnerability and collective rationalization and derives from cohesiveness and homogeneity. One of us also observed this same omnipotent air in several groups of five-year students in our Masters of Science in Accounting program where the students self-selected into small groups after working together for three years.

Several strategies could be used to increase the probability of students' conducting a methodological search. These strategies reduce the number of antecedents to groupthink and structure mechanisms to avoid the dynamic. To increase the probability of adequate deliberation, students may generate a written list of alternative solutions and evaluate these alternative ideas in writing. When students are responsible for reporting on alternative solutions discussed by the group, members consider multiple answers to the problem. Each group could maintain a journal or keep formal minutes of their group meetings to document how they evaluated each alternative. When students summarize in writing the process and resources they used to evaluate an alternative, they gather information from outside the group.

Strategies such as dialectic method programs are also effective in dealing with problems that are present when members come from similar backgrounds (Miranda, 1994, p. 111). The dialectic method programs conflict into the decision-making process by structuring debate between differing views in the group regardless of members' personal feelings.

GENERAL STRATEGIES TO COUNTERACT GROUPTHINK

Instructors may find that our observations hit a familiar chord and are similar to their own experiences. We have heard this reaction from colleagues when discussing the topic of groupthink at conferences. On the other hand, the examples we have provided may be too specific. In that case, we offer some general strategies that instructors can modify to fit most circumstances. The following strategies are based in part on Janis's general recommendations for preventing groupthink (1982, p. 262):

(1) *Encourage the flow of ideas within the group and interaction with outside influences.* We recommend that instructors require students to support assumptions with at least one outside source. This support may take the

form of research studies cited by the students on the particular issue or, as one of our colleagues currently requires, consultation with an outside expert/practitioner. The process will differ with the nature of the assignment.

(2) *Require students to consider alternative solutions.* We recommend that instructors provide students with a procedure to solve problems. For example, require the simple four-step procedure of (1) identifying the problem, (2) determining the causes of the problem, (3) identifying multiple solutions, and (4) evaluating and selecting among the alternatives and documenting these steps in the group's decision-making process. Emphasize the importance of steps 3 and 4 and require the students to document their problem-solving process in writing as part of the assignment.

(3) *Provide students sufficient time before a due date to allow them to both reach a conclusion and then to reconsider the original recommendation.* Because students are likely to delay working on a project until close to its due date, structure interim dates for stages of completion of their work if the nature of the assignment permits. These suggestions are practical strategies that improve student group process whether or not the reader accepts that the problems in group function result from the tenets of groupthink as a theory.

Groupthink as a Precursor of Unethical Business Decisions

Professional organizations are promoting the development of interpersonal skills in our classrooms, and instructors are responding. As a result of these external pressures, our academic programs now include the development of interpersonal skills in our list of student learning objectives submitted to accrediting organizations. The development of ethical behaviors also is on our list of developmental objectives at both the College of Business and accounting program levels. What strategies can we use to cover the development of such skills in our students when there is hardly enough time to teach the material in our courses and we are not trained as ethicists?

We suggest assigning the reading of an article written by Sims (1992) and published in the *Journal of Business Ethics*. He argues that inquiries into unethical behavior in corporations should consider the roles of corporate culture and groupthink. This article is equally relevant today given the consequences of the decisions by accounting professionals that resulted in scandals such as Enron and WorldCom.[1] Sims' proposition on the relationship between groupthink and ethics reflects the concerns of Marcia Angell as shared with university graduates in her graduation address: "... Groupthink leads not only to an intellectual dumbing down but also to an ethical dumbing down. Group think diffuses responsibility, sometimes in disastrous ways; group think leaves an important part of your mind idle, the part that wants to think" (Angell, 2003).

The reading exercise sensitizes business students to the existence of groupthink and its potential to contribute to unethical decisions by business groups. The article concludes with a review of Janis' own prescription for reducing the probability of groupthink – providing a handy reference for students to consider in both their group work and future professional lives.

Is Groupthink the Culprit?

Academic theories are subject to challenge over time, and this critical process improves the quality of theoretical constructs. This process of critical review is not unlike what we are suggesting to our own colleagues in connection with our decision as a profession to assign group work to our students. We understand and appreciate the fact that all groups do not result in "groupthink" occurring, and that many group decisions are excellent and provide very important results in the business world. However, we are also aware that groupthink can occur. Informing our students and making sure they are familiar with the concept and its implications can benefit them when involved in group decision-making.

Insufficient empirical research exists to confirm "point-by-point" the validity of groupthink theory (Ahlfinger & Esser, 2001, p. 32). All of the research suffers from this weakness (Schafer & Crichlow, 2002, p. 47). Difficulties exist with conducting such research, including operationalizing variables, measuring constructs, and testing all of the antecedents in the model simultaneously. Critics suggest adding variables to the original model or replacing the model with a more general decision-making model. Despite these and other criticisms, groupthink research has "considerable heuristic value" (Esser, 1998, p. 116).

Paulus (1998, p. 367) questions whether the goal of validating the complete groupthink model is too stringent a criterion for any theory. He maintains that all theories are "temporary guides to understanding reality on the way to discovering the truth" and are subject to modification from time to time.

Researchers will continue to validate the groupthink model and to question whether groupthink is actually the cause of poor group decisions. However, from a practical standpoint as instructors, the challenge we must address at this time is the issue of improving our students' decision-making process. If the symptoms attributable to groupthink are present, then the dynamics of our student groups require modification in order to improve the functioning of the group and the quality of their group decisions.

SUMMARY

Groupthink is a concept that has implications for students engaged in classroom group activities. It is imperative that we sensitize our students to the symptoms of groupthink and help them to develop strategies to discourage this phenomenon in their thinking. Without interventions, college-age students, trying to be acceptable to their peers, may easily fall victim to groupthink. Accounting instructors and students should understand its antecedents, symptoms, and consequences when designing effective classroom group activities. This awareness will help instructors to achieve their instructional objectives and students to be better problem-solvers. Instructors should inform their students of the potential for groupthink impacting future decisions in their professional lives.

This chapter introduces accounting educators to the underlying theory of the concept of groupthink, relates the topic to the environment of accounting education, and offers suggestions on counteracting its impact in student group activities. This chapter also may serve as a gentle reminder that it is important to subject our newer pedagogies to sufficient critical analysis. Otherwise, we too are the victims of groupthink.

NOTE

1. See Stephens and Behr (2002) and Scharff (2005), respectively, for articles contemplating the role of groupthink on the decision-making in these incidents.

REFERENCES

Ahlfinger, N. R., & Esser, J. K. (2001). Testing the groupthink model: Effects of promotional leadership and conformity predisposition. *Social Behavior and Personality*, *29*, 31–42.

Albrecht, W. S., & Sack, R. J. (2000). Accounting education: Charting the course through a perilous future. *Accounting Education Series*, *16*, 1–72.

Angell, M. (2003). James Madison University Commencement Address, December 12, 2003, James Madison Convocation, Harrisonburg, VA.

Auer-Rizzi, W., & Berry, M. (2000). Business vs. cultural frames of reference in group decision making: Interactions among Austrian, Finnish, and Swedish business students. *The Journal of Business Communication*, *37*, 264–292.

Bryant, S. M., & Albring, S. (2006). Effective team building: Guidance for accounting educators. *Issues in Accounting Education*, *21*, 241–265.

ERIC (Office of Educational Research and Improvement). (2007). Web-based resource accessed through EBSCO Host. Washington, DC: Education Resource Information Center.

Esser, J. K. (1998). Alive and well after 25 years: A review of groupthink research. *Organizational Behavior and Human Decision Processes*, *23*, 116–141.

Esser, J. K., & Lindoerfer, J. L. (1989). Groupthink and the space shuttle challenger accident: Toward a quantitative case analysis. *Journal of Behavioral Decision Making*, *2*, 167–177.

Flippen, A. R. (1999). Understanding groupthink from a self-regulatory perspective. *Small Group Research*, *30*, 139–165.

Glaser, R. (1993). Groupthink index. *Organizational Design and Development*. King of Prussia, Pennsylvania.

Hopper, K. B. (2003). In defense of the solitary learner: A response to collaborative, constructivist education. *Educational Technology* (March-April), 24–29.

Janis, I. L. (1972). *Victims of groupthink*. Boston: Houghton-Mifflin.

Janis, I. L. (1982). *Groupthink* (2nd ed.). Boston: Houghton-Mifflin.

Janis, I. L., & Mann, L. (1977). *Decision-making: A psychological analysis of conflict, choice and commitment*. New York: Free Press.

Johnson, S. D., & Weaver, R. L., II. (1992). Groupthink and the classroom: Changing familiar patterns to encourage critical thought. *Journal of Instructional Psychology*, *19*, 99–107.

Kramer, R. M. (1998). Revisiting the Bay of Pigs and Vietnam decision 25 years later: How well has the groupthink hypothesis stood the test of time? *Organizational Behavior and Human Decision Processes*, *73*(February/March), 236–271.

Longley, J., & Pruitt, D. G. (1980). Groupthink a critique of Janis's theory. *Review of Personality and Social Psychology*, 74–93.

Miranda, S. M. (1994). Avoidance of groupthink. *Small Group Research*, *25*, 105–136.

Montanari, J. R., & Moorhead, G. (1989). Development of the groupthink assessment inventory. *Educational and Psychological Measurement*, *49*, 209–219.

Moorhead, G., Neck, C. P., & West, M. S. (1998). The tendency toward defective decision making within self-managing teams: The relevance of groupthink for the 21st century. *Organizational Behavior and Human Decision Processes*, *73*, 327–351.

O'Connor, M. A. (2003). The Enron board: The perils of groupthink. *University of Cincinnati Law Review (Summer)*, *71*(4), 1233–1320.

Park, W. (2000). A comprehensive empirical investigation of the relationships among variables of the groupthink model. *Journal of Organizational Behavior*, *21*, 873–887.

Paulus, P. B. (1998). Developing consensus about groupthink after all these years. *Organizational Behavior and Human Decision Processes*, *73*, 362–374.

Raven, B. H. (1998). Groupthink, Bay of Pigs and Watergate reconsidered. *Organizational Behavior and Human Decision Processes*, *73*(February/March), 352–361.

Rebele, J. E., Apostolou, B. A., Buckless, F. A., Hassell, J. M., Paquette, L. R., & Stout, D. E. (1998). Accounting education literature review (1991–1997), Part I: Curriculum and instructional approaches. *Journal of Accounting Education*, *16*, 1–51.

Schafer, M., & Crichlow, S. (2002). The *Process-Outcome* connection in foreign policy decision making: A quantitative study building on groupthink. *International Studies Quarterly*, *46*, 45–68.

Scharff, M. M. (2005). Understanding WorldCom's accounting fraud: Did groupthink play a role? *Journal of Leadership and Organizational Studies*, *11*, 109–118.

Schwartz, J., & Wald, M. L. (2003). The nation: NASA's curse? Groupthink is 30 years old, and still going strong, *The New York Times*, March 9, Section 4, Page 5, Column 1, Week in Review Desk.

Sims, R. R. (1992). Linking groupthink to unethical behavior in organizations. *Journal of Business Ethics*, *11*, 651–662.

Social Science Citation Index. (2007). Institute for Scientific Information. Web-based resource. Philadelphia, PA: Web of Science.

Stephens, J., & Behr, P., (2002). Enron's culture fed its demise; groupthink promoted foolhardy risks, *The Washington Post*, January 27, Section A, p. 1.

Turner, M. E., & Pratkanis, A. R. (1998). Twenty-five years of groupthink theory and research: Lesson from the evaluation of a theory. *Organizational Behavior and Human Decision Processes*, *73*, 105–115.

T'Hart, P. (1991). Irving L. Janis's victims of groupthink. *Political Psychology*, *12*, 247–278.

Yetiv, S. A. (2003). Groupthink and the Gulf crisis. *British Journal of Political Science*, *33*(July), 419–442.

THE EFFECT OF FRAUD TRIANGLE FACTORS ON STUDENTS' CHEATING BEHAVIORS

Freddie Choo and Kim Tan

ABSTRACT

This study explores the effects of fraud triangle behaviors (pressure, opportunities, and rationalization) on students' self-reported propensity to cheat in class. We found each fraud triangle factor to be an influence on the students' propensity to cheat. Additionally, we observed a statistically significant three-way interactive effect indicating that all three factors jointly influence the students' propensity to cheat. These findings provide insights for accounting educators concerned with preventing classroom cheating. They also confirm the call by Statement on Auditing Standards No. 99 for auditor focus on fraud triangle variables. This exploratory study also suggests that future research is needed to examine the interactive effects of personality characteristics with fraud triangle factors to better understand student cheating behaviors.

Recent surveys suggest that cheating behavior among university students is widespread and may be increasing. In a 2006 survey of 5,331 students at 32

Advances in Accounting Education: Teaching and Curriculum Innovations, Volume 9, 205–220

ISSN: 1085-4622/doi:10.1016/S1085-4622(08)09009-3

graduate schools in the United States and Canada, 56 percent of business students admitted to cheating at least once in the previous year (McCabe, Butterfield, & Trevino, 2006). A 2005 survey of college students in general reported that 70 percent admitted to some sort of academic cheating, and 37 percent used the Internet to plagiarize (McCabe, 2005a). The University of California at Berkeley website (2003) found a 115 percent increase in reported cases of student dishonesty between 1995 and 2000.

Given the highly publicized accounting frauds of the past decade, there is a great deal of interest in the relationship between this increase in classroom cheating and unethical behavior in the corporate environment. Ogilby (1995) and Sims (1993) found that students who cheat are more likely to be dishonest in their professional behavior. Since the causes of student cheating may be important in understanding unethical behavior in the corporate world, this study hopes to contribute to the understanding by using the fraud triangle concept to investigate cheating behaviors among students.

Recently, in a field survey of 476 students, Becker, Connolly, Lentz, and Morrison (2006) used factor analysis to explore the influence of fraud triangle factors on students' cheating behavior. They found that each of the elements of the fraud triangle was a significant determinant of student cheating. Our study also hopes to contribute to the knowledge of these determinants by testing the robustness of Becker et al.'s (2006) findings by using an experimental survey, more powerful statistical methods, and different cheating behavior metrics.

This chapter is organized as follows. The first section describes the fraud triangle concept. This is followed by a review of the literature. The third section develops the research hypotheses and describes the study's methodology including design, materials, and subjects. Results and limitations are then discussed. The chapter concludes with a result summary and review of the study's implications for accounting instructors and future researchers.

FRAUD TRIANGLE CONCEPT

The fraud triangle concept originated from Donald R. Cressey's work about the psychology of embezzlers (Cressey, 1973). Cressey hypothesized that three variables (perceived financial need, perceived opportunities, and rationalization) led embezzlers to their illegal behaviors. In the early 1980s, the fraud triangle was adapted to auditing by Albrecht et al. (1984, p. 5) who suggested that three variables involved in occupational fraud were consistent with Cressey's fraud triangle concept. These elements were "a situational pressure, a perceived opportunity to commit and conceal the dishonest act, and some way to rationalize the act as being inconsistent with one's personal level of integrity." *Statement on Auditing Standards No. 99: Considerations of Fraud in a Financial Statement Audit* (SAS 99) (AICPA, 2002) later adopted much of Albrecht's work by recognizing that many fraud risks are associated with the three variables of the fraud triangle concept.

LITERATURE REVIEW

To date, there has been an enormous amount of research into students' cheating behavior across many disciplines. Our review of prior studies suggests that their focus has been primarily on the influence of either individual or situational factors on cheating behavior. Individual factors include perceived peer behavior (McCabe et al., 2006); ethics (Malone, 2006); religiosity (Rettinger & Jordan, 2005); beliefs (Lawson, 2004); self-image (Storch, Storch, & Clark, 2002); motivation (Murdock, Hale, & Weber, 2001); attitude (Jordan, 2001); deviance behavior (Blankenship & Whitley, 2001); areas of study (Cohen, Pant, & Sharp, 1998); grades (Burton & Near, 1995); gender (Bolin, 2004); age (Becker et al., 2006); Type-A behavior (Perry, Kane, Bernesser, & Spicker, 1990); degrees (Lane & Schaupp, 1989); and grade point average (Baird, 1980).

Situational factors include chance of being caught (Hugh & McCabe, 2006); classroom goal structure (Murdock, Miller, & Kohlhardt, 2004); in-class deterrent (Smith, Davy, Rosenberg, & Haight, 2002); student–instructor relationship (Stearns, 2001); teacher respect (Murdock et al., 2001); institutional policy (Whitley & Keith-Spiegel, 2001); faculty behavior (Kerkvliet & Sigmund, 1999); classroom environment (Pulvers & Diekoff, 1999); sanction threats (Harpp, Hogan, & Jennings, 1996); and honor codes (McCabe, 1993).

HYPOTHESES DEVELOPMENT AND RESEARCH METHODOLOGY

Research Hypotheses

Both individual and situational factor studies report findings that suggest the presence of a "pressure" variable as described in the fraud triangle concept. Ng, Davis, Bates, and Avellon (2003) found that students are more likely to cheat under peer pressure to increase their social acceptance. Burton and Near (1995) also report a higher incidence of cheating among students under pressure for better grades. Perry et al. (1990) indicated that Type-A students are more likely to cheat because they are under a constant pressure to compete with their peers. Lane and Schaupp (1989) reported that students engaged in unethical behavior were under pressure to complete their degrees. These past findings lead us to hypothesize:

H_{1a}. The presence of pressure will significantly increase the students' propensity to cheat.

The individual and situational factor studies also suggest the presence of an "opportunities" variable as described in the fraud triangle concept. Hugh and McCabe (2006) indicated that students are more likely to cheat if they perceive their chance of being caught for cheating is very low. Bolin (2004) found that students are more likely to cheat if they perceive an opportunity to do so. Smith et al. (2002) reported that there is a relationship between in-class deterrence and the students' future cheating behavior in class. Mohammed, Rawwas, and Isakson (2000) indicated that in-class opportunity to cheat explains most of the students' cheating behavior in comparison with other situational factors. These past findings lead us to hypothesize:

H_{1b}. The presence of opportunities will significantly increase the students' propensity to cheat.

Finally, prior research suggests the presence of a "rationalization" variable as described in the fraud triangle concept. McCabe et al. (2006) reported that students are more likely to cheat if they rationalize their cheating behavior to be a common peer behavior. Del Carlo and Bodner (2006) found that students are more likely to fudge laboratory data if they think that others inside the laboratory are doing the same. Lawson (2004) reported that students rationalize their unethical behaviors in business classes to be acceptable business practices. Similarly, McCabe and Trevino (1997), LaBeff, Clark, Haines, and Diekoff (1990), and Haines, Diekoff, LaBeff, and Clark (1986) all have found a positive relationship between rationalization and cheating behaviors among students. These past findings lead us to hypothesize:

H_{1c}. The presence of rationalization will significantly increase the students' propensity to cheat.

According to the fraud triangle concept, its three variables (pressure, opportunities, and rationalization) not only will exert independent effects on students' cheating behavior, but also will interact with one another to affect students' cheating behavior. Accordingly, we expect to find a significant statistical three-way interactive effect of the three variables (pressure × opportunities × rationalization):

> **H_2.** The presence of a three-way interactive effect (i.e., pressure × opportunities × rationalization) will significantly increase the students' propensity to cheat.

Research Method

We employed a full-factorial within-subjects ANCOVA design as we believe it is better for reducing demand effects. As Choo and Tan (2006, p. 156) explain, a full-factorial within-subjects ANCOVA attributes all that is common to the repeated measures on a subject to a "subject effect" and all that is common to the repeated measures at a point in time to the "time effect." What remains when the "subject effect" and "time effect" are removed is attributed to the "demand effect + error term." When the number of subjects is reasonably large (as it is in this study), there is a very low propensity for serial correlations between the "demand effect + error term." Therefore, there is a very low propensity of mistakenly attributing the "demand effect + error term" to the "subject effect."

The three independent variables were pressure, opportunities, and rationalization. In the survey instrument, we defined each independent variable by using examples.

- Pressure – "to meet student loan or other financial obligations, to enhance future job prospects, to graduate on time, etc."
- Opportunities – "lax controls in exam room, able to hide test answers in electronic devices, seats can be arranged to look at other students' exam papers, etc."
- Rationalization – "nothing to lose, everyone else has cheated, rules are meant to be broken, the exam is unfair, the instructor is a hard grader, the instructor does not seem to care, etc."

Each independent variable had two dichotomous levels: the presence or absence of that variable. We opted for dichotomous measurement because we used ANCOVA analyses in which the variables are implicitly discrete in nature. Therefore, dichotomous measurement is statistically robust in comparison to other research methodologies. Also, it is debatable as to whether continuous or dichotomous measures are more realistic since the variables of interest here are highly abstract and very complex.

According to research conducted by Farrell and Daniel (1995), the list of student cheating behaviors compiled by Fass (1990) is one of the most comprehensive. It includes cheating during examinations, inappropriate use of sources on papers and projects, inappropriate use of writing assistance and tutoring, dishonest collecting and reporting of data, unethical use of academic resources, tampering with the work of others, questionable practices regarding the use of computers, allowing misuse of one's academic work by others, and disregard of academic regulations. Based on this list, we defined the dependent variable (propensity to cheat) as broadly as possible:

> Cheating behavior in class is defined broadly as any conceivable cheating behavior such as cheating in test, plagiarism of assignment, electronic text messaging during exam, and so on.

Cheating behavior was measured on a scale of 0 percent (Never) to 100 percent (Absolutely) which was presented in five-point increments. While a student's self-reported propensity to cheat does not measure his/her actual cheating behavior, this widely used measure is useful because it neither entraps a student nor provides uninvited opportunities to cheat.

Materials

We constructed eight ($2 \times 2 \times 2$) context-free vignettes (versus context-specific vignettes) for the full-factorial within-subjects ANCOVA design. A context-free vignette is one in which a subject is instructed to respond to the dependent variable(s) based on his/her own vignette that matches the broad definition of the independent variable(s). On the other hand, a context-specific vignette is one in which a subject is instructed to respond to the dependent variable(s) based on a specific given vignette containing the independent variable(s). We did not use a context-specific vignette because it tends to entrap a subject into giving a false-positive cheating response, or restrict generalizing a subject's cheating response beyond the specific context that is given.

The eight context-free vignettes were randomized before they were compiled into one of eight sets of survey materials. Randomization was used to reduce a potential "order effect" that might be caused by the order in which the two dichotomous levels (presence or absence) of the three independent variables were presented to the subjects inside each set of the materials (Choo, 1984).

Subjects

Seven professors distributed and collected survey materials to 182 students in their classes who were majoring in accounting, finance, information systems, management, and marketing in the college of business of a large public university in California. The instructors provided students 10 min at the start of class to complete the survey. To minimize overlapping subjects, instructors asked students not to repeat the survey if they had already completed one. Although the sample included subjects from freshman to senior levels, the study did not control for age since prior literature has not specifically linked student age or level to cheating behavior. Additionally, given the low number of international students enrolled in the college, there was no need to control for possible effects of student culture and nationality.

RESULTS

Statistical Findings

Descriptive statistics of possible student factors affecting the propensity to cheat appear in Table 1. A Wilcoxon matched-pair signed-rank test on the frequency distribution of the sample demographic covariates against the frequency distribution of the same variables in a 2006 universitywide record confirmed that the sample is reasonably representative of the university.

Table 2 presents descriptive statistics for the dependent and independent variables. The sample consists of 1,345 usable scores out of a possible 1,456 (i.e., 182 students $\times$ 8 context-free vignettes each). A lower usable sample resulted primarily from our duplication of several questions in the instrument for a *posterior* consistency check. The test yielded an average correlation of 86 percent suggesting that student responses were reasonably consistent. The sample was also lowered by several missing cell values; however, since ANCOVA is statistically robust with missing cell scores, we did not randomly discard data to balance the cell scores in the analysis. Table 2 suggests that the missing cell scores are spread evenly across all the conditions. As suggested by a reviewer, the missing cell scores can be

Table 1. Student Demographics.

Variables	Frequency (%)
Gender ($N = 175$, mean 1.5, standard deviation 0.5)	
Male	45.1
Female	54.9
Level ($N = 175$, mean 3.5, standard deviation 0.7)	
Freshman	1.7
Sophomore	5.7
Junior	40.6
Senior	49.7
Graduate	2.3
Status ($N = 172$, mean 1.1, standard deviation 0.3)	
Full time	90.1
Part time	9.9
Grade point average ($N = 175$, mean 6.6, standard deviation 1.0)	
Less than 2.0	1.1
2.0 and 2.59	12.6
2.6 and 2.99	25.7
3.0 and 3.59	42.3
3.6 and 3.99	17.7
4.0	0.6
Credit units enrolled for the semester ($N = 175$, mean 2.6, standard deviation 0.7)	
1 and 6	5.2
7 and 12	37.7
13 and 18	53.1
19 and 24	2.9
25 and above	1.1

explained by subjects answering the survey questions in the order they were presented, and some just did not get to the last question in the allotted time.

According to Table 2, students' overall propensity to cheat was 19.8 percent, which appears low when compared to prior studies (e.g., McCabe et al., 2006; Hugh & McCabe, 2006). This is likely due to the fact that our study asked students to report their propensity to cheat with reference to specific conditions (i.e., pressure, opportunities, and rationalization), whereas prior studies did not. It also is interesting to note that the students' propensity to cheat was much lower (8.3 percent) when all three conditions were absent, than when all three conditions were present (33 percent). This suggests that the pattern of students' cheating behaviors was consistent with the manipulated present or absent conditions. In addition, the variance was

Table 2. Descriptive Statistics for Dependent and Independent Variables.

Scenario Independent Variables			Dependent Variable Propensity to Cheat		
Pressure	Opportunities	Rationalization	Mean	Standard deviation	Number of observations
Absent	Absent	Absent	8.3	17.7	166
Absent	Absent	Present	15.4	23.2	166
Absent	Present	Absent	19.0	25.6	170
Absent	Present	Present	19.2	24.0	166
Present	Absent	Absent	18.2	25.0	171
Present	Absent	Present	19.7	24.4	166
Present	Present	Absent	25.3	28.7	170
Present	Present	Present	33.0	33.2	170
		Total	19.8	26.4	1,345

Notes: Pressure variable – defined as "e.g., to meet student loan or other financial obligations, to enhance future job prospects, to graduate on time, etc."
Opportunities variable – defined as "e.g., lax controls in exam room, able to hide test answers in electronic devices, seats can be arranged to look at other students' exam papers, etc."
Rationalization variable – defined as "e.g., nothing to lose, everyone else has cheated, rules are meant to be broken, the exam is unfair, the instructor is a hard grader, the instructor does not seem to care, etc."
Propensity to cheat dependent variable – defined as "any conceivable cheating behavior such as cheating in test, plagiarism of assignment, electronic text messaging during exam, and so on." Measured on a scale of 0% (Never) to 100% (Absolutely).

lower (17.7 percent) when all three conditions were absent, than when all three conditions were present (33.2 percent). This suggests that preventing classroom cheating may be more effective than detection in reducing the extent of cheating when all three conditions are present.

Table 3 presents ANOVA analysis results with propensity to cheat as the dependent variable, the fraud triangle factors (PRESSURE, OPPORTUNITES, and RATIONALIZATION) as independent variables, and gender (GENDER), grade point average (GPA), university level (UNIVLEVEL), part/full-time (STATUS), and units taken (UNITS) as covariates.

Each of the three main effects (pressure, opportunities, and rationalization) was statistically significant and supports H_{1a}, H_{1b}, and H_{1c}. More importantly, these findings confirm prior studies which suggest that either pressure *alone* (e.g., Ng et al., 2003; Burton & Near, 1995), or opportunities *alone* (e.g., Bolin, 2004; Smith et al., 2002), or rationalization *alone*

Table 3. Full-Factorial ANOVA Results.

Source of Variation	Sum of Squares	df	Mean Square	*F*-Value	*P*-Value
Overall model	606,283.98	13	46,637.23	72.34	0.000
Pressure	24,950.65	1	24,950.65	38.70	0.000
Opportunities	25,661.795	1	25,661.795	39.81	0.000
Rationalization	5,628.99	1	5,628.99	8.73	0.003
Pressure × opportunities	707.09	1	707.09	1.09	0.295
Pressure × rationalization	75.916	1	75.916	0.118	0.732
Opportunities × rationalization	11.96	1	11.96	0.019	0.892
Pressure × opportunities × rationalization	3,748.12	1	3,748.12	5.81	0.016
Gender	6,325.88	1	6,325.88	9.81	0.002
GPA	6,561.34	1	6,561.34	10.18	0.001
Credit units	4,303.55	1	4,303.55	6.68	0.010
University level	0.01	1	0.01	0.00	0.997
Part/Full time	348.33	1	348.33	0.54	0.462
Error	858,731.01	1,332	644.69		
Total	1,465,015.00	1,345			

Notes: Adjusted $R^2 = 0.408$; Gender = male or female; University level = freshman, sophomore, junior, senior, or graduate; Part/Full time = full-time or part-time student.
GPA – grade point average classified in the following manner: 0.0–0.59, 0.6–0.99, 1.0–1.59, 1.6–1.99, 2.0–2.59, 2.6–2.99, 3.0–3.59, 3.6–3.99, and 4.0.
Credit units – enrolled credit units for the current semester classified in the following manner: 1–6, 7–12, 13–18, 19–24, and 25 and above.
Pressure variable – defined as "e.g., to meet student loan or other financial obligations, to enhance future job prospects, to graduate on time, etc."
Opportunities variable – defined as "e.g., lax controls in exam room, able to hide test answers in electronic devices, seats can be arranged to look at other students' exam papers, etc."
Rationalization variable – defined as "e.g., nothing to lose, everyone else has cheated, rules are meant to be broken, the exam is unfair, the instructor is a hard grader, the instructor does not seem to care, etc."

(e.g., Rettinger & Jordan, 2005; Storch et al., 2002) will significantly increase students' cheating behavior. The three-way interactive effect (pressure × opportunities × rationalization) also was statistically significant further supporting H_2.

While we did not hypothesize any two-way interactive effects, no two-way interactive effects were statistically significant. This is consistent with other recent studies of students' cheating behaviors that used other variables in context-specific vignettes (versus our context-free vignette) which also found only significant three-way interactive effects (e.g., significant competence × motivation × gender interaction) but no two-way interactive effect

(Rettinger & Jordan, 2005; Rettinger, Jordan, & Peschiera, 2004; Murdock et al., 2004).

Additional investigation of the significance of the gender covariate revealed that female students were more likely to cheat than male students in the study's sample. As for the significance of the GPA covariate, further examination using Tukey's HSD tests showed that lower GPA students, not surprisingly, had a higher propensity to cheat. The number of credits during a semester in which students were enrolled also appeared to affect their propensity to cheat. Additional analysis indicated that the more credits students took in a semester, the higher their propensity to cheat.

Finally, since our study also tests the robustness of Becker et al.'s (2006) findings, we summarize the major model differences and findings between the two studies in Table 4. Becker et al.'s study was a field survey of 476 students whereas we used an experimental survey in which 182 students participated. They focused on creating a predictive model while we designed a descriptive model of students' cheating behavior. Becker et al. (2006) extended Bolin's (2004) model in the psychology literature by adding the rationalization variable, whereas we built our model using the three variables of the fraud triangle concept. We used ANCOVA to study the interactive effects of the three variables whereas Becker et al. (2006) used factor analysis to identify their variables. Lastly, Becker et al. (2006) measured students' cheating behavior (the dependent variable) by asking them to indicate how often they have engaged in five cheating behaviors since beginning their college careers. We measured the dependent variable by asking students to indicate their propensity to cheat when given eight different scenarios.

We found a lower overall propensity to cheat in our sample (19.8 percent) than did Becker et al. in their sample (23.2 percent). This is likely due to the fact that we asked students to report their propensity to cheat with reference to specific conditions (i.e., pressure, opportunities, and rationalization), whereas their study did not. Both studies found the three independent variables to be statistically significant. Therefore, the fraud triangle model appears to be consistently robust in predicting and describing students' cheating behavior. In our sample, female students were more likely to cheat than male students, but in their sample, female and male student cheating behaviors were the same. Both findings appear inconclusive in light of the mixed results on this issue. Becker et al. (2006) found GPA not to be a significant factor in cheating behavior whereas we found it to be significant, which is consistent with most of the prior research. Lastly, Becker et al. were the first to identify age as a significant factor of student cheating behaviors,

Table 4. Comparison of Becker et al. (2006) with This Study.

	Becker et al. (2006)	This Study
Differences		
Method	A field survey	An experimental survey
Model	An extension of Bolin's (2004) model in psychology	An extension of a fraud triangle model in accounting
Sample	476 business students	182 business students
Independent variables	Incentive, opportunities, and rationalization	Pressure, opportunities, and rationalization
Dependent variable	Number of times students have engaged in five specific cheating behaviors since beginning of their college careers	Students' propensity to cheat on a scale of 0–100% in eight different scenarios
Analysis	Factor analysis	ANCOVA
Findings		
Dependent variable	An overall 23.2% propensity to cheat	An overall 19.8% propensity to cheat
Independent variables	All statistically significant at $p<0.01$ or less	All statistically significant at $p<0.01$ or less
Interactive effect	Not applicable	Statistically significant at $p<0.016$
Gender	Female and male student cheating behaviors were statistically the same at $p<0.84$	Female and male student cheating behaviors were statistically different at $p<0.002$
GPA	Not a statistically significant factor at $p<0.54$	A statistically significant factor at $p<0.001$
Age	A statistically significant factor at $p<0.04$	Not applicable
Credit units	Not applicable	A statistically significant factor at $p<0.01$

however, this finding seems counterintuitive and more research into the age factor is in order.

LIMITATIONS

Our study's findings must be interpreted with caution for several reasons. First, students' self-reporting of their cheating behavior may not be valid due to the potential for an over- or under-reporting bias. A second potential limitation of our study is that we did not use a context-specific vignette for the full-factorial within-subjects ANCOVA design. Next, the generalizability of our results is limited since our instrument did not provide incentives (e.g., extra credit) to approximate more closely student academic experiences. Finally, transparency of the survey instrument might have increased the likelihood of demand effects.

CONCLUDING REMARKS

This study's results affirm the need for instructors to reduce opportunities for cheating, minimize the pressure to cheat, and dispel misconceptions about cheating. They also suggest that preventing cheating may be more effective than detection, since so many instructors are unwilling to pursue cheaters due to the required time and effort (McCabe, 2005b). In fact, future pedagogical research should consider exploring which opportunity prevention measures are most effective, as well as identifying preventive measures for pressure and rationalization factors.

Recent research on the role of personality in cheating has yielded mixed results. We believe that students' possession of a particular set of personality characteristics per se does not necessarily translate into a propensity to cheat in class. Therefore, future investigations should consider examining the *interactive effect* of personality with the fraud triangle factors to better understand cheating behavior.

Finally, only two studies (Ogilby, 1995; Sims, 1993) to date have suggested that students who cheat are more likely to be dishonest in their future professional behavior. Accordingly, there is a need for more research on how students' academic dishonesty translates into corporate dishonesty when graduates experience the interactive influences of the fraud triangle factors in the corporate world.

ACKNOWLEDGMENTS

We appreciate the constructive comments from two anonymous reviewers and the editor, Anthony H. Catanach, Jr., for their help in further developing the chapter. We are grateful for Dr. Harriet Blodgett's help in proofreading the revised chapter. We also thank participants at the 2006 Asian Pacific International Accounting Conference and the 2005 American Accounting Association Annual Meeting for their helpful suggestions.

REFERENCES

Albrecht, W. S., Howe, K. R., & Romney, M. B. (1984). *Detecting fraud: The internal auditor's perspective*. Altamonte Springs: The Institute of Internal Auditors Research Foundation.

American Institute of Certified Accountants (AICPA). (2002). *Consideration of fraud in a financial statement audit, Statement on Auditing Standards No. 99*. New York.

Baird, J. (1980). Current trends in college cheating. *Psychology in the Schools*, (17), 515–522.

Becker, D., Connolly, J., Lentz, P., & Morrison, J. (2006). Using the business fraud triangle to predict academic honesty among business students. *Journal of the Academy of Educational Leadership*, *10*(1), 37–55.

Blankenship, K. L., & Whitley, B. E., Jr. (2001). Relationship of general deviance to academic dishonesty. *Ethics & Behavior*, *10*(1), 1–12.

Bolin, A. (2004). Self-control, perceived opportunity, and attitudes as predictors of academic dishonesty. *Ethics & Behavior*, *138*(2), 101–114.

Burton, B. K., & Near, J. P. (1995). Estimating the incidence of wrongdoing and whistle-blowing: Results of a study using randomized response technique. *Journal of Business Ethics*, (14), 17–30.

Choo, F. (1984). Split-plot repeated measures designs in internal control judgment research. *Accounting and Business Research*, (14), 83–84.

Choo, F., & Tan, K. (2006). A commentary on sample design issues in behavioral accounting experiments. *Accounting Research Journal*, *19*(2), 153–158.

Cohen, J., Pant, L., & Sharp, D. (1998). The effect of gender and academic discipline diversity on the ethical evaluations, ethical intentions and ethical orientations of potential public accounting recruits. *Accounting Horizons*, *12*(3), 250–270.

Cressey, D. R. (1973). *Other people's money*. Montclair: Patterson Smith.

Del Carlo, D., & Bodner, G. (2006). Dishonesty in the biochemistry classroom laboratory. *Biochemistry and Molecular Biology Education*, *34*(5), 338–342.

Farrell, C. M., & Daniel, L. G. (1995). A frame of reference for understanding behaviors related to the academic misconduct of undergraduate teacher education students. *Research in Higher Education*, (36), 345–375.

Fass, R. A. (1990). Cheating and plagiarism. In: W. W. May (Ed.), *Ethics and higher education* (pp. 170–184). New York: Macmillan.

Haines, V. J., Diekoff, G. M., LaBeff, E. E., & Clark, R. E. (1986). College cheating: Immaturity, lack of commitment, and the neutralizing attitude. *Research in Higher Education*, *25*(4), 342–354.

Harpp, D. N., Hogan, J. J., & Jennings, J. S. (1996). Crime in the classroom. *Journal of Chemical Education*, *73*(4), 349–351.

Hugh, J. C., & McCabe, D. L. (2006). Academic misconduct in Canada. *Canadian Journal for Higher Education*, *36*(3), 122–134.

Jordan, A. E. (2001). College student cheating: The role of motivation, perceived norms, attitudes, and knowledge of institutional policy. *Ethics and Behavior*, *11*(3), 233–247.

Kerkvliet, J., & Sigmund, C. L. (1999). Can we control cheating in the classroom? *Journal of Economic Education*, (30), 331. Retrieved from the EBSCOhost database.

LaBeff, E. E., Clark, R. E., Haines, V. J., & Diekoff, G. M. (1990). Situational ethics and college student cheating. *Sociological Inquiry*, *60*(2), 190–198.

Lane, M. S., & Schaupp, D. (1989). Ethics in education: A comparative study. *Journal of Business Ethics*, (8), 943–949.

Lawson, R. A. (2004). Is classroom cheating related to business students' propensity to cheat in the "Real World? *Journal of Business Ethics*, *49*(2), 179–189.

Malone, F. L. (2006). The ethical attitude of accounting students. *The Journal of American Academy of Business*, *8*(1), 142–146.

McCabe, D. L. (1993). Faculty responses to academic dishonesty: The influence of student honor codes. *Research in Higher Education*, *34*(5), 647–658.

McCabe, D. L. (2005a). Cheating among college and university students: A North American perspective. *International Journal for Academic Integrity*, *1*(1), 1–11.

McCabe, D. L. (2005b). It takes a village: Academic dishonesty. *Liberal Education*, (Summer/ Fall), 26–31.

McCabe, D. L., Butterfield, K. D., & Trevino, L. K. (2006). Academic dishonesty in graduate business programs: Prevalence, causes, and proposed action. *Academy of Management Learning & Education*, *5*(3), 203–211.

McCabe, D. L., & Trevino, L. K. (1997). Individual and contextual influences on academic dishonesty: A multi-campus investigation. *Research in Higher Education*, *38*(3), 379–396.

Mohammed, Y., Rawwas, A., & Isakson, H. R. (2000). Ethics of tomorrow's business managers: The influence of personal beliefs and values, individual characteristics, and situational factors. *Journal of Education for Business*, *75*(6), 311–321.

Murdock, T. B., Hale, N. M., & Weber, M. J. (2001). Predictors of cheating among early adolescents: Academic and social motivations. *Journal of Educational Psychology*, *26*(1), 96–115.

Murdock, T. B., Miller, A., & Kohlhardt, J. (2004). Effects of classroom context variables on high school students' judgments of the acceptability and likelihood of cheating. *Journal of Educational Psychology*, *96*(4), 765–777.

Ng, W., Davis, G., Bates, I., & Avellon, M. (2003). Academic dishonesty among pharmacy students. *Pharmacy Education*, *3*(4), 261–269.

Ogilby, S. M. (1995). The ethics of academic behavior: Will it affect professional behavior? *Journal of Education for Business*, *71*(2), 82–92.

Perry, A. R., Kane, K. M., Bernesser, K. J., & Spicker, P. T. (1990). Type-A Behavior, competitive achievement-striving, and cheating among college students. *Psychological Reports*, (66), 459–465.

Pulvers, K., & Diekoff, G. M. (1999). The relationship between academic dishonesty and college classroom environment. *Research in Higher Education*, *40*(4), 487–498.

Rettinger, D., & Jordan, A. E. (2005). The relationships among religion, motivation and college cheating: A natural experiment. *Ethics & Behavior*, *15*(2), 107–129.

Rettinger, D., Jordan, A. E., & Peschiera, F. (2004). Evaluating the motivation of other students to cheat: A vignette experiment. *Research in Higher Education*, *45*(8), 873–890.

Sims, R. L. (1993). The relationship between academic dishonesty and unethical business practices. *Journal of Education for Business*, (69), 207–211.

Smith, K. J., Davy, J. A., Rosenberg, D. L., & Haight, G. T. (2002). A structural modeling investigation of the influence of demographic and attitudinal factors and in-class deterrents on cheating behavior among accounting majors. *Journal of Accounting Education*, *20*(1), 15–25.

Stearns, S. A. (2001). The student-instructor relationship's effect on academic integrity. *Ethics & Behavior*, *11*(3), 325–342.

Storch, J. B., Storch, E. A., & Clark, P. (2002). Academic dishonesty and neutralization theory: A comparison of intercollegiate athletes and non-athletes. *Journal of College Student Development*, (November/December), 1–11.

University of California at Berkeley website. (2003). First search for http://www.executiveforum.net/pdfs/; then click Creating Business Value for either the PDF file of www.executiveforum.net/pdfs/jennings_summary.pdf or the slides file of www.executiveforum.net/pdfs/kunath_slides.pdf

Whitley, B. E., Jr., & Keith-Spiegel, P. (2001). Academic integrity as an institutional issue. *Ethics & Behavior*, *11*(3), 325–342.

CURRENT FACTORS AND PRACTICES RELATED TO INSTRUCTIONAL APPROACH IN THE INTRODUCTORY FINANCIAL ACCOUNTING COURSE

Christie L. Comunale, Thomas R. Sexton and Stephen C. Gara

ABSTRACT

For nearly two decades, accounting educators have debated whether to continue with a preparer approach, or adopt a user perspective, or a blended model in the introductory financial accounting course. We examine the extent to which accounting programs have chosen to employ each approach, the factors that influenced their selection, as well as the relative importance of each factor. We also explore institutional and course characteristics associated with the choice of instructional method.

Our results indicate that one-third of programs employ the user perspective, and one-fifth the traditional preparer approach, while nearly half use a blend of the two. Programs using the preparer approach tend to focus on the accounting major (e.g., performance and career goals). In contrast, user approach institutions appear to emphasize performance issues and career paths of non-accounting majors.

Advances in Accounting Education: Teaching and Curriculum Innovations, Volume 9, 221–232

ISSN: 1085-4622/doi:10.1016/S1085-4622(08)09010-X

Fifteen years ago, the Accounting Education Change Commission (AECC, 1992) encouraged educators to replace the traditional preparer approach with a user perspective in the introductory financial accounting course. Generally, the traditional preparer approach emphasizes record keeping and information preparation functions, while the user perspective focuses on how various parties use information for economic decision-making. Not surprisingly, a third model has evolved: a blended solution which captures certain aspects of both the preparer and user approaches.

The choice of instructional philosophy is important for several reasons. First, it potentially can impact skill development (communication, problem-solving, and technical), as well as student performance in future accounting and business courses. This is particularly important since introductory accounting courses generally serve two audiences: accounting majors for whom the course is a foundation for more advanced work, and non-accounting majors for whom the class may be their one and only accounting course. Additionally, this course often serves as a major recruiting tool for accounting majors (Riordan, St Pierre, & Matoney, 1996, p. 129).

In this chapter, we examine both the choice of instructional approach and the factors affecting selection of the teaching method. We also explore the relative importance of these factors, as well as the course characteristics associated with the choice of instructional approach. Our study's results provide insights to administrators and faculty who are considering changing their introductory financial accounting courses.

LITERATURE REVIEW

The AECC's position statement entitled "The First Course in Accounting" (1992) called for a greater emphasis on the use of accounting information. Albrecht and Sack (2000, p. 63) also stressed the need to move the introductory accounting course from a preparer focus to more of a user perspective.

Proponents of the user perspective have asserted that the preparer approach does not accurately reflect the current business environment (Diller-Haas, 2004, p. 60). According to Pincus (1997, pp. 576–578), the preparer approach suffers from a number of drawbacks: new software applications have effectively eliminated journal entries, students are led to believe that there exists only one correct solution to a problem, and it perpetuates the accountant stereotype. However, Vangermeersch (1997, pp. 581–583) asserts that the user perspective suffers from its own drawbacks: reduction in the rigor of the introductory accounting course, as well as a failure to prepare accounting majors for upper-level coursework.

In the mid-1990s, several researchers surveyed universities to determine how accounting programs were responding to the AECC's recommendations. Wilson and Baldwin (1995, pp. 157–159) found that approximately 50 percent of respondents had switched from a preparer to a user approach. Meanwhile, Holt and Swanson (1995, pp. 348–350) reported adoption of a user approach by less than 40 percent of respondents. Jordan and Clark's study (1995, pp. 68–71) indicated that over 80 percent of faculty members at two-year colleges were using the preparer approach, although respondents were evenly split over the need to change to a user approach. More recently, Diller-Haas (2004, p. 61) found that 71 percent of accounting programs in the New York metropolitan area still used the preparer approach.

This study builds on the research of Diller-Haas (2004) by examining approach adoptions on a national basis during the mid-2000s to assess the longer term impact of the AECC's proposal. Our research also examines those factors affecting the decision to adopt a particular approach in the introductory accounting course.

RESEARCH QUESTIONS

Our study seeks to answer three questions:

- What is the current state of the user versus preparer perspective in the introductory accounting course?
- What factors determine accounting programs' choice in instructional method for the introductory accounting course?
- Which of these factors are more influential in the approach adoption decision?

Identifying these factors and their respective weights are relevant to curriculum designers who are choosing an approach at their institution. Our study also provides those involved with curriculum design with insights into how other institutions have addressed the adoption issue, including which factors most influenced their decisions.

METHODOLOGY

In the spring of 2005, we designed and pre-tested an online survey containing 46 questions to examine our study's research questions. We used online surveys because of their many potential advantages including shorter response times, lower large sample cost, and convenience for respondents. We distributed the survey to accounting department chairpersons and deans at 825 colleges and universities using contact information obtained from Hasselback (2004).

Five questions requested information about the institution and the individual completing the survey. The next 13 questions asked about certain characteristics of the introductory financial accounting course including average class size, the percentage of accounting majors, textbook used, and the school's current instructional approach. We specifically asked respondents to describe their current approach as either preparer, user, or blended. Rather than providing strict definitions of each term, we allowed respondents to reply based on their perception of which approach their accounting program used. The next 14 questions determined which factors were considered in adopting the current approach, and the remaining 14 questions evaluated the relative importance of each factor. All factor related questions used a five-point scale ranging from -2 (strongly disagree) to $+2$ (strongly agree).

Since online surveys often yield lower response rates than mailed paper surveys (Cook, Heath, & Thompson, 2000, p. 832), approximately one month after distributing the initial survey we sent a reminder to initial non-respondents. Ultimately, we received 120 useable responses: a response rate of 14.5 percent. Of these, 113 reported their academic position. Seventy-eight held administrative positions (73 accounting program chairs or coordinators, 3 deans or associate deans, and 2 graduate program directors). Thirty-five were accounting faculty, one of whom was retired. To address our research questions, we used descriptive statistics, χ^2 tests, multinomial tests, and one-way ANOVA's. In those cases where evidence existed that group standard deviations were not all equal, we also applied the Kruskal–Wallis one-way nonparametric procedure.

RESULTS

Sample Characteristics

Table 1 reports that 20 percent of surveyed programs use a preparer approach when teaching the introductory financial accounting course, while

Table 1. Summary Sample Characteristics.

	Preparer Approach	User Perspective	Blended Model	Overall
Number (%)	23 (20.0%)	37 (32.2%)	55 (47.8%)	115 (100%)
Mean years using approach	35.0	8.8	10.7	14.8
Policy existed on approach	52.2%	81.1%	50.9%	60.9%
Percent accounting majors	19.9%	14.9%	15.7%	16.9%
Ownership				
Public	60.9%	59.5%	61.8%	60.9%
Private	39.1%	40.5%	38.2%	39.1%
Accreditation				
Business and accounting	21.7%	37.9%	20.0%	26.1%
Business only	34.8%	35.1%	38.2%	36.5%
Neither	43.5%	27.0%	41.8%	37.4%
Highest accounting degree				
Ph.D.	8.7%	10.8%	7.4%	8.8%
Masters	43.5%	51.4%	37.0%	43.0%
Bachelor	47.8%	35.1%	50.0%	44.7%
No degree	0.0%	2.7%	5.6%	3.5%
Class size				
11–25 students	26.1%	10.8%	12.7%	14.8%
26–40 students	26.1%	51.4%	58.2%	49.5%
41–60 students	47.8%	18.9%	21.8%	26.1%
>60 students	0.0%	18.9%	7.3%	9.6%

32.2 percent adopt a user perspective, and 47.8 percent programs employ a blended model. All observed proportional differences are statistically significant at *P*-values ranging from .0003 to .0707.

A one-way ANOVA indicates that adopters of the preparer approach have been using that approach for significantly longer (mean 35 years) than adopters of the blended model (10.7 years) or the user perspective (mean 8.8 years) approach (*P*-value <0.00005). Table 1 also indicates that 60.9 percent of respondent programs have either an explicit or implicit policy regarding their particular instructional approach. We find that 81.1 percent of user perspective programs have a policy, while only 52.2 percent of preparer approach programs and 50.9 percent of blended model programs report a policy regarding approach. A χ^2 test confirmed observed percentage differences in policies across approaches (*P*-value $= 0.0092$).

Table 1 also indicates that 16.9 percent of students enrolled in the introductory financial accounting course were accounting majors. Tukey's HSD test for pairwise comparisons revealed that the preparer approach mean (19.9 percent) was significantly greater than the user perspective mean (14.9 percent), but we could not distinguish either of these from the blended model mean. Only two institutions reported offering separate introductory financial accounting courses for accounting and non-accounting majors.

Table 1 also reports ownership, accreditation, degree offering, and class size data for all sample institutions by each instructional approach. While none of these characteristic differences are statistically significantly across approach, it is interesting that the user perspective appears more widely accepted at institutions with both business and accounting accreditation, and which offer graduate degrees. Additionally, the preparer approach appears more prevalent in larger classes of 41–60 students, while the user perspective and blended model are used more frequently in mid-sized classes of 26–40 students.

Factors Affecting the Choice of Teaching Approach

Table 2 reports those factors that are statistically significant as to differences across choice of teaching approach. When asked to evaluate factors affecting their decision to adopt a particular instructional method, we find that preparer approach programs generally agree that (relative to the user perspective):

- accounting majors perform better in the introductory accounting course;
- accounting majors perform better in future accounting courses; and
- accounting majors find the course more relevant to their career path (programs that use the blended model also cited this factor relative to the user perspective).

Conversely, programs that adopt the user perspective generally agree that (relative to the preparer approach):

- non-accounting majors perform better in the introductory financial accounting course;
- non-accounting majors perform better in future business courses;
- students improve their writing and oral communication skill more;
- non-accounting majors find the course more interesting; and
- non-accounting majors find the course more relevant to their career path.

Table 2. Statistically Significant Factors in Decision to Adopt an Instructional Approach.

Question	Mean Response			
We adopted current approach because we believe that, relative to other approaches	Preparer approach	User perspective	Blended model	Overall
Accounting majors perform better in the Introductory Financial Accounting Course	0.826	0.114	0.415	0.455[a]
Non-accounting majors perform better in the Introductory Financial Accounting Course	−0.409	0.556	0.057	0.089[a]
Accounting majors perform better in future accounting courses	1.435	0.229	0.642	0.699[b]
Non-accounting majors perform better in future business courses	0.130	0.714	0.321	0.415[a]
Students improve their writing and oral communication skills more	−0.318	0.200	0.113	0.074[a]
Non-accounting majors find the course more interesting	−0.652	1.060	0.154	0.238[c]
Accounting majors find the course more relevant to their career path	1.217	0.235	0.717	0.689[d]
Non-accounting majors find the course more relevant to their career path	−0.565	1.111	0.170	0.290[c]

Note: All factor related questions used a five-point scale ranging from −2 (strongly disagree) to +2 (strongly agree).

[a]Preparer approach mean was statistically different from the user perspective mean.

[b]Preparer approach mean was statistically different from both user perspective and blended model means.

[c]All pairwise differences among means were statistically significant.

[d]Preparer approach mean was statistically different from the user perspective mean, and the blended model mean was statistically different from the user perspective mean.

Importance of Factors in Choice of Teaching Approach

Table 3 reports the importance of factors that are statistically significant as to differences across choice of teaching approach. Consistent with Table 2's results, we find that preparer approach programs generally place more importance (relative to the user perspective) on:

- performance of accounting majors in the introductory accounting course;
- performance of accounting majors in future accounting course;
- performance of accounting majors in future business courses; and

Table 3. Statistically Significant Factors on Importance Dimension.

Question	Mean Response			
Please indicate the importance of the following factor in selecting your approach	Preparer approach	User perspective	Blended model	Overall
Performance of accounting majors in the Introductory Financial Accounting Course	1.217	0.514	0.774	0.797[a]
Performance of accounting majors in future accounting courses	1.609	0.667	1.113	1.089[b]
Performance of accounting majors in future business courses	1.217	0.600	0.846	0.852[a]
Increasing interest in the course among non-accounting majors	0.591	1.222	0.868	0.886[a]
Retaining accounting majors in the accounting major	1.217	1.086	0.755	0.943[c]
Increasing accounting major's perception of the course relevance to their career path	1.522	0.886	0.943	1.081[d]

Note: All importance related questions used a five-point scale ranging from −2 (strongly disagree) to +2 (strongly agree).
[a]Preparer approach mean was statistically different from the user perspective mean.
[b]All pairwise differences among means are statistically significant.
[c]Preparer approach mean was statistically different from the blended model mean.
[d]Preparer approach mean was statistically different from both the user perspective and blended model means.

- increasing accounting major's perception of the course's relevance to their career path.

On the other hand, user perspective programs generally place more importance (relative to the preparer approach) on increasing interest in the course among non-accounting majors. Finally, programs that utilize the preparer approach generally place more importance (relative to the blended model) on retaining accounting majors in the accounting major.

Our study also noted no statistically significant differences among the instructional approaches for a number of decision choice factors (Panel A, Table 4), and importance level factors (Panel B, Table 4). However, we observe that the mean levels reported for many of these items are of comparable magnitude to those reported for items that did differ across instructional approaches. This suggests that these items may be equally important considerations across instructional approaches.

Table 4. Statistically Insignificant Factors.

Panel A: Statistically Insignificant Factors in Decision to Adopt an Instructional Approach

We adopted our current approach because we believe that, relative to other approaches	Overall mean
Accounting majors perform better in future business courses	0.645
Accounting majors find the course more interesting	0.636
Non-accounting majors are more motivated to become accounting majors	0.341
Accounting majors are more likely to remain accounting majors	0.780
Students acquire a greater degree of understanding of the course material	0.959
Instructors are more enthusiastic	0.545

Panel B: Statistically Insignificant Factors (Importance Dimension)

Please indicate the importance of the following factor in selecting your approach	
Performance of non-accounting majors in Introductory Financial Accounting course	0.855
Performance of non-accounting majors in future business courses	0.919
Improvement of student writing and oral communication skills	0.311
Increasing interest in the course among accounting majors	0.754
Motivating non-accounting majors to become accounting majors	0.811
Increasing student's degree of understanding of the course material	1.390
Increasing non-accounting major's perception of course relevance to their career path	0.992
Increasing the enthusiasm of the instructor	0.496

Note: All factor and importance related questions used a five-point scale ranging from −2 (strongly disagree) to +2 (strongly agree).

LIMITATIONS AND FUTURE RESEARCH

Our study is a first step toward understanding the choice that institutions face when orienting their introductory financial accounting course. In that sense, it is exploratory rather than confirmatory, and provides a general review of the current state of this issue in accounting education. We have identified the perceptions associated with each teaching approach; the next step may be to establish the validity of those perceptions. For example, do:

- Accounting majors really perform better in the introductory financial accounting course when the course is taught using the preparer approach?
- Students really improve their writing and oral communication skills more when the course is taught utilizing the user perspective?
- Accounting majors really stay in the major when the preparer approach is used?

Like most surveys, we received responses from only one person at each institution. Therefore, our data reflect the views of only one person, and do not shed any light on the diversity of opinion that may exist within each institution. However, we did ask about the existence of a departmental policy regarding how the introductory financial accounting course is taught as a way of determining the degree to which faculty members are consistent in their teaching approach.

We did not attempt to define the terms "preparer," "blended," and "user." Instead, we allowed each respondent to indicate their approach based on their own perception, as we felt that strict definitions might not be universally accepted, and might confuse the respondents. We found no indication that the absence of definitions caused problems.

Finally, although we treated the teaching approach as a categorical variable, we did provide respondents with the opportunity to elaborate on the nature of their approach. While no respondent indicated that the categorical variable caused any misunderstanding, we might have obtained a more refined response had we measured the approach as a continuous variable on a finite scale.

IMPLICATIONS AND CONCLUSION

After two decades of repeated calls for a shift to the user perspective in the introductory financial accounting course, only one in five programs continues to utilize the traditional preparer approach. Not surprisingly, these preparer-focused programs have the highest percentage of accounting majors in their introductory financial accounting course, and they value the performance of accounting majors in current and future accounting courses, as well as their career paths. We also find that one in three programs currently utilizes the user perspective. These programs have the lowest percentage of accounting majors in their introductory financial accounting course and they focus on the current and future performance and career paths of the non-accounting major.

These findings suggest that the accounting program's perceived role within the business school largely determines the teaching approach adopted. Accounting programs that have fully adopted the user perspective are likely to see themselves as providing a service course to non-accounting majors. Conversely, preparer-focused institutions may view their mission as preparing professional accountants, and are less concerned about the non-accounting major's needs.

Almost half of the programs have developed a blended model, apparently in an attempt to satisfy the demands of both the accounting and non-accounting majors. However, the fact that our sample institutions have used the blended model slightly longer than the user perspective suggests that the blended model may simply be a transition from the preparer approach to the user perspective.

We find it interesting that only two programs in our sample have chosen to offer separate introductory financial accounting courses to accountants and non-accountants. Educational effectiveness argues for separate courses for accounting majors (employing the preparer approach) and non-accounting majors (employing the user perspective). Indeed, such a practice is common in statistics and economics for their respective majors and non-majors. However, resource limitations may limit the feasibility of this option. Additionally, separate courses for accounting majors could adversely affect students who decide to change their majors, as well as transfer students.

In deciding on an approach, accounting educators and administrators might consider viewing their decision within the four-part process for accounting curriculum change introduced by Ainsworth (2001, p. 282). This process consists of environmental, program, and curriculum analyses, as well as an assessment element. Step one consists of an evaluation of the accounting program's environment, including student demographics and faculty resources. The next two steps, program and curriculum analyses, consist of analyzing the role of the introductory accounting course as it prepares students for both subsequent accounting coursework, as well as coursework in other disciplines. The final step, assessment, determines subsequent student performance in later courses. The assessment step also could include eliciting feedback on students' interest in accounting as a career option.

While we cannot offer specific guidance to curriculum designers, we can say that it appears that programs generally select an approach based on the population that they serve. This suggests that as long as accounting programs face the inherent conflicts between the demand to prepare professional accountants and the needs of the non-accounting major, it is unlikely that we will ever see a complete shift to the user perspective.

ACKNOWLEDGMENTS

The authors acknowledge the helpful comments and suggestions from our editor, Anthony H. Catanach Jr, two anonymous reviewers, and attendees at the 2007 Northeast Regional Meeting and the 2007 Annual Meeting of the American Accounting Association. The authors also thank the Teaching and Curriculum section for selecting this study for the Best Paper Award at the 2007 American Accounting Association Northeast Region Meeting.

REFERENCES

Accounting Education Change Commission. (1992). *The first course in accounting: Position statement number two*. Sarasota, FL: Accounting Education Change Commission.

Ainsworth, P. (2001). Changes in accounting curricula: Discussion and design. *Accounting Education*, *10*(September), 279–297.

Albrecht, W. S., & Sack, R. J. (2000). *Accounting education: Charting a course through a perilous future*. Sarasota, FL: American Accounting Association.

Cook, C., Heath, F., & Thompson, R. (2000). A meta-analysis of response rates in web or Internet-based surveys. *Educational and Psychological Measurement*, *60*(December), 821–836.

Diller-Haas, A. (2004). Time to change introductory accounting. *The CPA Journal* (April), 60–62.

Hasselback, J. R. (2004). *Accounting faculty directory 2002–2003*. Upper Saddle River, NJ: Prentice-Hall.

Holt, D. L., & Swanson, J. G. (1995). Use of AECC directives and cooperative learning theory in introductory accounting classes. *Journal of Education for Business*, *70*(July/August), 348–350.

Jordan, C. E., & Clark, S. J. (1995). Two-year college accounting faculty: Their opinions on the first course in accounting. *Journal of Education for Business*, *71*(November/December), 68–71.

Pincus, K. V. (1997). Is teaching debits and credits essential in elementary accounting? *Issues in Accounting Education*, *12*(Fall), 575–579.

Riordan, M. P., St Pierre, E. K., & Matoney, J. (1996). Some initial empirical evidence regarding the impact of the introductory accounting sequence on the selection of accounting as a major. *Accounting Education (JAI)*, *1*(Summer), 127–136.

Vangermeersch, R. G. (1997). Dropping debits and credits in elementary accounting: A huge disservice to students. *Issues in Accounting Education*, *12*(Fall), 582–583.

Wilson, T. E., & Baldwin, E. F. (1995). The accounting education change commission and accounting principles courses: A survey of accounting programs. *Journal of Education for Business*, *70*(January/February), 157–159.

DOES ETHICS INSTRUCTION MAKE A DIFFERENCE?

John Delaney and Martin J. Coe

ABSTRACT

It is broadly accepted that ethics should be incorporated into accounting programs. Most CPA firms rely on colleges and universities to teach ethical behavior. Utilizing a quasi-experimental approach, this chapter examines the effectiveness of ethics instruction delivered via a combination of lecture and active learning methods. Specifically, the impact of ethics instruction on behavior in business settings is investigated. Though similar studies have addressed this issue, this study tests the effectiveness of a particular curriculum in a post-Enron environment. Further, a new instrument to measure moral reasoning ability in work situations is introduced. The study's findings suggest that ethics instruction is effective in increasing moral reasoning ability, particularly in upper-level accounting courses such as accounting information systems and auditing.

It is broadly accepted that ethics should be incorporated into accounting programs. Recently, Armstrong, Ketz, and Owsen (2003, p. 1) have suggested that "the sheer number of accounting abuses serves as prima facie evidence that something more is needed in terms of accounting ethics" in the classroom. However, it remains unclear as to how best to include ethics in the accounting curriculum. Anecdotal evidence suggests that

Advances in Accounting Education: Teaching and Curriculum Innovations, Volume 9, 233–250

ISSN: 1085-4622/doi:10.1016/S1085-4622(08)09011-1

accounting educators wrestle with how to incorporate ethics into an already-full curricula without compromising coverage of technical topics. Thus, if scarce resources are used to add ethics into accounting programs, the ultimate question that must be asked is: *Does ethics instruction make a difference*?

Dellaportas (2006, p. 393) reports that ethics generally is introduced in the classroom using either the discrete method or the pervasive approach. The discrete method requires a separate course devoted to ethics, while the pervasive approach integrates ethical issues into several accounting courses. Armstrong (1993, p. 89) concludes that the ideal curriculum should use both instructional approaches. While such a comprehensive approach may be appealing, the required investment of faculty resources and the potential negative impact on coverage of traditional topics cannot be ignored.

Consequently, this study explores whether or not accelerated ethics instruction imbedded in an existing accounting course positively impacts moral reasoning in business settings. More specifically, we use a quasi-experimental approach to examine the effectiveness of ethics instruction when it is delivered via a combination of lecture and active learning methods. Though similar studies have addressed this issue, our study tests the effectiveness of a particular curriculum in a post-Enron environment. Additionally, we introduce a new instrument to measure moral reasoning ability in work situations. Our results indicate that ethics instruction is effective in increasing moral reasoning ability (MRA), particularly in upper-level accounting courses such as accounting information systems (AIS) and auditing.

The chapter begins with a brief literature review which is followed by a hypothesis development section and a discussion of the research methodology. Results are then reported and discussed. These are followed by a summary of the findings and their implications, the study's limitations, and proposals for future research. The authors finish with concluding remarks.

LITERATURE REVIEW

Moral Reasoning Ability and Behavior

Many studies have investigated the factors that influence auditor's ethical reasoning in work situations (Jones, Massey, & Thorne, 2003). Most of these studies are based on either Lawrence Kohlberg's cognitive development theory of moral reasoning or James Rest's model of ethical action (Coyne, Massey, & Thibodeau, 2005).

Following Kohlberg (1981, p. 173), MRA is defined as the degree to which an individual differentiates the self from others, and defines his or her values in terms of self-chosen ethical principles. In other words, MRA is the degree to which an individual uses a principled, moral thought process in solving an ethical dilemma. He argues that as one matures, he or she is able to reason at higher levels, ultimately peaking at some point. Given Kohlberg's view that MRA is developmental, then successful ethics instruction should lead to higher levels of MRA.

Rest's model of ethical action indicates that moral failure can occur for any one of four reasons: (1) failure to identify an ethical dilemma; (2) failure to formulate an ethical judgment; (3) failure to determine an intention to act ethically; or (4) failure of an ethical action/behavior (Rest, 1994, p. 22). If one accepts Rest's view, then successful ethics instruction would lead to sensitivity to ethical dilemmas, better ethical decision-making processes, and ultimately, ethical action. Therefore, this study attempts to impact the ethical decision-making process reflected by Rest's model through an intervention (ethics instruction).

Studies that examine factors leading to ethical action provide evidence that higher MRA is linked to pro-social behavior (Rest, Narvzez, Bebeau, & Thoma, 1999). Further, in a widely cited lab study of 88 staff-level auditors working for a large U.S. accounting firm, Ponemon (1992, p. 185) provides evidence that MRA is related to actual behavior.

Ethics Instruction

With respect to the MRA of accounting students specifically, Earley and Kelly (2004, p. 61) found that while the level of MRA applied in considering general hypothetical moral dilemmas does not differ from the level applied in work-related (context-specific) situations, ethics instruction did significantly increase the students' MRA in context-specific situations. More recently, Massey and Thorne (2006, p. 113) found that an intervention using task information feedback was both effective in increasing both auditor and student MRA. Both of these studies suggest that properly designed accounting ethics instruction can make a difference.

HYPOTHESIS DEVELOPMENT

Prior research has proposed that the manner of integrating ethics into accounting courses affects the effectiveness of the instruction. While there seems to be consensus that case study is essential to ethics instruction (Loeb & Rockness, 1992; Ponemon, 1993; Kerr & Smith, 1995), other suggested methods include: introduction to ethical theory utilizing philosophy texts and lecture (Ferris, 1996, p. 347); readings from published articles; use of educational novels and professionally prepared videotape presentations dealing with ethical issues; and a group assignment in which students prepare their own video presentations involving an ethical issue (Kerr & Smith, 1995).

With the exception of the educational novel, we incorporated all of these methods in our accounting ethics program. Similar to Ponemon (1993), we also used a game to create a Prisoners' Dilemma to test the propensity of students to bargain in good faith.

Consistent with the call by Armstrong et al. (2003, p. 12) to investigate the linkage between ethics content, method, and course, we seek to determine if our curriculum is effective by testing the following hypothesis:

H_1. Students who receive comprehensive, theory-based ethics instruction (CTBEI) integrated within an accounting course will display better MRA than students who do not receive such ethics instruction.

Because the same ethics instruction is used in various accounting courses (Principles, AIS, Auditing), we expect the same results regardless of course. Consequently, we also tested the following hypotheses:

H_{2a}. Students who receive (CTBEI) integrated within a Principles course will display better MRA than students who do not receive such ethics instruction.

H_{2b}. Students who receive (CTBEI) integrated within an AIS course will display better MRA than students who do not receive such ethics instruction.

H_{2c}. Students who receive (CTBEI) integrated within an Auditing course will display better MRA than students who do not receive such ethics instruction.

RESEARCH METHOD

A quasi-experimental design was used for this study. One group served as a control group, while another received the ethics instruction treatment. The non-equivalent control group design was appropriate for this study because students were not randomly assigned to control and treatment groups within the same class. This design ensured that students within a particular class were treated equally since they were exposed to the same curriculum.

All groups were given a pre- and post-test. Other data was collected via a separate survey administered at the same time as the post-test. This data included the participant's age, gender, and year in school. Further, the participants were asked to indicate whether or not they previously received any form of ethics instruction.

Sample

The groups were composed of separate accounting classes meeting for accounting principles, AIS, and auditing courses at a large state university (approximately 25% of the sample) and a small liberal arts college (approximately 75% of the sample) located in the Midwest. The classes were composed of both younger traditional students and older non-traditional students. Like Coyne et al. (2005, p. 182), we attempted to draw our sample from a wide spectrum of students to assess the robustness of the intervention.

A total of 138 students participated in the study. However, in nine cases a student was absent on either the day of the pre- or post-test, and in eight cases the survey responses did not pass an internal consistency check. Consequently, usable pairs of surveys (pre- and post-test) were obtained from 121 individuals (61 women and 60 men, mean age = 23.2 years, age range 19–48 years) which included responses from 47 seniors, 37 juniors, and 37 sophomores. Sixty students had received prior ethics instruction. Fifty-four of the usable surveys came from students in the control group while 67 came from the experimental group. Of the demographic characteristics, a statistically significant difference was noted only between the experimental and control groups for age ($p = .08$, experimental mean = 22.34 years, control mean = 24.3 years), and was dealt with in the analysis by inclusion of an age variable as a covariate. Table 1 presents a summary of the sample's demographic characteristics.

Table 1. Sample Descriptive Statistics.

	Total	Experimental	Control	*t*-Test Significance (2-Tailed)
Females				
Number	61	31	30	.31
Percent	50	46	56	
Age				
Mean	23.21	22.34	24.30	.08
Range	19–48	19–47	19–48	
Level				.78
Sophomores				
Number	37	22	15	
Percent	31	33	28	
Juniors				
Number	37	21	16	
Percent	31	31	30	
Seniors				
Number	47	24	23	
Percent	39	36	43	
Prior ethics instruction				
Number	60	37	23	.17
Percent	50	55	43	
Institution				.37
Private				
Number	90	52	38	
Percent	74	78	70	
Public				
Number	31	15	16	
Percent	26	22	30	

Although students at the same institution received differential treatments (i.e., some received the intervention and others did not), the experimental design was ethically appropriate as there was no deliberate attempt to deceive the participants (Gibbins, 1992). Both control group and experimental group members were offered the same extra credit to complete the research instruments. Informed consent was obtained following guidelines established by the lead author's human research review committee. Ethics instruction was delivered over a three-week period. During the three-week intervention classes met either three times per week for 75 min or twice per week for 110 min.

Two separate principles of accounting classes at the liberal arts college participated in the study. Participants in these classes (primarily sophomores) included business and accounting majors. One class served as a control group receiving no ethics instruction. This group received instruction on management accounting concepts during the three-week instruction period. The other class received ethics instruction during this time. The same principal investigator was the instructor for both classes. Procedures were used to ensure proper matching of pre- and post-test scores without the identity of the student being disclosed to the principle investigators.

Two separate AIS classes at the state university participated in the study. Participants in these classes were junior and senior accounting majors. One class served as a control group receiving no ethics instruction. The control group received instruction on team building, while the other class received ethics instruction. Both classes were co-taught by the principal investigators of this study. Since the objective of the study was to determine if MRA scores improve after exposure to ethics instruction, it was necessary to match scores on the pre- and post-test by individual. We used the same procedures to preserve response confidentiality in the pre- and post-test.

Two separate upper-level auditing classes at the liberal arts college also participated in the study. Participants in these classes were junior and senior accounting majors. One class served as a control group receiving no ethics instruction. This group received instruction on statistical sampling and fraud detection during the three-week instruction period. The inclusion of fraud detection in the control group curriculum is justified considering Bernardi (1994, p. 77) found no relationship between fraud detection and moral development of auditors. The other class received the ethics instruction during this period. The same principal investigator was the instructor for both classes and the pre- and post-test were administered in the same manner as for the principles and AIS classes.

Measuring Moral Reasoning Ability

Massey (2002, p. 202) points out "probably because of demand effects, there is no known standardized measure of moral behavior." Another pervasive problem of ethics research is a social desirability response bias, otherwise referred to as a halo effect (Cohen, Pant, & Sharp, 1995). Though observation and measurement of business ethics is difficult, questionnaires are nonetheless very commonly used as an observation technique in business ethics research (Randall & Fernandes, 1991).

Instruments used to measure MRA in accounting and business situations (Earley & Kelly, 2004; Massey, 2002) are patterned after the Defining Issues Test (DIT) developed by James Rest in the 1970s. The DIT is a reasoning test that uses general hypothetical moral dilemmas. We created an accounting version of the DIT for this study: the Accounting Moral Reasoning Test (AMRT). This instrument measures respondent MRA when confronted with accounting/business hypothetical moral dilemmas. The AMRT is similar to instruments used in previous ethics research (Massey, 2002) in that the dilemmas address ethical issues commonly encountered by auditors (i.e., premature sign-off of audit procedures and whistle-blowing).

However, the AMRT is different in two ways. First, it was constructed in a post-Enron environment, thus some of the dilemmas reflect elements of actual accounting scandals of the recent past. Second, the dilemmas described in the prior studies pertain almost exclusively to situations facing auditors of public accounting firms, whereas the AMRT includes ethical dilemmas faced by a greater range of accounting professionals (public accountants, internal auditors, cost accountants, and accounting supervisors). Our belief is that the AMRT will add robustness to the prior research by including issues currently facing both auditors of public accounting firms and other accounting professionals. Table 2 compares each AMRT dilemma actor and topic with instruments used by other recent studies. The order in which the dilemmas appear in Table 2 matches the order in which they appear in their respective instrument.

Similar to the DIT, the AMRT includes six moral dilemmas, each followed by 12 statements used to measure moral reasoning level. The participants were required to rate the importance of each of these statements in resolving the accounting/business dilemma. The AMRT was administered to all of the study participants during both the pre- and the post-test. The Principled Score (*P*-score) from these two tests, reflecting the degree to which higher-stage moral reasoning is utilized in resolving the dilemmas, was used to measure MRA in the accounting/business situations. A higher *P*-score reflects a greater preference for using higher-stage moral reasoning.

Since the AMRT was constructed specifically for this study, we checked validity and reliability using procedures that mirror the work performed by Massey (2002, pp. 206–207). The AMRT was developed using Kohlberg's well-established theory of cognitive moral development, thus suggesting construct validity. We established the face validity of our instrument by engaging a panel of two philosophy and three business professors familiar with Kohlberg's work to review the content and scoring matrix of the AMRT. The philosophers have taught business ethics for several years and

Table 2. Comparison of Ethical Dilemmas and Actors by Research Study.

Dilemma	AMRT	Brugman and Weisfelt (2000)	Thorne (2000)	Massey (2002)
1 Actor	Auditor	Auditor	Auditor	Auditor
1 Topic	Premature sign-off on audit procedure	Disclose confidential information	Fail to disclose severe control weaknesses	Underreport audit time
2 Actor	Internal auditor	Auditor	Audit partner	Audit partner
2 Topic	Suppress audit findings from final report	Disclose confidential information	Waive audit adjustments	Waive audit adjustments
3 Actor	Cost accountant	Auditor	Auditor	Auditor
3 Topic	Whistle-blow on the company	Accept a questionable client	Conflict of interest	Premature sign-off on audit procedure
4 Actor	Accounting supervisor	Auditor	Auditor	Auditor
4 Topic	Manipulate earnings	Owner sells products off the books	Disclose confidential information	Whistle-blow on a client
5 Actor	Audit partner	Auditor	Audit partner	NA
5 Topic	Shred audit documents	Suppress disclosure of a material amount	Disclose exorbitant management fee	NA
6 Actor	Auditor	NA	Audit partner	NA
6 Topic	Opinion shopping by client	NA	Failure to require client record asset impairment	NA

one of the business professors has published extensively in the field of business ethics. The other two business professors are familiar with the work of Kohlberg and Rest through their service on dissertation committees. These individuals identified cases where the scoring matrix did not appear to agree with the level of moral reasoning reflected by some of the statements. In these cases the statements were revised until the panel agreed that all of the statements represented the level of moral reasoning intended by the scoring matrix. Two iterations were needed to complete this process.

We evaluated the test–retest reliability of the AMRT on a separate sample of 46 junior and senior accounting students that did not participate in the study. The test–retest was conducted over a three-week interval. The Pearson correlation for the *P*-scores on the test–retest is .65. This reliability measure compares favorably to that of both Massey's (2002, p. 207) instrument (.72) and Thorne's (2000, p. 149) prescriptive instrument (.71). We evaluated internal consistency by calculating Cronbach's α from the responses to the AMRT by participants of this study. Cronbach's α is .65 for this study which again is comparable to instruments used by both Bernardi, Downey, Massey, and Thorne (2002, p. 79) and Massey (2002, p. 207).

Ethics Curriculum Intervention

The learning objectives of the accounting ethics program examined in this study are as follows:

- To understand some of the philosophical base for ethics, particularly those of Aristotle, Kant, and Bentham.
- To grow in appreciation for the importance of acting with honesty, fairness, and integrity in all business transactions.
- To begin to understand one's own set of moral standards of behavior and ethical systems of belief.
- To reflect on problematic ethical dilemmas that people face in business (accounting) and consider possible steps that one should take in these situations.
- To consider how institutional structures and peer pressure impact decision-making.

The ethics instruction was centered on certain seminal readings in business ethics suggested by Jennings (2004). These readings (Asch, 1958; Carr, 1968; Milgram, 1963; Nash, 1981) were incorporated into the ethics instruction, along with other readings that provide a philosophical base for ethics.

Consistent with Jennings' approach, cases addressing the accounting scandals at Enron, Sunbeam, Tyco, and WorldCom also were discussed as they related to the class readings and exercises. To further illustrate the impact of peer pressure on group decision-making, the students were required to view the movie *Twelve Angry Men*. Additionally, the students were required to view the documentary *Obedience*, a depiction of Milgram's studies during the 1960s. This documentary illustrates a person's tendency to follow orders from those perceived to be in authority. A considerable amount of time was spent in class reviewing various business and general hypothetical dilemmas through group activities, an active learning approach consistent with the pedagogy suggested by Coyne et al. (2005, p. 177).

The ethics instruction used a combination of lecture and active methods such as case study, small group discussion, small group project, and role-playing. The students first read about recent high profile accounting scandals, then discussed the impact of these scandals on the accounting profession. Later in the course we discussed the roles of various individuals in the scandals and how one might perceive them as role models (e.g., internal auditor Cynthia Cooper at WorldCom) or villains (e.g., Bernie Ebbers and accounting staff at WorldCom). This approach is consistent with the suggestion by Armstrong et al. (2003, p. 12) to use exemplars to contextualize the issues and provide role models to follow.

Next, students were introduced to ethics via required readings and lectures covering such topics as virtue, universalism, utilitarianism, normative stockholder theory, and stakeholder theory. This approach mirrors Ponemon's (1993, p. 197) assignment of readings dealing with ethics and professionalism, and lectures on classic and contemporary philosophies on ethics and morality. Then, students reviewed several moral dilemmas (cases) both individually and in groups with the intent of solving the dilemmas from multiple perspectives.

Instructors then required students to participate in role-playing exercises designed to test their MRA. This was followed by a student requirement to write a short paper to document individual reactions to the readings, lectures, and exercises.

Finally, students participated in a group project in which they identified and acted out on videotape an accounting ethics dilemma (Kerr & Smith, 1995). Student groups presented their projects to the class, after which the groups led discussions on how to resolve the ethical dilemmas. The same curriculum was used for all the experimental groups.

RESULTS

Control group scores on the AMRT pre-test (Mean = 39.33) were not statistically different ($p = .462$) from those of the experimental group (Mean = 41.21). However, the results of the surveys indicate that average AMRT scores move in opposite directions. The experimental groups scored higher on the post-test (Mean = 42.87) than on the pre-test, while the control groups scored higher on the pre-test than on the post-test (Mean = 34.11). This decline is consistent with the results (assessed using the DIT) reported by Massey and Thorne (2006).

Two tests were conducted to test H_1. First, an independent samples *t*-test for equality of means (control versus experimental) yielded significant results for the AMRT post-test *P*-score ($p<.01$). The experimental group scores (Mean = 42.87) were significantly greater than the control group scores (Mean = 34.11), thus supporting H_1. Further analysis of the data reveals that post-test *P*-scores were significantly greater for experimental group subjects than control group subjects ($p<.10$) at each school.

For the second test, we used ANCOVA to control for the effects of the pre-test score, age, gender, year in school, previous ethics instruction, course, and school type on MRA scores. These results are reported in Table 3. Once again, group membership (control versus experimental) significantly impacted the AMRT post-test *P*-score ($p<.05$), thus supporting H_1. Gender also is significant which is consistent with some prior research that links gender to scores on tests of MRA (Enyon, Hill, & Stevens, 1997; Shaub, 1994).

In order to test hypotheses 2a, 2b, and 2c, we again used ANCOVA to control for the effects of pre-test score, age, gender, year in school, and previous ethics instruction on MRA scores. Tables 4 through 6 report the ANCOVA results. Group membership (control versus experimental) significantly impacted the AMRT post-test *P*-score ($p<.05$) for both the AIS and auditing classes, but not the principles course, thus supporting H_{2b} and H_{2c}, but not H_{2a}.

Further analysis revealed that AMRT post-test scores actually declined for both control and experimental groups in the principles class. Given this finding, we attempted to determine if the increase in scores noted in both the AIS and auditing classes was statistically significant. If so, there would be evidence that the instruction was particularly effective in the case of

Table 3. ANCOVA Test of H_1: MRA $= f$ (Ethics Instruction).

Source of Variation	Sum of Squares	df	Mean Square	*F*	*p*-Value
AMRT pre-test score (covariate)	9539.446	1	9539.446	66.861	.000
Age (covariate)	2.652	1	2.652	.019	.892
Gender (covariate)	588.849	1	588.849	4.127	.045
Year in school (covariate)	19.807	1	19.807	.139	.710
Prior ethics instruction (covariate)	20.784	1	20.784	.146	.703
Course (covariate)	97.844	1	97.844	.686	.409
School type (covariate)	30.752	1	30.752	.216	.643
Group	570.501	1	570.501	3.999	.048
Residual error	15979.747	112	142.676		

Table 4. ANCOVA Test of H_{2a}: MRA for Principles Class = f (Ethics Instruction).

Source of Variation	Sum of Squares	df	Mean Square	F	p-Value
AMRT pre-test score (covariate)	1865.454	1	1865.454	15.665	.000
Age (covariate)	103.011	1	103.011	.865	.358
Gender (covariate)	585.887	1	585.887	4.920	.032
Year in school (covariate)	258.582	1	258.582	2.171	.149
Prior ethics instruction (covariate)	22.743	1	22.743	.191	.665
Group	196.133	1	196.133	1.647	.207
Residual error	4644.271	39	119.084		

Table 5. ANCOVA Test of H_{2b}: MRA for AIS Class = f (Ethics Instruction).

Source of Variation	Sum of Squares	df	Mean Square	F	p-Value
AMRT pre-test score (covariate)	4016.361	1	4016.361	21.966	.000
Age (covariate)	63.544	1	63.544	.343	.561
Gender (covariate)	.02091	1	.02091	.000	.992
Year in school (covariate)	84.740	1	84.740	.463	.503
Prior ethics instruction (covariate)	6.241	1	6.241	.034	.855
Group	986.890	1	986.890	5.397	.029
Residual error	4388.335	24	182.847		

Table 6. ANCOVA Test of H_{2c}: MRA for Auditing Class = f (Ethics Instruction).

Source of Variation	Sum of Squares	df	Mean Square	F	p-Value
AMRT pre-test score (covariate)	2929.344	1	2929.344	18.889	.000
Age (covariate)	.163	1	.163	.001	.974
Gender (covariate)	317.588	1	317.588	2.048	.161
Year in school (covariate)	196.281	1	196.281	1.266	.268
Prior ethics instruction (covariate)	14.694	1	14.694	.095	.760
Group	920.697	1	920.697	5.937	.020
Residual error	5738.017	37	155.082		

upper-level classes. However a paired samples t-test of the AIS and auditing experimental group means (pre-test paired to post-test) revealed that although the scores increased following ethics instruction, the differences were not statistically significant.

SUMMARY AND IMPLICATIONS

Statistically significant differences in MRA scores between those receiving ethics instruction and those not receiving ethics instruction were noted. Those receiving ethics instruction scored higher on the AMRT, thus supporting H_1. Those who participated in the ethics intervention had higher scores on the post-test AMRT, but only by less than two points on average. In contrast, those who did not participate in the ethics intervention had lower scores on the post-test AMRT, by more than five points on average. If the intervention was successful, then we would expect the increase for the experimental group subjects. The observed change for the experimental group subjects is small, but it is, indeed, an increase. This may be due to the brevity of the intervention (only three weeks), which may suggest that our results are understated.

With regard to H_{2a}, H_{2b}, and H_{2c}, the findings provide some evidence that the ethics instruction was effective in raising the AMRT scores of students in the AIS and auditing classes. Since the AIS and auditing classes were composed of juniors and seniors, whereas the principles class was primarily composed of sophomores, it appears that the effectiveness of ethics instruction may be a function of student level. Our findings are consistent with an assertion by Lucas (1990, pp. 108–109) that first and second-year college students function at a lower stage of intellectual development than upper-level students, mainly due to lack of experience. The principles students attended a liberal arts college which does not allow students to take business courses until sophomore year. Thus, it is also possible that the principles students showed no improvement because they had relatively little prior business coursework from which to draw, compared to the students in the upper-level classes. To support this point, prior research shows that students' understanding about the requirements and responsibilities of auditors converges with that of practicing auditors following completion of the introductory audit course (Gramling, Schatzberg, & Wallace, 1996; Ferguson, Richardson, & Wines, 2000). Perhaps upper-level students are more sensitive to ethics instruction because they have a "frame" to put around the instruction. If this were true, an individualized approach to ethics instruction as suggested by Massey and Thorne (2006, p. 114) seems prudent, instead of a one-size-fits-all approach.

LIMITATIONS

There are several limitations to this study that should be noted when considering its results. First, the number of subjects (121) is relatively small, and the study includes students from only two institutions in the Midwest. Future research should consider introducing an intervention at more schools so as to yield a wide spectrum of students from across the country. Another potential limitation is that the principal investigators of the study conducted the instruction. It may not be appropriate to assume that other instructors would obtain the same results under similar circumstances.

FUTURE RESEARCH

More research is needed to determine the most effective content and duration of ethics instruction. In this study, a relatively short amount of class time was devoted to ethics instruction, yet statistically significant results were obtained. Others have used different instructional techniques that also appear to be beneficial. It would be valuable to determine if a stand-alone accounting ethics course yields equal or better results, than simply incorporating ethics instruction in existing accounting classes.

Additionally, longitudinal studies of accounting students and practitioners should be conducted. If ethics instruction does in fact impact a student's MRA, can this effect be sustained throughout one's career? If so, would practitioner ethics instruction on an ongoing basis be necessary? These are important questions that need to be addressed possibly through longitudinal studies that track the accounting careers of accounting professionals.

In this study we did not attempt to determine which particular teaching methods (active or passive) have the greatest effect on MRA. While, the ethics curriculum tested shows promise, future research also should focus on determining which techniques (e.g., active versus passive) are most effective.

CONCLUSION

Our belief is that ethics instruction should be incorporated into the accounting curriculum. This study provides additional support for investing in ethics instruction for accounting students, as well as directions for future research. As accounting educators continue to refine methods and techniques for teaching ethics, our students will benefit. In turn, ethics instruction will benefit the firms that employ our students. The ethics curriculum tested in this study, significantly based on Jennings (2004), provides a framework for delivering ethics instruction that shows promise. By using active learning methods along with seminal ethics readings within an existing accounting course, we find that ethics instruction does make a difference.

ACKNOWLEDGMENT

We would like to thank Dr. Dan Ebener, Dr. Monica Forret, Dr. Joseph McCaffrey, Dr. David O'Connell, and Dr. Craig VanSandt for their help with this manuscript. In particular, their review and suggested improvements to the AMRT are greatly appreciated.

REFERENCES

Armstrong, M. (1993). Ethics and professionalism in accounting education: A sample course. *Journal of Accounting Education*, *11*, 77–92.

Armstrong, M., Ketz, J., & Owsen, D. (2003). Ethics education in accounting: Moving toward ethical motivation and ethical behavior. *Journal of Accounting Education*, *21*(1), 1–16.

Asch, S. (1958). Effects of group pressure on the modification and distortion of judgment. In: E. E. Maccoby, T. M. Newcomb & E. L. Hartley (Eds), *Readings in social psychology* (pp. 566–569). New York: Holt, Rinehart, and Winston.

Bernardi, R. (1994). Fraud detection: The effect of client integrity and competence and auditor cognitive style. *Auditing: A Journal of Practice and Theory*, *13*, 68–84.

Bernardi, R., Downey, A., Massey, D., & Thorne, L. (2002). Critical thinking and the moral reasoning of intermediate accounting students. *Research on Accounting Ethics*, *8*, 73–102.

Brugman, D., & Weisfelt, M. (2000). Moral competence and professional reasoning by Dutch Auditors. *Research on Accounting Ethics*, *7*, 103–140.

Carr, A. Z. (1968). Is business bluffing ethical? *Harvard Business Review*, *46*(January/February), 2–8.

Cohen, J. R., Pant, L. W., & Sharp, D. J. (1995). An exploratory examination of international differences in auditors' ethical perceptions. *Behavioral Research in Accounting*, *7*, 37–64.

Coyne, M., Massey, D., & Thibodeau, J. (2005). Raising students' ethical sensitivity with a value relevance approach. *Advances in Accounting Education: Teaching and Curriculum Innovations*, *7*, 171–205.

Dellaportas, S. (2006). Making a difference with a discrete course on accounting ethics. *Journal of Business Ethics*, *65*(4), 391–404.

Earley, C., & Kelly, P. (2004). A note on ethics educational interventions in an undergraduate auditing course: Is there an Enron effect? *Issues in Accounting Education*, *19*(1), 53–71.

Enyon, G., Hill, N., & Stevens, K. (1997). Factors that influence the moral reasoning abilities of accountants: Implications for universities and the profession. *Journal of Business Ethics*, *16*(12), 1297–1309.

Ferguson, C. B., Richardson, G. D., & Wines, G. (2000). Audit education and training: The effect of formal studies and work experience. *Accounting Horizons*, *14*(2), 137–167.

Ferris, W. P. (1996). The effectiveness of teaching business ethics using moral philosophy and personal ethical codes. *Journal of Management Education*, *20*(3), 341–357.

Gibbins, M. (1992). Deception: A tricky issue for behavioral research in accounting and auditing. *Auditing: A Journal of Practice and Theory*, *11*(2), 113–126.

Gramling, A. A., Schatzberg, J. W., & Wallace, W. A. (1996). The role of undergraduate auditing coursework in reducing the expectations gap. *Issues in Accounting Education*, *11*(1), 131–161.

Jennings, M. (2004). Incorporating ethics and professionalism into accounting education and research: A discussion of the voids and advocacy for training in seminal works in business ethics. *Issues in Accounting Education*, *19*(1), 7–26.

Jones, J., Massey, D., & Thorne, L. (2003). Auditors' ethical reasoning: Insights from past research and implications for the future. *Journal of Accounting Literature*, *22*, 45–103.

Kerr, D. S., & Smith, M. L. (1995). Importance of and approaches to incorporating ethics into the accounting classroom. *Journal of Business Ethics*, *14*(12), 987–995.

Kohlberg, L. (1981). *Essays on moral development: The philosophy of moral development*. New York: Harper and Row.

Loeb, S. E., & Rockness, J. (1992). Accounting ethics and education: A response. *Journal of Business Ethics*, *11*(7), 485–490.

Lucas, A. F. (1990). Using psychological models to understand student motivation. *New Directions for Teaching and Learning*, *42*, 103–114.

Massey, D. (2002). The importance of context in investigating auditors' moral abilities. *Research on Accounting Ethics*, *8*, 195–247.

Massey, D., & Thorne, L. (2006). The impact of task information feedback on ethical reasoning. *Behavior Research in Accounting*, *18*, 103–116.

Milgram, S. (1963). Behavioral study of obedience. *Journal of Abnormal and Social Psychology*, *67*, 371–378.

Nash, L. (1981). Ethics without the sermon. *Harvard Business Review*, *59*(November/December), 79–89.

Ponemon, L. (1992). Auditor underreporting of time and moral reasoning: An experimental lab study. *Contemporary Accounting Research*, *9*(1), 171–189.

Ponemon, L. (1993). Can ethics be taught in accounting? *Journal of Accounting Education*, *11*, 185–209.

Randall, D. M., & Fernandes, M. F. (1991). The social desirability response bias in ethics research. *Journal of Business Ethics*, *10*, 805–817.

Rest, J. (1994). Background: Theory and research. In: J. Rest & D. Narvaez (Eds), *Moral development in the professions*. Hillsdale, NJ: Lawrence Erlbaum Associates.

Rest, J., Narvzez, D., Bebeau, M., & Thoma, S. (1999). *Postconventional moral thinking: A neo-Kohlbergian approach*. Mahwah, NJ: Lawrence Erlbaum Associates.

Shaub, M. (1994). An analysis of the association of traditional demographic variables with the moral reasoning of auditing students and auditors. *Journal of Accounting Education*, *12*(1), 1–26.

Thorne, L. (2000). The development of two measures to assess accountants' prescriptive and deliberative moral reasoning. *Behavioral Research in Accounting*, *12*, 139–169.

USING THE ALBRECHT AND SACK STUDY TO GUIDE CURRICULUM DECISIONS

Steve Johnson, Bunney Schmidt, Steve Teeter and Jonathan Henage

ABSTRACT

This study replicates the portion of Albrecht and Sack's "Perilous Future" monograph (AAA, 2000) that examines the knowledge, skills, and abilities desired by employers of entry-level accounting graduates. Its purpose is to determine if Albrecht and Sack's (A&S) results are sufficiently generalizable to guide curriculum development in meeting stakeholder needs at a regional state college. We administered a survey instrument similar to that used by A&S to employers of accounting graduates to determine what knowledge, general skills, and technology abilities are important to their hiring decisions.

Our findings reveal that large, national, and international employers desire knowledge and skills that are different from those required by smaller, local, and regional employers. The study also found that desired knowledge and skills differ between employer industries. Finally, significant differences also were noted in the knowledge, general skills, and technology ability requirements. These results suggest that A&S findings should be interpreted in the context of each educational institution's own unique environment.

Advances in Accounting Education: Teaching and Curriculum Innovations, Volume 9, 251–266

ISSN: 1085-4622/doi:10.1016/S1085-4622(08)09012-3

"Accounting Education: Charting the Course through a Perilous Future," authored by Albrecht and Sack (AAA, 2000) addresses the need to improve the academic preparation of accountants for entry into the profession. Their study specifically encourages accounting educators to revise curriculums to meet the changing requirements of business employers, and potentially serves as a guide in curriculum revision decisions. Albrecht and Sack (A&S) also focus their attention on addressing student deficiencies in the knowledge, skills, and abilities possessed by entry-level accountants. Our study builds on A&S's work by examining the generalizability of their results to a unique institutional setting.

Our research used a survey similar to A&S's instrument to collect data from Utah employers regarding the knowledge, business skills, and technical abilities employers most desired in accounting graduates. Our findings were not consistent with those of the A&S study. Instead, we found that smaller, local, and regional employers generally require a broader range of knowledge, skills, and abilities than do national or international employers. This difference arises because the job responsibilities of those employed by smaller, local, and regional firms are broader, and much less specialized than in larger firms. Our study also reports large differences in the knowledge and skills required by employers in different industries. These results suggest that each educational institution must evaluate the needs of their own employer stakeholders in order to provide a relevant accounting education for their students.

This chapter begins with a brief review of the relevant literature. Next, we provide a description of the institutional setting of our college, Utah Valley State College (UVSC). The research methodology then is discussed. The chapter concludes with a summary of results and a review of the study's implications for accounting educators.

LITERATURE REVIEW

Motivated by criticism that the A&S study had a "national school, Big 5" bias, Burnett (2003) tested the validity of this criticism. He administered a streamlined version of the A&S study questionnaire twice to employers of graduates at a regional university in the Texas Panhandle. Employers included private corporate firms, non-Big 5 accounting firms, as well as local CPAs. The response rate for each survey was 27.6% and 21.7%, respectively. The study compared the rankings of professional skills and technology abilities of these surveys with the A&S rankings. Burnett determined that his overall results from the two surveys were similar to those reported in the A&S monograph, thus appearing to validate A&S's findings. We believe that our institutional context may be sufficiently different from Burnett (2003) to warrant a new investigation of the generalizability of A&S.

INSTITUTIONAL SETTING

Our institution, UVSC, is a public coeducational college based in Orem, Utah that evolved from a vocational/trade technical school to a state college. UVSC is primarily a commuter school with approximately 24,000 students and 400 accounting majors. The school of business recently received accreditation from the Association to Advance Collegiate Schools of Business (AACSB).

UVSC's accounting department strives for continuous improvement in its accounting curriculum to provide a quality education that will meet the needs of stakeholders, particularly employers, and enable accounting graduates to succeed. To address this mission, we decided to examine the knowledge, skills, and abilities that our students are developing within our current curriculum. We initially used the A&S study to determine where our curriculum might fall short. However, we questioned the usefulness of this study in guiding our curriculum decisions given its apparent orientation to large national/international employers, and the reality of our institution's demographics and placement experience.

An internal survey of UVSC accounting majors revealed that more than half were married, and had started a family. More than two-thirds worked part-time and 24% worked full time. Upon graduation, approximately 80% planned to attend graduate school, and 77% anticipated obtaining a professional accounting designation. UVSC accounting graduates were employed primarily by six different types of organization: local CPA firms (both staff and bookkeeping positions), government (primarily the Internal Revenue Service and the State Tax Commission), local manufacturers, a variety of retail and service businesses, and software development firms. Clearly, UVSC provides accounting graduates primarily for a smaller, more local, regional employer base.

Given this student profile, we questioned whether the knowledge and skill needs of employers were the same at all educational institutions (i.e., generalizability of A&S's study), or if employer needs differed across geographical regions, or between industries. Since each educational institution operates in a somewhat unique context and environment, we decided to conduct a study similar to A&S to determine what knowledge and skills are desired by employers of UVSC accounting graduates.

RESEARCH METHODOLOGY

Sample

To gather data, we created a questionnaire based on the knowledge and skills portions of the A&S instrument, and mailed it to 170 employers from throughout the State of Utah. We drew our sample from two different employer directories: the Utah County Employers Directory and an online business directory located at www.firmfind.dws.state.us. We selected a random sample of 110 employers from those businesses employing more than 100 employees in Utah County, and the remaining 60 came from businesses employing more than 300 employees in the State of Utah. Both samples included past and potential employers of UVSC accounting graduates with no duplication of companies in either group. The questionnaire was purposefully silent as to how many UVSC graduates the employer had hired in the past.

Before mailing the questionnaires, we contacted each employer by telephone to inform them about our study and enlist their participation. We requested the name of an individual familiar with the knowledge, skills, and abilities required for their accounting positions, and then sent the questionnaire to this individual at each company. Ninety-four employers responded and six questionnaires returned as undeliverable. This yielded a response rate of 57.3%.

Survey Instrument

Our survey used the same four-point scale to assess knowledge content and the same five-point scale to assess skills and abilities as the A&S study. However, we expanded the list of knowledge topics beyond those listed in the A&S study to provide us with a more detailed breakdown of content in six areas: auditing (AUD), financial accounting (FACT), finance (FIN), information systems (IS), management accounting (MACT), tax (TAX), and other (OTH). This classification scheme enabled us to more closely examine the subject matter of each course and better assess the demand for subtopics within the traditional major accounting discipline, other accounting topics, and finance.

The A&S study did not provide sample sizes or standard deviations, making a statistical comparison of means impossible to perform. Therefore, we used a *t*-test to produce a 95% confidence interval on the UVSC mean results to determine whether the A&S study results can be generalized to describe the qualities important to our regional employers.

RESULTS

Rankings of Accounting and Finance Topics

Table 1 reports the mean responses on a four-point scale identifying only the *accounting and finance* topics and subtopics most desired by respondents. FACT, FIN, and AUD account for nine of the first 10 knowledge topics most desired by employers. In fact, financial statement preparation and analysis, including an understanding of generally accepted accounting principles (GAAP) occupy three of the top five positions. Cash management and finance topics follow at numbers three and six, respectively. These preferences suggest an emphasis on the knowledge and skills needed to finance and run a small to midsize business.

MACT topics occupy four of the top 13 topics with budgeting at number four and management control, product costing, and performance measurement and evaluation occupying positions 11 through 13. The rankings reveal a clear preference for financial accounting knowledge over management accounting information for decision-making. These results are consistent with the common smaller business practice of relying primarily on financial statement information systems for internal management decision-making. Similarly, the 17 ranking for long-term financing/capital structure when compared to general finance (ranked at 7) suggests the need for a simple capital structure in the small to medium-sized business, versus a more complex capital structure for larger business.

Other financial accounting topics such as leases, deferred taxes, pensions, Financial Accounting Standards Board (FASB) pronouncements, consolidations, and government/non-profit accounting, commonly found in the second intermediate and advanced financial accounting courses, rank in the lower half of the 37 surveyed topics. There also is a large divergence in the auditing results with internal/operational auditing ranked at 7, and financial statement auditing and EDP auditing ranked at 24 and 26, respectively. These results

Table 1. Mean Ratings for Surveyed Topics.

	Topics	Means
1	Financial statement preparation (FACT)	3.55
2	Financial statement analysis (FACT)	3.55
3	Cash management (FIN)	3.22
4	Budgeting (MACT)	3.13
5	GAAP (FACT)	3.03
6	Finance (FIN)	2.99
7	Internal/operational auditing (AUD)	2.98
8	Accounting theory (FACT)	2.90
9	Asset management/capital budgeting (FIN)	2.88
10	Working capital management (FACT)	2.87
11	Management control systems (MACT)	2.86
12	Product costing (MACT)	2.83
13	Performance measurement/evaluation (MACT)	2.79
14	Systems analysis (IS)	2.79
15	Corporate tax (TAX)	2.78
16	Controllership (MACT)	2.78
17	Long-term financing/capital structure (FIN)	2.75
18	Strategic cost management (MACT)	2.74
19	Leases, deferred taxes, pensions, capital transactions (FACT)	2.71
20	Financial accounting research (OTH)	2.70
21	Taxation (TAX)	2.70
22	FASB pronouncements (FACT)	2.69
23	Database management (IS)	2.68
24	Financial statement auditing (AUD)	2.67
25	Operations/supply-chain management (OTH)	2.67
26	EDP auditing (AUD)	2.64
27	CPA/CMA review (OTH)	2.60
28	Consolidations (FACT)	2.59
29	Information systems design (IS)	2.56
30	Public finance/tax policy (TAX)	2.44
31	Personal finance (FIN)	2.30
32	Individual tax (TAX)	2.27
33	Tax research (TAX)	2.21
34	International accounting (OTH)	2.06
35	Government/non-profit accounting (FACT)	2.01
36	Estate & gift tax (TAX)	1.88
37	Accounting history (OTH)	1.82

suggest that the majority of respondents rely on external public accountants to perform financial statement and EDP auditing. The bottom half ranked topics appear to identify knowledge areas more likely required in a large business organization rather than a small or medium-sized business.

Comparison of Rankings of Business Topics with A&S

Table 2 compares the rankings for all accounting and business topics at UVSC with the A&S study. To make this comparison, we averaged the means for the subtopics within each of the broad accounting areas. For example, the means for all of the topics in Table 1 followed by FACT were averaged to obtain an overall mean for financial accounting. The final means and ranking for each of the seven accounting and finance topics are as follows: financial accounting (2.88, 1); management accounting (2.86, 2); finance (2.83, 3); auditing (2.76, 4); information systems (2.68, 5); tax (2.38, 6); and other (2.37, 7). These averages indicate a clear preference among our sample for students that are knowledgeable in FACT, MACT, and FIN.

Several noticeable differences exist between our study and that of A&S. The three largest differences are in taxation, ethics, and information

Table 2. Topical Comparison between Studies.

Rank		Topic	Means		Confidence Intervals	
A&S	This study		A&S	This study	Lower	Upper
1	3	Financial accounting	3.57	2.88	2.80	2.93
2	10	Information systems	3.56	2.68	2.58	2.77
3	5	Finance	3.28	2.83	2.75	2.91
4	17	Taxation	3.28	2.38	2.30	2.46
5	2	Business strategy	3.15	2.90	2.75	3.06
6	7	Auditing/assurance services	3.06	2.76	2.67	2.86
7	4	Managerial accounting	3.05	2.86	2.79	2.92
8	8	Technology topics	3.01	2.72	2.56	2.88
9	13	E-commerce	3.00	2.57	2.40	2.74
10	6	Business law	2.95	2.81	2.64	2.98
11	18	Global/international business	2.92	2.17	1.99	2.35
12	1	Ethics	2.89	3.39	3.24	3.54
13	14	Economics	2.81	2.56	2.40	2.72
14	15	Statistics/quantitative methods	2.73	2.52	2.35	2.69
15	9	Accounting research methods	2.50	2.70	2.52	2.87
16	11	Operations/supply chain management	2.48	2.67	2.50	2.84
17	12	Organizational behavior/ human resources	2.46	2.66	2.49	2.82
18	16	Marketing	2.45	2.41	2.24	2.58

Note: A&S denotes the Albrecht and Sack study.

systems. Why did this likely occur? A public accounting firm that provides tax services would require a stronger knowledge of taxation than a small to midsize non-accounting business. In fact, a smaller business likely would outsource its tax services, while a large organization would perform a large share of the tax functions itself. The Internal Revenue Service and the State Tax Commission also would require a strong knowledge of tax. Public accounting firms and government employers only comprised 13.5 percent of the sample of responding firms, which likely contributes to the low tax ranking.

Also, respondents ranked ethics first in our study compared to 12 in the A&S investigation. The timing of the two studies could account for this difference as the A&S conducted their study in a pre-Sarbanes–Oxley world before the well-publicized business failures of Enron and WorldCom, and the demise of Arthur Andersen. According to Haas (2005, p. 66), "recent corporate accounting scandals have brought ethics back into the limelight," resulting in many schools increasing their coverage of ethical issues. If A&S repeated their study today, ethics likely would rank higher. Also, Utah's culture may account for the high ethics ranking. Since religion plays a prominent role in the lives of state and county residents, this likely contributed to the high ranking of ethics as well.

Additionally, the A&S study ranked information systems at two, while our respondents ranked it at 10. Again, business size likely impacts respondent perception of the importance of the information system within an organization. While all businesses require information to run effectively and efficiently, smaller organizations generally require much simpler information systems that rely on data gathered through often informal, face-to-face communication. Conversely, larger, more complex organizations generally rely on more sophisticated technologies to provide them with decision-making information.

Employers in our study also appeared to value several non-accounting and finance topics very highly. For example, ethics and business strategy were rated ahead of financial accounting, managerial accounting, and finance, and business law was ranked higher than auditing/assurance services. Additionally, all business topics, except for international business, were valued more than taxation in our study. These findings are noteworthy because the A&S study ranked all business and non-accounting topics *below* accounting and finance topics (except for business strategy). These results suggest that our employers prefer a broader business education, than those surveyed in the A&S study. In short, large firms may prefer more specialization in the accountants they hire.

Employer size also appears responsible for smaller differences noted between the two studies in business strategy, managerial accounting, operations/supply chain management, and organizational behavior/human resources. Our study ranked each of these topics slightly higher than A&S. It also should be noted that A&S means fell within reported confidence intervals for only two topics, business law and marketing, suggesting that A&S study results were not generalizable to the UVSC population in most instances.

Industry Effects: Topical Coverage

Employers in different industries may require different knowledge and skills for their new hires. Therefore, we ranked each knowledge topic and skill within each industry after calculating industry means. Table 3 reports our results.

A review of the top five topics for each industry shows that employers in each value the knowledge and skills needed to successfully accomplish work for that particular industry. For example, one would expect an accountant working in public accounting to have a strong knowledge base in financial accounting, auditing, tax, and business law. On the other hand, an accountant working in a manufacturing environment would need a foundation in managerial accounting, finance, and business strategy. The top five topics for each of the six industries comprise 10 of the 18 topics in Table 3, illustrating the diversity and variety of knowledge required by employers. This appears to confirm that industry sample composition can affect surveys of desired knowledge, skills, and abilities. Therefore, when designing an accounting curriculum for an educational institution's stakeholders, faculty must consider the needs of each industry it serves.

We also noted large differences in six topical areas. Information systems, business strategy, auditing/assurance services, technology topics, business law, operations and supply chain management, all were ranked very high by some industries, and very low by other industries. For example, government, retail, and software industries appear to require knowledge of information systems, but accounting, manufacturing, and service employers do not appear to value these topics very highly.

The similarities in Table 3 also are interesting. For example, every industry ranked ethics first. After ethics, three topics rank high across all six industries: financial accounting, finance, and managerial accounting. These results are consistent with each main topic ranking in Table 2.

Table 3. Topical Rankings by Industry.

Topics	Industry (Sample Size)					
	Acct (4)	Govt (8)	Manuf (32)	Retail (16)	Service (22)	Software (7)
Financial accounting	3	2	5	9	7	3
Information systems	14	6	9	5	12	5
Finance	10	9	3	6	2	7
Taxation	7	17	16	16	17	18
Business strategy	11	4	4	3	3	2
Auditing/assurance services	2	3	14	4	8	12
Managerial accounting	8	8	2	7	4	4
Technology topics	5	5	10	11	13	16
E-commerce	15	16	12	12	15	8
Business law	4	13	6	15	5	6
International business	17	18	17	18	18	13
Ethics	1	1	1	1	1	1
Economics	12	10	11	14	16	14
Statistics	6	11	15	17	9	9
Accounting research methods	9	7	8	8	10	10
Operations & supply chain management	18	14	7	10	6	17
Organizational behavior & human resources	13	12	13	2	11	15
Marketing	16	15	18	13	14	11

Note: Acct, Accounting; Govt, Government; Manuf, Manufacturing.

Comparison of Rankings of Business Skills with A&S

Table 4 reports comparative rankings for business skills. Both studies show the same top 10 skills for the 22 examined, but in a different order. Oral communication, interpersonal skills, and decision-making ranked higher in our study. As before, the smaller size of our employer sample appears to be driving these results. The smaller firm would likely use simpler information systems characterized by more frequent interpersonal contacts which require better oral communication and interpersonal skills. Also, the likelihood of interaction with customers and other individuals important to the success of the business becomes much more critical in a smaller firm. While decision-making is an important skill for any accountant, smaller firm employers generally assign a broader range of responsibilities, thus elevating the importance of decision-making.

Table 4. Skills Comparison between Studies.

Rank		Topic	Comparative Means		Confidence Intervals	
A&S	This study		A&S	This study	Lower	Upper
1	5	Written communication	4.32	4.22	4.08	4.35
2	3	Analytical/critical thinking	4.29	4.24	4.10	4.37
3	1	Oral communication	4.27	4.28	4.14	4.41
4	7	Computing technology	4.07	4.13	3.99	4.27
5	6	Teamwork	4.02	4.15	4.02	4.28
6	2	Decision-making	3.96	4.27	4.14	4.40[a]
7	4	Interpersonal skills	3.89	4.24	4.11	4.37[a]
8	8	Leadership	3.83	3.86	3.70	4.03
9	9	Continuous learning	3.70	3.85	3.66	4.04
10	10	Personal demeanor	3.66	3.85	3.69	4.00[a]
11	14	Project management	3.66	3.39	3.23	3.55[a]
12	12	Business decision modeling	3.65	3.40	3.22	3.58[a]
13	15	Risk analysis	3.39	3.28	3.14	3.42
14	17	Change management	3.36	3.18	3.03	3.34[a]
15	13	Negotiation	3.35	3.40	3.23	3.56
16	11	Customer orientation	3.34	3.74	3.55	3.94[a]
17	18	Resource management	3.32	3.11	2.95	3.27[a]
18	19	Research	3.26	3.07	2.87	3.26
19	20	Entrepreneurship	3.24	3.02	2.82	3.23[a]
20	16	Measurement	3.12	3.28	3.11	3.48
21	21	Salesmanship	2.79	2.89	2.69	3.10
22	22	Foreign language	2.56	2.17	1.98	2.36[a]

[a]The A&S study mean cannot be generalized to the UVSC population as it falls outside the confidence interval.

Within the bottom ranked 12 skills, customer orientation showed the largest difference between the two studies, ranked at 11 in our study and at 16 by A&S. The likelihood of greater contact in a smaller firm between employees and customers likely makes customer orientation a more valued skill to our sample.

Unlike Table 2's results, almost half of the skill's mean responses from the A&S study cannot be generalized to the UVSC population (i.e., A&S means outside the confidence interval). While the bottom 15 skills show little difference in rankings, 8 of the 10 significant differences in means appear in the bottom 13 skills. Of the 10 skills where the A&S mean fell outside of the UVSC confidence interval, project management, business decision modeling, change management, resource management, entrepreneurship, and foreign language all have higher means in the A&S study, skills which generally are more characteristic of large firms (except for entrepreneurship). In contrast, our study's employers value personal demeanor and customer orientation more highly than do A&S employers. In summary, Table 4's results indicate fewer differences between the two studies in business skills, than in knowledge topics.

Industry Effects: Business Skills

Table 5 reports rankings of business skills by industry. Survey responses to several skills within an industry were the same, resulting in identical rankings within that industry. For example, the accounting industry ranked both written communication and interpersonal skills as third in importance. An average ranking of each skill across the six industries identifies the most

Table 5. Skills Ranking by Industry.

Skills	Industry					
	Acct	Govt	Manuf	Retail	Service	Software
Written communication	3	2	6	1	3	4
Analytical/critical thinking	5	2	1	5	6	8
Oral communication	1	4	3	2	1	4
Computing technology	9	7	4	3	7	1
Teamwork	6	6	7	7	3	1
Decision-making	1	4	2	5	1	6
Interpersonal skills	3	1	5	4	3	1
Leadership	13	7	8	7	11	13
Continuous learning	9	10	9	9	8	8
Personal demeanor	6	7	10	11	8	10
Project management	15	12	13	12	18	13
Business decision modeling	17	14	11	15	13	10
Risk analysis	13	14	15	19	15	17
Change management	15	14	17	18	17	21
Negotiation	9	13	16	12	13	13
Customer orientation	6	11	12	10	8	7
Resource management	20	18	18	20	15	17
Research	9	19	19	21	19	10
Entrepreneurship	17	20	20	15	20	17
Measurement	17	14	14	14	12	20
Salesmanship	21	21	21	15	21	13
Foreign language	22	22	22	22	22	22

Note: Acct, Accounting; Govt, Government; Manuf, Manufacturing.

important skills as oral communication, interpersonal skills, decision-making, written communication, analytical/critical thinking, teamwork, computing technology, and interpersonal skills.

Not surprisingly, the most important skills for each industry relate to the type of work performed. Accountants value oral communication, decision-making, and written communication skills, suggesting a need to communicate effectively with clients so as to make good auditing and tax decisions. Government employers stress interpersonal skills, written communication, and analytical/critical thinking, indicating a need to communicate successfully with taxpayers and coworkers. Similarly, manufacturing firms appear to focus on communication skills, as well as the analytical/critical thinking and decision-making abilities needed to compete successfully in today's complex business environment. Both retail and service employers stress communication abilities given the major role that they play in effectively and efficiently meeting customer demands. Software industry respondents cite computing technology, teamwork, and interpersonal skills as important. These abilities likely are key to software development activities.

Comparison of Rankings of Technology Skills with A&S

Table 6 reports results for comparing 23 different technology skills evaluated in A&S with our employer sample. Little variance exists in the rankings of the top 10 technology skills except for presentation software (ranked six places higher in the A&S study) and database software (ranked four places higher in our study). Basic personal computer applications all ranked high in both studies. However, the A&S study places more value on the World Wide Web, technology terminology, and presentation software, while our study places more value on database software and file and directory management. Similar to knowledge and business skills, work differences between large and small firms likely explain the variance in these rankings. Formal, less spontaneous communication found in larger firms might require greater use of formal presentation software. Conversely, strong database software, and file and directory management skills likely are required in smaller firms. Consistent with the business skill findings, the A&S study also ranked e-commerce skills higher than our study. Since UVSC uses tax software extensively in its tax courses, our study included this technology skill in our investigation, even though it did not appear in A&S.

Table 6. Technology Skills Comparison between Studies.

Rank A&S	Rank This study		Means A&S	Means This study	Confidence Intervals Lower	Confidence Intervals Upper
1	1	Spreadsheet software	2.89	2.99	2.97	3.01[a]
2	2	Windows	2.80	2.82	2.74	2.91
3	3	Word-process software	2.76	2.76	2.67	2.85
4	5	World Wide Web	2.47	2.46	2.35	2.56
5	7	Technology terminology	2.47	2.39	2.28	2.50
6	12	Presentation software	2.42	2.32	2.20	2.43
7	6	File and directory management	2.42	2.41	2.29	2.52
8	4	Database software	2.41	2.52	2.42	2.62[a]
9	9	Technology security and controls	2.37	2.36	2.22	2.50
10	10	Communications software	2.33	2.34	2.23	2.45
11	8	Project management	2.29	2.38	2.26	2.50
12	16	Information system planning and strategy	2.28	2.21	2.08	2.34
13	18	Electronic commerce	2.28	2.12	2.02	2.22[a]
14	13	Technology management and budgeting	2.13	2.30	2.16	2.43[a]
15	17	Systems analysis	2.04	2.17	2.05	2.30[a]
16	15	Intra/extranets	2.02	2.25	2.14	2.36[a]
17	20	Computer operations management	2.02	2.08	1.97	2.20
18	11	Computer hardware	1.95	2.33	2.22	2.43[a]
19	21	Graphics software	1.89	1.86	1.73	1.98
20	14	Other operating systems	1.83	2.27	2.16	2.38[a]
21	22	HTML and other web programming	1.60	1.78	1.68	1.88[a]
22	23	Programming languages	1.52	1.74	1.64	1.84[a]
23	18	Tax preparation software	NA	2.12	2.00	2.24

[a]The A&S study mean cannot be generalized to the UVSC population as it falls outside the confidence interval.

Ten of the 23 technology skill means from the A&S study fall outside of our investigation's confidence intervals. Of these 10 skills, A&S employers value only electronic commerce higher. On the other hand, our study's employers more highly value the remaining nine skills: spreadsheet software, database software, technology management and budgeting, systems analysis, intra/extranets, computer hardware, other operating systems, HTML and other web programming, and programming languages. As witnessed with the business skills results, the smaller firms in our sample appear to focus on having a well-rounded employee. The smaller firms are less likely to have their own IT department and specialists, so employees with a broad range of computer skills are more highly valued.

CONCLUSION

Although A&S's study provides a general guide to begin the discussion of curriculum issues among accounting faculty, their results may not be generalizable across institutions, since the pool of potential employers is not homogeneous. This study questions whether knowledge and skills differ between large, national, and international employers, and smaller, local, and regional employers. It also investigates whether knowledge and skills differ across industries.

Although Burnett (2003, pp. 129–134) validated the A&S results and found "no glaring contradictions" between the two studies, our study provides only limited support for the A&S study. Our study highlights the differences in knowledge required by the large national and international employers (the A&S study sample) and smaller, local, and regional employers (our study sample). Smaller, local, and regional employers appear to prefer students with a broader education that focuses on the knowledge needed to manage the whole business, and that emphasizes ethics, strategy, budgeting, cash and working-capital management, internal audit, and decision-making. On the other hand, larger, national, and international employers appear to prefer a more focused, specialized education.

Additionally, industry differences appear to affect the knowledge required for employment. Each industry emphasizes and prefers the knowledge tailored to the type of work performed within that industry. However, common areas of knowledge also exist that are important to any organization and any industry. For example, an accounting curriculum grounded in financial accounting, managerial accounting, and finance address the fundamental needs of most employers.

A critical first step in curriculum design is to consider whether your accounting department will be reactive or proactive. Gabbin (2002, pp. 81–86) addresses the differences between reactive and proactive and argues for a proactive approach for colleges or universities when implementing changes into their curriculums. Business schools and accounting departments must consider the needs and desires of the employer stakeholder in the job market they serve. Differences in industry requirements must be addressed. It cannot be assumed that results of national studies are generalizable across all colleges and universities. On the other hand, the desire to modify an accounting curriculum to reflect the desires of employers must be tempered by caution and common sense. As indicated by both A&S and our study, foundation topics and skills such as financial reporting, assurance services, communication, and analytical skills will always be in demand. Generally, business and society prefer that we graduate students with a broad educational background rather than a narrow, specialized education that meets a temporary need or trend. Like most businesses today, we cannot afford to sacrifice long-run educational objectives for short-run, possibly temporary desires of employers. The dynamic business environment affects both business skills and the content of accounting and business education, and students must become prepared to address change in business. This study can be used as a model to address the mission of your school's accounting curriculum, so that it more closely meets the needs of the employers of your accounting graduates.

REFERENCES

Albrecht, W. S., & Sack, R. J. (2000). *Accounting education: Charting the course through a perilous future*. Accounting Education Series, *16*, 1–72.

Burnett, S. (2003). The future of accounting education: A regional perspective. *Journal of Education for Business*, *78*(3).

Gabbin, A. L. (2002). The crisis in accounting education. *Journal of Accountancy*, *193*(4).

Haas, A. (2005). Now is the time for ethics in education. *The CPA Journal*, *75*(6).

USING A TECHNOLOGY-MEDIATED APPROACH TO CREATE A PRACTICE–FEEDBACK–INTERACTION PROCESS FOR USE WITH ACCOUNTING COURSES

Richard E. Lillie

ABSTRACT

Teaching Net Generation accounting students is a challenging experience. They anticipate that technology will be an integral part of the teaching–learning processes that we offer them. This chapter focuses on how to use technology tools to create innovative course materials, delivery methods, and collaborative processes.

The chapter explains how I combined traditional instructional methods and technology-mediated learning (TML) techniques to create a practice–feedback–interaction process for use with two undergraduate auditing courses. I taught the first course (Auditing) during Fall Quarter 2006 and the second course (Advanced Auditing) during Winter Quarter 2007. I taught both courses in a blended instructional format.

This chapter shows how I used the practice–feedback–interaction process with individual and team writing assignments in the two auditing courses. I explain how the TML process works and describe technology

Advances in Accounting Education: Teaching and Curriculum Innovations, Volume 9, 267–286

ISSN: 1085-4622/doi:10.1016/S1085-4622(08)09013-5

tools used at each step of the process. Student comments provide feedback about how they reacted to using the technology-mediated teaching–learning process.

Today's university learning environment is changing due to the arrival of the Net Generation, students born after 1981 (Oblinger, 2003, p. 38). Most of these students are younger than the personal computer; more comfortable using a keyboard than writing things down by hand, and prefer to read from a screen rather than reading from traditional printed text (Frand, 2000, p. 15).

Frand (2000, pp. 16–22) identified 10 attributes of Net Generation students. He describes the attributes as the *mindset of the information-age learner* (Frand, 2000, p. 16). Table 1 presents a summary of the attributes of the information-age learner.

Oblinger and Oblinger (2005, p. 14.1) suggest that Net Generation students expect learning processes to move beyond traditional lecture, note taking, and face-to-face contact with instructors and peers. Net Generation students prefer that instructors keep pace with rapidly changing technologies, include them in their course designs, and use them to communicate their expertise in more creative and efficient ways (Roberts, 2005, p. 3.6).

Net Generation students, particularly Millennials, seem to be more technology savvy than previous student generations and expect that computers, the Internet, online resources, and instant access to information will shape their education (Oblinger & Oblinger, 2005, pp. 2.4–2.7). To meet student expectations, the face-to-face teaching–learning model, the cornerstone of traditional higher education for students before the Net Generation, needs to take advantage of new instructional technologies (Surry, 2005, p. 934). As educators, we need to transform the teaching–learning process so that it is meaningful to the Net Generation information-age learner (Frand, 2000, p. 24).

Technology-mediated learning (TML) makes it possible to engineer innovative learning environments where instructors and learners use advanced information technologies to interact with learning materials and each other (Alavi & Leidner, 2001, p. 2). TML provides a way to add technology tools and instructional strategies to course design (Hardaway & Scamell, 2005, p. 144).

Table 1. Attributes of the Information-Age Mindset.

Attribute No.	Attribute	Description
1	Computers are not technology	Technology, to the information-age generation, is everything that surrounds computers and is made possible by computers but only incidentally the computers themselves. Young people make the devises work without a manual, without the instruction set, as if the devises are hardwired into their psyche.
2	Internet better than TV	Net generation students are using the Web as their primary information source. They are drawn by the interactivity enabled by the Internet and opportunities for socializing.
3	Reality no longer real	For the Net Generation, a virtual reality simulation may be as real as the real experience. Things that appear real over the Internet may not be.
4	Doing rather than knowing	Net Generation students live in a world where digital technologies have made events occur in real time, effects are immediate, and reaction times are short. Results and actions are more important than accumulation of facts.
5	Nintendo over logic	Net Generation students prefer to take an active trial and error approach to problem solving, rather than thinking their way through a problem before taking action.
6	Multitasking way of life	Net Generation students do not concentrate on one activity at a time, rather they multitask (i.e., do multiple things at the same time). Multitasking may be a response to information overload.
7	Typing rather than handwriting	For Net Generation students, the keyboard has replaced the pen or pencil. It is not the typing but the power of the technology tools behind the typing that is important to the student.
8	Staying connected	Advanced telecommunication connectivity (e.g., beepers, cell phones, email, and instant messaging) is standard operating procedure. Not being in touch anytime, anywhere, anyhow is unthinkable.
9	Zero tolerance for delays	For the Net Generation student, the concept of time (and time compression) have changed. Technology has enabled quick response that may be both immediate, as well as, at your convenience.
10	Consumer/creator blurring	To the Net Generation student, there is no distinction between the owner, the creator, and the user of information. Technology tools support sharing/borrowing/taking of other's intellectual property.

Source: Frand (2000).

MOTIVATION FOR THE STUDY

In 1983, Richard E. Clark suggested that THE instructional method rather than THE instructional media causes learning to occur (Clark, 1983, p. 457). Clark's "it's-the-method, not-the-medium" argument started a debate that is not yet resolved. In 1994, Robert A. Reiser, a professor of Instructional Systems at Florida State University, offered a response to Clark's argument (Reiser, 1994).

Reiser suggested that while Clark is correct that instructional method contributes to learning processes, he fails to acknowledge that instructional media also contributes to learning processes (Reiser, 1994, p. 45). Reiser suggested that media and method are both important to learning processes (Reiser, 1994, p. 46).

Reiser called for educators to examine how to use media delivery to solve instructional problems, rather than simply accepting Clark's "it's-the-method, not-the-medium" argument (Reiser, 1994, p. 47). For example, Reiser suggested that instructors should know whether a student's beliefs about a media delivery system might affect how a student learns. He suggested that a student's perceptions about an instructional media might affect the amount of effort that a student puts into a study process (Reiser, 1994, p. 47). Reiser suggested that finding answers to questions like these should be important to instructors as they attempt to design course materials and learning activities (Reiser, 1994, p. 48).

I thought about Reiser's concerns as I considered characteristics of Net Generation students enrolling in my accounting courses. I felt it important to learn whether technology-mediated methods and techniques like the ones that I create will satisfy the educational expectations of my Net Generation accounting students.

The TML-based process that I created for two undergraduate auditing courses combines benefits of face-to-face instruction with flexibility of technology-mediated delivery and interaction strategies used in distance learning courses. Students used TML tools to complete writing assignments and submit them for grading. I used TML tools to grade the writing assignments and give students personalized feedback about their performance. Assignments included individual and team-based writing activities.

By sharing information about my approach, I hope to motivate accounting instructors to use TML techniques when designing their courses and instructional materials. I believe use of TML techniques should improve or enhance the learning process of students.

LITERATURE REVIEW

This literature review focuses on relationships and interactions between instructional method and delivery media as they relate to the design of the practice–feedback–interaction approach I used. The review considers instructional design models, basic elements of instructional design, and issues affecting use of TML methods and techniques.

Continuum of Instructional Design Models

Instructional design models range from traditional face-to-face to fully online formats (Dziuban, Hartman, & Moskal, 2004, p. 2). Between the two extremes lies a range of blended or mixed-mode instruction models that include both face-to-face and online activities. These blended or technology-mediated instruction models use technology tools to varying degrees (Dziuban et al., 2004, p. 2).

In Fig. 1, I show that design emphasis of an instruction model changes by moving left or right along the continuum. Technology tools mediate the learning process to the extent needed (e.g., a face-to-face course may enhance instruction through use of technology without reducing classroom contact time). Clark (2003, pp. 13–14) suggests that technology per se does not promote learning. Rather, she suggests that innovative use of technology may improve the instructional process.

Basic Elements of an Instructional Design Model

Clark (2003, p. 4) states that there are three common models of learning (e.g., absorption, behavioral, or cognitive). Each model makes different

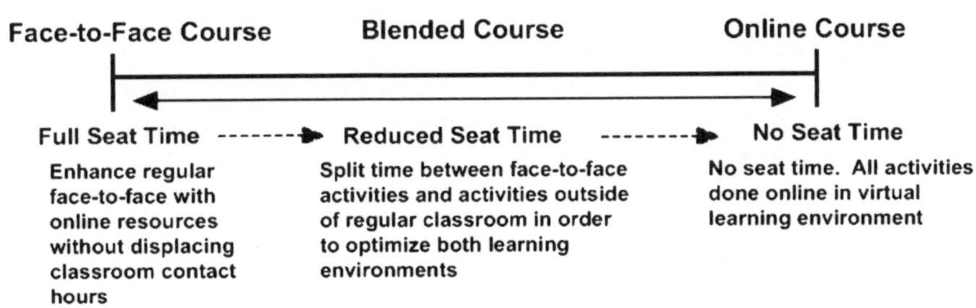

Fig. 1. Continuum of Instructional Models.

assumptions about how and when learning occurs and emphasizes one or more of the basic elements of instructional design (i.e., content, practice, and feedback) (Clark, 2003, pp. 4–5).

The learning model used by an instructor provides a framework for designing a teaching–learning experience (Clark, 2003, p. 4). The framework guides selection of instructional methods that in turn help guide the learner's transformation of content into internal knowledge and skills (Clark, 2003, p. 13). The transformation process involves interaction between the learner, instructor, content, and the learning environment (Boettcher, 2007).

Boettcher (2007) suggests that innovative use of technology can dramatically affect how an instructor and learner communicate with each other during a course. Boettcher (2007) suggests that an instructor's innovative use of technology may enable a learner to make better use of the instructor as a source of specialized guidance and feedback.

Issues Affecting Use of Technology-Mediated Learning Methods and Techniques

Four technology-mediation issues relate to the practice–feedback–interaction process presented in this chapter. The four issues are practice, feedback, synchronicity, and instructor immediacy.

Issue No. 1: Practice

No matter whether it occurs in a face-to-face, blended, or online learning environment, practice (i.e., learning by doing) enhances learning dramatically (Boettcher, 2007). A key element of effective practice is frequent instructor–student interaction both in and out of class. Interaction is an important factor in student motivation and involvement (Chickering & Gamson, 1987, p. 2). Chickering and Gamson (1987) state that, "Learning is not a spectator sport. Students do not learn much just by sitting in classes listening to teachers, memorizing pre-packaged assignments, and spitting out answers. They must talk about what they are learning, write about it, relate it to experiences and apply it to their daily lives. They must make what they learn part of themselves" (p. 3).

Issue No. 2: Feedback

Feedback is the exchange of information between instructor and student about an action, event, or process that results in improved student learning (Chickering & Gamson, 1987, p. 3). Whether provided in a face-to-face, blended, or online environment, instructors need to provide students with timely feedback in order to keep them engaged in the learning process. Students need to know how they are progressing, as well as, receive suggestions for improving performance (Thurman & Wambach, 2004).

Tsutsui (2004, p. 379) suggests there are three types of feedback: interactive feedback (immediate between student and instructor), intrusive feedback (immediate feedback between student and instructor that interrupts the student's performance), and delayed feedback (occurs after performance by providing comprehensive comments). He suggests that technology tools such as audio, video, email, text chat, and video-conferencing may be effective when providing delayed feedback (Tsutsui, 2004, p. 389).

Issue No. 3: Synchronicity

Keefe (2003) says that synchronicity refers to the timing or synchronization of communication transfers between a sender and a receiver. It is either immediate (synchronous) or delayed (asynchronous). He says (2003) that synchronous communication does not have to be face-to-face, but it does have to be immediate (e.g., "live" text chat through a service such as MSN, AOL, or Skye would be an example of synchronous communication that is not face-to-face). Synchronous technology includes tools such as online chat, audio and video-conferencing.

Keefe (2003) says that asynchronous communication is delayed rather than immediate. Asynchronous communication could be a recorded audio or video message, email, or written document. Asynchronous technology includes tools such as message boards, discussion boards, and email.

Issue No. 4: Instructor Immediacy

Instructor immediacy deals with communication between instructor and student (Baker & Woods, 2004, p. 4). Immediacy includes both nonverbal and verbal signals and behaviors between the instructor and the student (Arbaugh, 2001, p. 43).

In TML environments, immediacy is somewhat controlled by including both synchronous and asynchronous communication methods, each being used when most appropriate (Larose & Whitten, 2000, p. 332). Graphic images such as the "talking paper clip" in Microsoft Windows are a type of TML communication (Larose & Whitten, 2000, p. 333).

Instructor immediacy is a special concern in TML. Instructors need to pay attention to this issue when designing TML experiences (Richardson & Swan, 2003, p. 81).

Relating the Literature Review to the Design of Two Auditing Courses

The TML-based instructional design approach presented in this chapter emphasizes two basic elements of instructional design (i.e., practice and feedback). The approach emphasizes the TML issues of practice, feedback, synchronicity, and instructor immediacy.

DESIGN OF TWO AUDITING COURSES

General Information about the Courses

During Fall Quarter 2006, I taught *Auditing*, a senior-level, undergraduate course required of all accounting students. During Winter Quarter 2007, I taught *Advanced Auditing*, a senior-level, undergraduate elective course.

I used *Blackboard*, a learning management system supported by the university, to create course websites. Each course used a blended format for the overall course design. As depicted in Fig. 1, blended format means that the course included both traditional face-to-face lecture-discussion class sessions and TML-based outside-of-class learning activities. Each course met two times per week.

Assignments for both courses included two examinations, topic quizzes, individual writing assignments, and self-study questions. Students used the TML-based practice–feedback–interaction process described in this chapter to complete individual and team writing assignments.

Before enrolling in a course, students accessed an online course information page that described how the course worked, listed textbook information, explained technology requirements, included links to software download websites, explained the need for using a headset/microphone and webcam, and included a link to a pre-course survey. The page concluded with a statement regarding student and instructor responsibilities.

After reviewing the course information page, students completed an online pre-course survey questionnaire designed to gather demographic information about prospective students. Certain questions asked whether a student had the necessary technology needed for the course, and gave a student the opportunity to indicate whether there might be a need for special assistance in order to participate in the class. I monitored survey forms as submitted and called students if I had questions about their responses.

Throughout both courses, I offered four traditional office hours per week. I also offered virtual online office hours on an "as available basis."

Students used *Skype*, a free online audio/video-conferencing service to contact me during virtual office hours. Students were able to talk with me before and after class, see me during regular office hours, contact me on Skype, and send me an email, or post questions and comments in the Blackboard discussion forums.

Course Enrollments, Class Size, and Student Composition

During Fall Quarter 2006, 24 students enrolled in *Auditing*. Of the 24 students, 22 continued their studies by enrolling in *Advanced Auditing* during Winter Quarter 2007. Six additional students enrolled in *Advanced Auditing* resulting in a total enrollment of 28 students. The size of each class was typical for upper-level accounting courses at my university.

I used the 22 students who completed both courses (i.e., Auditing and Advanced Auditing) as the focus group for my study. These students had the most experience with the TML methods and techniques used in both courses. I felt these students would be in the best position to provide me with meaningful feedback.

Of the 22 students, 64 percent were 30 years old or younger, which placed them in Net Generation category. The remaining 36 percent of the students were Baby Boomers.

More than 77 percent of the 22 students rated their computer skills as either good or excellent. The remaining 23 percent rated their computer skills as acceptable. When I set up study teams, I used this information to balance teams so that each team possessed computer skills needed to complete assignments.

Oblinger (2003, p. 38) observed that some generation trends are emerging about how learners view technology, and that technology is becoming a natural part of the learning environment. Table 2 compares how Boomers, Generation Xers, and Millennials view technology.

About the TML Approach Used to Design Writing Aspects of the Courses

To help make the TML concept clearer, I present it in equation form (i.e., Desired Instructional Outcome $= \text{T1}+\text{T2}+\cdots+\text{T}n$; where T represents individual technology tools). To create a learning experience, a technology tool can work by itself or link with other tools to create an instructional medium that makes it possible to achieve a desired instructional outcome.

Table 2. Comparative Views of Technology Boomer, Generation X, and Millennial.

Boomer	Generation X	Millennials
Instrument for improving personal productivity	Instrument for saving time and effort	Default way to think and work
Something new to learn	Something new to figure out, master, and find the limitations of	The inevitable next cool thing

Source: Salkowitz (2008).

I believe this is what Reiser (1994, p. 47) intended when he called for educators to examine how media can be employed to solve instructional problems.

For the two auditing courses, I created a learning experience using the TML equation previously presented. Through use of technology tools, students completed and submitted writing assignments for grading. I used technology tools to grade writing assignments and to provide personalized feedback. When we needed to communicate outside of class or scheduled office hours, we used technology tools that best fit the needs of the moment (e.g., email, chat, *Skype*, or the telephone).

Technology Tools Used in the Practice–Feedback–Interaction Process

Technology Tools Used by Both Instructor and Students

Everyone involved with both the auditing classes used basic technology tools (e.g., computer, the Internet, email, and Blackboard). Additionally, everyone used a headset/microphone, webcam, and a free web-based audio–video communications service called *Skype*.

For most students (and the instructor), the basic technology tools required little or no introduction or start-up time. The headset/microphone and webcam are plug-and-play tools (i.e., plug the headset/microphone and webcam into a USB port on the computer and the computer's operating system automatically handles installation).

Since many TML-based technology tools are web-based, they work with both PC and Apple computers. This versatility helps to reduce the chance that a TML-based teaching–learning method or tool may not work for a student.

Technology Tools Used by Students

All students used a writing and collaboration tool called *Google Docs and Spreadsheets*, a free service provided by *Google*.

Google Docs and Spreadsheets offers versatility and functionality not offered by Microsoft *Word* or *Excel*. For example, the Google tools are web-based which makes them readily available from any web browser connected to the Internet. Web accessibility makes Google tools more versatile and better suited for teamwork collaboration. Google tools are compatible with other web-based software tools such as online audio and video-conferencing (e.g., *Skype* and *Yugma*).

Creating a *Google Docs and Spreadsheets* personal account takes just a few moments. *Google* provides short tutorial programs that explain how to work with Google tool features. Since most students are familiar with *Microsoft Office* tools, getting a student up and running with *Google Docs and Spreadsheets* usually takes less than 30 min.

Google Docs is an open-source writing tool compatible with *Microsoft Word. Google Spreadsheets* is an open-source spreadsheet tool compatible with *Microsoft Excel*. Google automatically updates Google tools so students always use the latest version and there is no concern about version compatibility or the ability to share documents among users.

Documents created with the Google tools are accessible by one individual or multiple individuals without the need for file transfer (i.e., sharing documents as email attachments among team members). Students may save, share, or transfer Google documents in a variety of formats (e.g., *Adobe Acrobat* (.pdf) format).

Google Docs and Spreadsheets enables a student to create a virtual (web-based) workspace accessible from any web browser and invite others by email to join the workspace as collaborators. Each member of the workspace can have full edit and modification permissions for a document.

A virtual workspace may include an unlimited number of documents. *Google* automatically saves documents to its servers. As a best practice, I encourage students to save documents to an alternative backup source (e.g., the hard drive of their individual computer or to a portable USB flash drive memory stick).

Technology Tools Used by the Instructor

I used an IBM ThinkPad X41 Tablet PC computer running the Microsoft *Windows XP* operating system. With the Tablet PC's digital inking feature, I was able to use the tablet's pen to write directly on the computer screen in my own handwriting. Combining digital inking technology with a software program called *PDF Annotator* made it possible to digitally mark up Adobe Acrobat (.pdf) formatted documents submitted by students. Doing this enabled me to convert the grading process from a traditional paper-based process to a digital paperless process.

To make the grading-feedback process more personal for a student, I used a web-based, video-messaging service called *SightSpeed* to record a brief video commentary about the student's paper. To record a video message, I used a webcam and headset/microphone. Typically, the video commentary lasted three minutes or less. *SightSpeed* saved the video message on its web server and provided me with a web link to the video message.

I used Blackboard's email feature to return the graded paper and video commentary to the student. I attached the graded paper in Adobe Acrobat (.pdf) format to the email and included the web link to the video message in the text of the email.

As with any new computer, it took me a couple of hours to learn how to use the features of the Tablet PC. Both *PDF Annotator* and *SightSpeed* were easy to learn since they work through use of icon symbols similar to the icon symbols displayed at the top of a web browser screen or at the top of each of the *Microsoft Office* tools (e.g., *Word*, *Excel*, and *PowerPoint*).

Table 3 summarizes information about the technology tools we used.

Table 3. Technology Tools used by the Instructor and Students.

Technology Tools	Type of Tool (Web-Based or Personally Owned)	Tool Used by	Tool Provided by
Adobe Acrobat v7	Personally owned software	Instructor	Adobe, Inc.
Blackboard	Free Web-based software	Instructor and students	University
Digital Drop Box (Blackboard)	Free Web-based software	Instructor and students	University
Email	Part of computer operating system or free Web-based email service.	Instructor and students	Various sources
Google Docs and Spreadsheets	Free Web-based software	Students	Google
PDF Annotator	Personally owned software	Instructor	Grahl Software Design
Sight Speed	Personally owned online subscription	Instructor	SightSpeed.Com
Skype	Free Web-based audio-video messaging and conferencing service	Instructor and students	Skype.com

STEPS IN THE TML-BASED PRACTICE–FEEDBACK–INTERACTION PROCESS

Fig. 2 shows the seven steps of the TML-based process and highlights three considerations about each step: (1) the nature of the activity (i.e., asynchronous or synchronous), (2) when the activity occurs (e.g. one time versus multiple times), and (3) time estimate needed to complete the step. A brief description of each step follows.

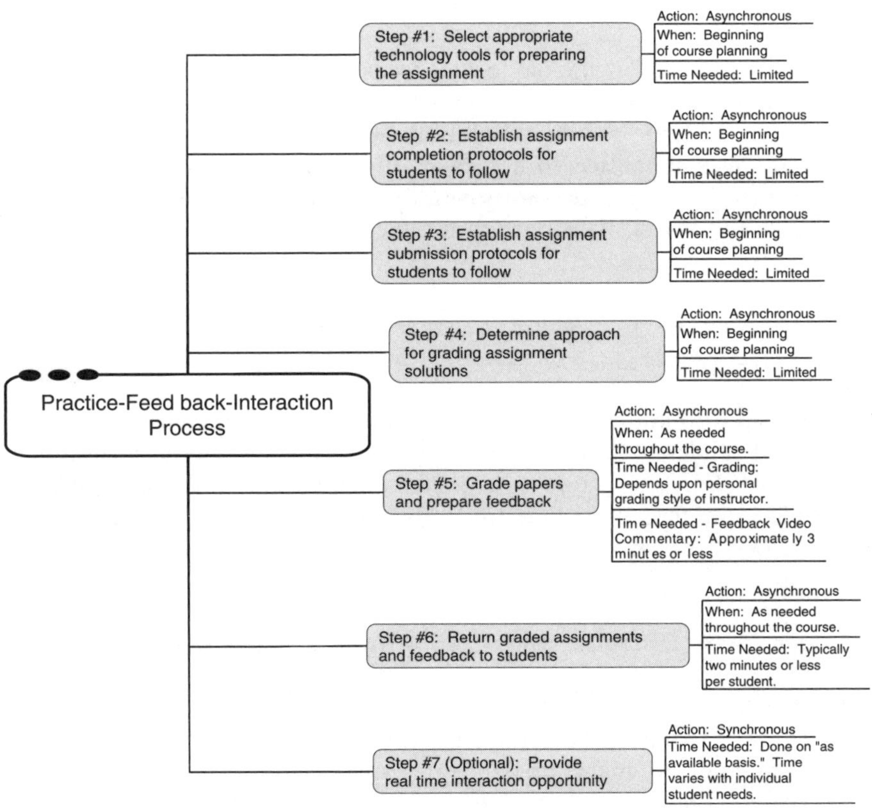

Fig. 2. Technology-Mediated Practice–Feedback–Interaction Process.

Step No. 1: Select an Appropriate Technology Tool for Preparing the Assignment Solution

This is a one-time task typically completed at the beginning of course planning. The task requires little time to complete. For this study, I selected *Google Docs and Spreadsheets* for essay writing, spreadsheet, and collaboration-type assignments. For instructors who do not want to use *Google Docs and Spreadsheets*, alternative technology tools might include *Microsoft Word*, *Microsoft Excel*, and/or other free open-source products like *Zoho Writer or Zoho Sheet.*

Step No. 2: Establish Assignment Completion Protocols for Students to Follow

Students need to know the file format to use when saving assignment files. I required students to submit assignments in Adobe Acrobat (.pdf) format in order to facilitate the digital grading-feedback process. For instructors who want files submitted in a format other than Adobe Acrobat (.pdf), *Google Docs and Spreadsheets* saves files in a variety of formats (e.g., HTML, RTF, Word, Excel, or Open Office).

Step No. 3: Establish Assignment Submission Protocols for Students to Follow

Students need to know how to hand in completed assignments for grading. I required students to use *Digit Drop Box*, the file transfer feature in *Blackboard.* For instructors who prefer an alternative transfer protocol, other file transfer tools include free web-based file transfer/storage services like *File-Sharing.com.*

Step No. 4: Determine Approach for Grading Assignment Solutions

I decided to grade papers digitally. I used my Tablet PC's digital inking technology in conjunction with an inexpensive software program called *PDF Annotator* to mark up student papers. I wanted the warmth of handwritten comments rather than the coldness of typewritten comments. For instructors without access to a Tablet PC computer, an alternative way to mark up papers is the annotation/tracking changes feature in Microsoft *Word.*

Step No. 5: Grade Papers and Prepare Feedback

I combined digital mark up and video messaging to perform grading and provide personalized feedback comments to students for writing assignments. Using digital inking technology to mark up student writing assignments did not reduce grading time. Rather, the digital inking technology enabled me to use software features to enhance the way that I marked up student papers. For example, I could insert a web link to a support resource that supported a grading comment.

Using *Sightspeed*, a video messaging tool, enabled me to give personal comments in addition to handwritten comments. I felt that combining these two technologies improved the overall quality of the grading process.

Using technology tools to convert the grading-feedback process to a full digital process made it possible to change interaction with students. We were no longer limited to face-to-face class time or traditional office hours. By using the technology tools, we could work together asynchronously or synchronously in response to each student's needs.

Step No. 6: Return Graded Assignments and Feedback to Students

In this step, everything comes together. I attached a graded assignment (i.e., in Adobe Acrobat .pdf format) to an email. I included the hyperlink to my video commentary in the text of the email message. The email message asked the student to print a copy of the graded assignment. It also asked the student to review the graded paper while viewing the video commentary. Typically, this step took two minutes or less for me to complete.

Step No. 7 (Optional): Provide Real-Time Interaction Opportunity

The final (optional) step is where I used *Skype* to work one-on-one with a student. Step No. 7 is the only synchronous (i.e., "live") step in the process. All others are asynchronous (i.e., "delayed"). If a student wanted to talk "live" with me about a graded paper, we used *Skype*, a free online videoconferencing service. When a student called, if I answered the call, we would begin a one-on-one, live video conversation. If I was not available, a student could leave me an audio voice message indicating the best time for me to return the call.

STUDENT FEEDBACK

After completing the *Advanced Auditing* course, I asked the 22 students who completed both auditing courses to complete a post-course online survey questionnaire. Summarized survey responses from the 22 students appear in Table 4.

Respondents to the post-course survey questionnaire did three things.

1. They rated the TML technology tools they used during the two auditing courses.
2. They expressed their personal beliefs about the efficiency and effectiveness of the practice–feedback–interaction process they used in the two auditing courses.
3. They offered overall general feedback about the two auditing courses.

Survey responses were anonymous. Students completed the online survey after they completed the second course (*Advanced Auditing*) and had received course grades.

Each survey question required a response. The survey system would not accept a survey form if there were unanswered questions.

I calculated percentages in order to make responses to questions more understandable. All 22 students completed the post-course survey. Therefore, percentages reflect 22 responses per question.

All students used the same technology tools during the two auditing courses and met the same course requirements. There were no alternative tools used by the 22 students. Student responses relate to the same technology tools (e.g., use of *Google Docs and Spreadsheets*).

I realize that 22 respondents is not a large survey. However, I believe the student comments presented in Table 4 should prove helpful to accounting instructors interested in incorporating TML techniques into their course design.

PERSPECTIVE REGARDING THE TML APPROACH

The technology-mediated practice–feedback–interaction process discussed in this chapter is illustrative of innovative ideas that instructors can do to

Table 4. Summary of Student Feedback Responses.

Survey Questions	Summarized Responses	
How would you rate the features of Google Docs and Spreadsheets?	Very easy or easy to use: 70% Somewhat easy to use: 30%	
How easy was it for you to use course technology to submit your assignment for grading and feedback?	Very easy or easy to do: 90% Somewhat easy to do: 10%	
How easy was it for you to have graded assignments and feedback returned to you in digital format?	Very easy or easy to do: 86% Somewhat easy or difficult to do: 14%	
How easy was it to receive and access the video feedback commentary?	Very easy or easy to do: 91% Somewhat easy or difficult to do: 9%	
How would the instructor's technology-based approach to grading assignments and feedback compare to feedback approaches used in other accounting classes you have taken?	Hand-graded digital papers: • More effective: 59% • Equally effective: 32% • About same or less effective: 9% Personalized video feedback comments: • More effective: 73% • Equally effective: 18% • About the same or less effective: 9%	
When you wanted to talk with the instructor about an assignment or other course issue, how easy was it for you to contact the instructor on Skype ?	Very easy or easy to do: 86% Somewhat easy to do: 14%	
How effective is talking with an instructor online (e.g., meeting on Skype) as compared to meeting face-to-face during traditional office hours?	More effective than meeting face-to-face during traditional office hours	32%
	Equally as effective as meeting face-to-face during traditional office hours	55%
	OK but not as effective as having face-to-face contact during office hours	14%
How effective is talking with an instructor online (e.g., meeting online on Skype) as compared to talking with an instructor on the telephone during office hours?	More effective than talking with an instructor on the telephone during office hours	77%
	Equally effective as talking with an instructor on the telephone during office hours	23%
How convenient is talking with an instructor online (e.g., meeting online on Skype) compared to coming to traditional office hours?	More convenient than coming to traditional office hours	96%
	About as convenient as coming to traditional office hours	4%

Table 4. *(Continued)*

Survey Questions	Summarized Responses
Do you prefer a course that incorporates Web-based technology into the course design?	Yes: 91% No: 9%
Do you prefer a course that incorporates audio/video communication into the course design (e.g., Skype)?	Yes: 86% No: 14%
Would the fact that a technology is "free" affect your opinion about using the technology in a course (e.g., Skype)?	Yes: 86% No: 14%
Do you feel that the instructor used too much technology in the design of the auditing courses?	Yes: 9% No: 91%

enliven the ways that they create and deliver course content, interact with their students, and meet student expectations that technology will be an integral part of their learning process. Learning how to include technology tools in instructional design may involve trial and error. Instructors must be patient with the process and learn from their efforts and student feedback.

LIMITATIONS OF THE APPROACH

The TML-based method described in this chapter is a work in process. The method needs further testing with other accounting course designs in order to demonstrate broader applicability.

Students provided useful qualitative belief-type feedback for this study. However, qualitative feedback by itself limits the ability to draw conclusions that might apply to other studies.

I used the TML-based method and technology tools with two auditing courses. The size of each class was typical for an upper-level accounting course at my university. While the TML-based method and technology tools appear to work with a class size of 20–30 students, I have not used the method and tools with a much larger class size (e.g., 50 or more students). The instructor of a larger class may need to modify the TML-based design (e.g., an instructor may need assistance from a graduate assistant).

CONCLUDING COMMENTS

My study used a technology-mediated (TML) approach to design aspects of two auditing courses. Cutting-edge technology tools played a key role in the TML-based process. The way that I used technology tools pushed the boundaries of traditional accounting course design.

As stated earlier, Reiser suggested that a student's perceptions about an instructional media might affect how a student reacts to a learning process (1994, p. 48). Following are comments made by students about TML methods and techniques used in the two auditing classes.

- "It is great to be in a class where innovative methods are at our hands. The exposure to new technologies will definitely benefit us in our careers."
- "I thought one of the greatest aspects of being able to use Skype and speak to the instructor was that I could speak to you and see your computer screen and I could physically see exactly how to perform a certain operation on the computer with no confusion."

Student feedback was positive regarding my use of the TML-based method and technology tools. I believe this outcome suggests that use of a TML-based approach and technology tools may contribute to meeting learning expectations of Net Generation information-age accounting students.

ACKNOWLEDGMENTS

I would like to thank Conrad Shayo, Montgomery Van Wart, and Wayne Johnson for guiding me through the writing of this chapter and for offering extensive edit and review comments and encouragement.

Comments and suggestions from independent reviewers of this chapter helped me to revise the chapter and to make it more understandable.

REFERENCES

Alavi, M., & Leidner, D. (2001). Research commentary: Technology-mediated learning – A call for greater depth and breadth of research. *Information Systems Research*, *12*, 1–10.

Arbaugh, J. B. (2001). How instructor immediacy behaviors affect student satisfaction and learning. *Business Communication Quarterly*, *64*(4), 43.

Baker, J. D., & Woods, R. H., Jr. (2004). Interaction and immediacy in online learning. *International Review of Research in Open and Distance Learning*, *5*(2).

Boettcher, J. (2007). Ten core principles for designing effective learning environments: Insights from brain research and pedagogical theory. *Innovate*, *3*(3)Retrieved on February 19, 2008. Available at www.innovateonline.info/index.php?view = article&id = 54.

Chickering, A., & Gamson, Z. (1987). Seven Principles for Good Practice in Undergraduate Education. Accessed on July 28, 2007. Available at www.csuhayward.edu/wasc/pdfs/End%20Note.pdf.

Clark, R. (1983). Reconsidering research on learning from media. *Review of Educational Research*, *53*, 445–459.

Clark, R. C. (2003). *Building expertise, cognitive methods for training and performance improvement*. Silver Springs, MD: International Society for Performance Improvement.

Dziuban, C., Hartman, J., & Moskal, P. (2004). Blended learning (ID: ERB0407). *Educause Research Bulletin*, *2004*(7), 1–12Retrieved on February 2, 2008. Available at http://ecampus.nl.edu/resources/webct/BlendedLearningUCFStudy.pdf.

Frand, J. L. (2000). The information-age mindset: Changes in students and implications for higher education. *Educause Review* (September/October), 15–24.

Hardaway, D., & Scamell, R. (2005). Use of a technology-mediated learning instructional approach for teaching an introduction to information technology course. *Journal of Information Systems Education*, *16*, 137–145.

Keefe, T. (2003). Enhancing a Face-to-Face Course with Online Lectures: Instructional and Pedagogical Issues. Murfreesboro, Tennessee: Eighth Annual Mid-South Instructional Technology Conference. Retrieved on February 19, 2008. Available at http://www.mtsu.edu/~itconf/proceed03/109.html.

Larose, R., & Whitten, P. (2000). Re-thinking instructional immediacy for web courses: A social cognitive exploration. *Communication Education*, *49*, 320–338.

Oblinger, D. (2003). Boomers, Gen-Xers, Millennials: Understanding the new students. *Educause Review* (July/August), 38–47.

Oblinger, D., & Oblinger, J. (2005). Is it age or IT: First steps toward understanding the Net Generation? In: D. G. Oblinger & J. L. Oblinger (Eds), *Educating the Net Generation*, Educause. Retrieved on July 24, 2007. Available at http://www.educause.edu/educatingthenetgen/.

Reiser, R. (1994). Clark's invitation to dance: An instructional designer's response. *Educational Technology Research and Development*, *42*, 45–48.

Richardson, J. C., & Swan, K. (2003). Examining social presence in online courses in relation to students' perceived learning and satisfaction. *Journal of Asynchronous Learning Networks*, *7*(1), 66–88. Available at http://www.sloan-c.org/publications/JALN/v7n1/v7n1_richardson.asp.

Roberts, G. R. (2005). Technology and learning expectations of the Net Generation. In: D. G. Oblinger, & J. L. Oblinger (Eds), *Educating the Net Generation*. Educause. Retrieved on July 24, 2007. Available at http://www.educause.edu/educatingthenetgen/.

Salkowitz, R. (2008). *Generation blend: Managing across the technology age gap* (p. 60). New Jersey: Wiley.

Surry, D. (2005). Editorial. *British Journal of Educational Technology*, *36*(6), 933–935.

Thurman, V. A., & Wambach, K. (2004). Understanding interactions in distance education: A review of the literature. *International Journal of Instructional Technology & Distance Learning*, *1*(1)Retrieved on February 19, 2008. Available at http://itdl.org/journal/Jan_04/index.htm.

Tsutsui, M. (2004). Multimedia as a means to enhance feedback. *Computer Assisted Language Learning*, *17*(3/4), 377–402.

STUDENT TURNED CONSULTANT: TEACHING THE BALANCED SCORECARD USING EXPERIENTIAL LEARNING

Noah P. Barsky, Anthony H. Catanach and C. Andrew Lafond

ABSTRACT

This instructional tool provides management accounting instructors with an efficient and practical way to teach the Balanced Scorecard using experiential learning. This exercise requires students to visit their college or university bookstore, meet with store managers, and develop a Balanced Scorecard for the business. Students address contemporary performance measurement issues in a simulated consulting engagement as they research industry trends, analyze store operations, interview employees, and prepare a written report for store management.

The requirements of this active learning assignment address many of the analytical, communication, and experiential competencies recommended in widely discussed calls for accounting education change. Instructors appreciate the convenience, practicality, and rigor offered by this exercise. Students value the opportunity to engage in a realistic exercise that allows them to draw upon their own consumer experiences. The authors used these materials in both undergraduate and graduate

Advances in Accounting Education: Teaching and Curriculum Innovations, Volume 9, 287–305

ISSN: 1085-4622/doi:10.1016/S1085-4622(08)09014-7

accounting courses, and received positive feedback from students and bookstore managers alike.

The Balanced Scorecard (Scorecard) is a widely recognized performance management tool that has become a prominent topic in management accounting education over the past decade. Brewer (2000, p. 229) describes how the Scorecard can be taught in an advanced course in the management accounting curriculum. More recently, Barsky and Catanach's (2005, p. 40) Business Planning Model uses the Balanced Scorecard framework to organize management accounting topics into a topical delivery approach. Yet, to date, cases appear to be the preferred method for teaching this topic.

However, most Scorecard cases are ill-suited for undergraduate courses, and many graduate classes as well. These cases generally are based on successful Scorecard implementations at large, well-known, global businesses such as Wells Fargo (Kaplan & Tempest, 2001) and Coors Brewing Company (Grove, Cook, & Richter, 2000). In these cases, students develop a Balanced Scorecard to address specific issues facing the multinational enterprise. Class discussion typically centers on comparing student-generated solutions to the actual Scorecard implementation at the firm. While these cases certainly provide valuable "real-world" examples that illustrate the Scorecard's use, they generally are best suited for top-tier, full-time MBA courses which discuss complex industries and business processes that are usually unfamiliar to most students. Additionally, these cases are based on specific companies that are likely to be geographically distant. Therefore, it is virtually impossible for students to visit them, thus forcing reliance on the case authors' written descriptions of the business setting.

In contrast, the instructional tool described in this chapter builds on Grove and Rudebusch's (2004, p. 105) Westlake Bookstore Case by requiring students to develop a complete Scorecard for their own campus bookstore, a very real and readily accessible business whose industry and processes are familiar to most students. This active learning assignment also differs from traditional Scorecard cases in that it re-positions the student as a consultant charged with showing how performance measurement can help address identified operating problems. Students typically are well suited for this role given their frequently voiced frustrations with the campus bookstore over such issues as high book costs, low buyback prices, and limited services. Finally, most colleges and universities have on-campus bookstores as well as off-campus competitors, making a visit to these operations a convenient and relatively costless exercise in experiential learning.

The store tour, management interview, and subsequent Scorecard deliverable highlight the complicated nature of what often appears to be a simple campus business. This local, small operation example illustrates the inherent complexity in performance measurement in business enterprises, given the depth of issues that students encounter at a campus store. Students also gain valuable insights into the challenges of applying "classroom theory" in "live" business settings, and develop the analytical, communication, and teamwork skills demanded in today's dynamic business environment. The remaining sections of this chapter present the instructional tool, implementation guidance, assessment results, and conclusions about its benefits. Detailed teaching instructions also are provided for instructors.

THE BALANCED SCORECARD ASSIGNMENT

Learning Objectives

The primary learning objective of this instructional tool is to provide students with an opportunity to apply what they have learned in the classroom about the business value chain, performance measurement, and the Balanced Scorecard in a real, yet familiar, business setting. The assignment also promotes student development of oral and written communication skills in a business-consulting context. Finally, the exercise fosters teamwork through its required collaboration.

Institutional Context

We used the assignment at two private universities in the Mid-Atlantic region of the United States in a required undergraduate introductory managerial accounting course, a traditional cost accounting class at the first institution, and again in a Masters of Accountancy (MAC) performance evaluation course at the other university. Students visited the store on their respective campus. The first institution enrolls approximately 3,000 students with SAT/ACT scores in the 25–75th percentiles ranging from 970 to 1160. The second university enrolls approximately 9,000 students with SAT/ACT scores in the 25–75th percentile ranging from 1180 to 1360.

Initially, we pilot-tested the assignment in a small traditional cost accounting course with nine students. Based on preliminary student feedback, the materials were revised and subsequently used in an introductory managerial accounting course with 28 students and in a MAC performance measurement course with 21 students. Teams consisted of three or four students. The undergraduates included sophomores, juniors, and seniors, while the graduate students were in the first semester of a MAC program. Each student was provided with a detailed Scorecard assignment which is illustrated in the appendix. As recommended by Stocks, Stoddard, and Waters (1992, p. 198) and Schofield and Combes (1993, p. 73), this handout reviews the assignment and justifies its importance. It also provides questions to guide student planning in preparing for their consulting engagement.

The assignment also gives students detailed instructions to guide report preparation. Student teams are instructed to include in their final report the following items: (1) a brief summary of the consulting engagement and scope of work, (2) a detailed discussion of the work product (the Scorecard prepared by each team), (3) suggestions on how the client can implement the Scorecard, and (4) a review of any relevant limitations that may impact the engagement and resulting recommendations. While these instructions potentially limit student creativity, they are critical to using this instructional tool given that the assignment is much less structured than traditional text-driven homework problems or published case studies.

IMPLEMENTATION GUIDANCE

Prior to beginning the course, the instructor should meet with the campus bookstore manager to provide background on this assignment and obtain agreement to participate in the student project. The instructor should emphasize to the manager that little preparation is required on his/her part, since the manager will only be directing a tour of the campus store. It is expected that during the tour, the manager will provide some limited background store information, however, it is the students that will be asking the questions needed to gather the required Scorecard data. During this preliminary planning visit, the instructor also should determine whether a review of the Scorecard for the manager is necessary to promote the potential benefits that the store may gain from the assignment's final reports.

Ideally, this project should be assigned after students have reviewed their text's coverage of the Scorecard and related topics. Additionally, completing text exercises and problems on Scorecards will increase students' confidence and ability to complete this simulated consulting exercise. When the scheduled assignment date has arrived, the instructor should distribute appendix to students in class, and its requirements should be thoroughly reviewed. A preliminary class discussion of the campus bookstore operations usually elicits numerous criticisms and complaints from the student-customer. If not already in groups, the instructor should put students in "consulting" teams of three or four students, and encourage them to meet and construct questions for the store manager that will elicit the information needed to complete the assignment's requirements. The instructor should emphasize that the manager will only provide limited background information on the campus store, and that it is the student questions that will drive the interview. Ultimately, the students' reports will draw on data collected from both the interview and industry sources.

Students should be encouraged to visit the campus store's website, and also research industry information about college bookstores. The store's website can provide students with insights into its mission, organization, product and service offerings, and other retailing initiatives. The National Association of College Stores (NACS) website (www.nacs.org) reinforces the concept of industry benchmarking, and highlights the information value of industry trade associations. NACS provides industry research and statistics, including retail market facts and figures, margin data, industry financial reports, and satisfaction survey services. Instructors should point out that although NACS offers a limited amount of benchmarking information (financial, customer satisfaction, faculty satisfaction, and compensation) on its website, students should determine if the store is considering industry averages or standards when evaluating its operating performance. Table 1 offers a list of suggested readings and resources that the instructor can use to supplement the course text. The instructor should emphasize that the assignment requires students to identify the financial and non-financial measures needed to manage the store's operations, rather than specific quantitative targets or benchmarks.

The student consulting visit consists of both a store tour and manager interview. It is ideally suited for one 75 min class, but also can easily be adapted to two 50 min sessions (one class for the store tour and a second for the manager interview). Student teams can expect preparation and completion of the learning activity each to last three times the amount of dedicated class time. The student teams should conduct their manager interview only after the tour.

Table 1. Suggested Readings and Resources.

Readings

Ittner, C.D., & Larcker D.F. (2003). Coming up short on non-financial performance measurement. *Harvard Business Review, 81*(11), 88–95.

Kaplan, R.S., & Norton D.P. (2001). Transforming the balanced scorecard from performance management to strategic management: Part I. *Accounting Horizons, 15*(1), 87–104.

Kaplan, R.S., & Norton D.P. (2004). Strategy maps. *Strategic Finance 85*, 27–35.

Internet resources

The Balanced Scorecard Institute (www.balancedscorecard.org)

The Palladium Group (formerly Balanced Scorecard Collaborative) (www.thepalladiumgroup.com)

Bookstore and industry resources

National Association for College Stores (www.nacs.org)

Institution-specific college or university campus bookstore website

Naturally, a large class size or other factors may prevent a formal store tour. However, several alternatives exist to accommodate instructors with large class sizes that would allow students to collect the necessary data to complete their report. For example, instructors can divide the class into smaller groups that can more easily tour the store. Alternatively, on one of our class visits, half the students from each team toured the store with the general manager, while the other half interviewed the textbook manager. After a set amount of time, the groups then switched roles so that each student had a similar exposure and experience.

Since multiple visits will require more of the store managers' time, the instructor may instead require student teams to visit the store on their own to observe operations and then prepare a list of questions in advance of an in-class question and answer session with store managers. In this case, the instructor may collect student questions in advance of class so that a selected sample of high quality questions may be directed to store managers.

Given their consulting role, students should treat their bookstore "client" in a professional manner. Therefore, the instructor should emphasize the importance of proper attire and conduct for the tour and subsequent interview. Additionally, instructors should encourage students to obtain the manager's email address or business card, to facilitate mailing of their final reports. This simple task reinforces upon students the importance of professional contact information in effecting timely and effective business communication.

During the class immediately following the bookstore visit, each student team should be prepared to discuss the information gathered during the tour and manager interview. This classroom debrief reinforces what was learned during the store visit, addresses any questions students may have at this stage of the assignment, and prepares them for the report preparation phase.

If time permits, students should be encouraged to submit drafts of their consulting reports so that instructors can offer improvement opportunities. Once initial report drafts have been edited and revised, students should prepare two copies of their final consulting report: one for the instructor and another for the store manager. Requiring students to share their report with the manager generally motivates them to craft a higher quality report. Moreover, the notion of an "external" review seems to increase the assignment's realism beyond that of a typical academic course assignment. If the instructor has a large number of reports, it may be advisable to forward the best reports and to reward those student teams in some manner. Our experience also indicates that store managers greatly appreciated the students' report findings.

SUGGESTED RESPONSES AND GRADING

Requirement 1: Identifying Strategic Objectives and Related Measures

There is no one correct answer for this requirement since each campus bookstore faces challenges and measurement issues unique to its own institution and business setting. For each of the four dimensions of the Scorecard, students should identify short- and long-term strategic objectives of the campus store. Once they have determined the strategic objectives of the store for each dimension (learning and growth, internal business process, customer, and financial), students should link financial and non-financial measurements that appropriately evaluate the performance of the campus store in meeting this objective. Table 2 presents sample strategic objectives and performance measures proposed by students after their tours and interviews.

Requirement 2a: Preparing the Introductory Paragraph of the Consulting Report

For this requirement students should describe the purpose of their team report, the nature of their assignment, and the scope of their work (i.e., how and when data were collected). Students also should provide general

Table 2. Suggested Balanced Scorecard Objectives and Measures.

Scorecard Dimension	Strategic Objectives	Performance Measures
Financial	Increase sales revenue Increase profitability Increase sales of new products Reduce holding period of inventory as a means to improve cash flow	• Sales revenue growth percentage • Net income as a percentage of revenue • Percentage of sales from new products • Inventory turnover ratio
Customer	Increase customer satisfaction Increase repeat customers and frequency of visits Reduce the number of customer complaints	• Customer satisfaction ratings • Purchase frequency and amounts • Number and nature of customer service transactions
Internal business process	Increase orders placed online Maximize checkout efficiency	• Online sales as a percentage of total sales • Number of register transactions (dollar and amount) per register per hour, differentiating between peak and slow times
	Improve relationships with faculty	• Percentage of book adoption submissions submitted on time • Faculty satisfaction ratings
Learning and growth	Enhance employee commitment and satisfaction	• Employee turnover
	Improve employee skills and abilities	• Number of hours of training • Employee cross-training hours by department
	Empower workforce	• Percentage of employee suggestions implemented

Note: These strategic objectives and performances have been adapted from student submissions. They do not necessarily represent a complete Balanced Scorecard, but illustrate the types of suggestions students are likely to offer.

background information on the Scorecard as well as a specific recommendation about its applicability to the bookstore operation that they analyzed. In this section students should demonstrate proper written communication skills by providing a good introductory paragraph which explains the purpose of the consulting engagement, how implementation of the Scorecard can improve the campus store's operation and ultimately the profitability of the campus store. Since most campus store managers are probably unfamiliar with the Scorecard, the memo to the store manager should also explain how it can help the manager evaluate the store's performance using both financial and non-financial measures along the four Scorecard dimensions. The length of the report is typically a minimum two to three single-spaced pages (as indicated in appendix), but some instructors may vary expectations depending on course time allocated to the experience.

Requirement 2b: Communicating Recommendations in the Consulting Report

Responses to this requirement should include a discussion of each Scorecard dimension created in requirement 1. The solution should begin by describing each of the four dimensions as well as the causal relationship present in the Scorecard. For example, investments in trained workers (learning and growth dimension) lead to better business processes, which then improve customer satisfaction, which finally increase profitability.

For each dimension, students should recommend specific metrics for each strategic objective and justify their recommendations accordingly. Each strategic objective should be measurable or be able to be quantified in some way by the campus store in order to accurately gauge the store's performance within that dimension. For example, customer satisfaction might be quantified using customer satisfaction surveys.

Student solutions should describe how performance measures will be operationalized. Students should specifically consider the key bookstore stakeholders (i.e., the university, students, faculty, employees, and suppliers) in their reports, and explain the importance and applicability of each measure.

Requirement 2c: Discussing Scorecard Implementation Barriers

Each team report should discuss the four common mistakes companies make when implementing non-financial performance measurements, as identified by Ittner and Larcker (2003). They report that companies encounter difficulty when: (1) measures are not explicitly linked to strategy; (2) no meaningful attempt has been made to validate the asserted links between measures and business outcomes; (3) management has not set credible performance targets; and (4) measurements do not reliably indicate when performance has changed. Students should review this article when preparing for this experiential learning exercise. Their report should provide specific advice to the campus store manager as to how each of these four common pitfalls can be avoided when implementing the Scorecard.

Requirement 2d: Concluding with Limitations and Recommendations

Finally, each consulting team should review any limitations to their engagement analysis, and summarize any recommendations previously made in their report. A discussion of engagement limitations makes students aware of the assumptions, judgments, and subjectivity inherent in any such consulting project. Instructors should stress to the students that the campus store manager is expecting specific recommendations to improve the campus store. This heightens the realism of the consulting engagement and forces students to exercise critical thinking skills, and take the assignment seriously. For instructors with large class sizes and many resulting team submissions, the instructor may elect to forward the best reports.

Grading Worksheet

Catanach and Rhoades (1997) provide practical guidance on developing and evaluating collaborative writing assignments in accounting courses. Consistent with their recommendations, a grading worksheet to assess report content, analysis, writing quality, organization, and overall presentation was created and appears in Table 3.

The grading worksheet divides student work assessment into four categories to evaluate the substance, scope, and professionalism of student work. Points are awarded for the clarity and appropriateness of selected measures, as well as the quality of student discussion including the justifications and explanations of their choices. It further rewards students for their ability to read and apply content from assigned readings, as well as any other sources they may have found. Lastly, this grading worksheet allows instructors to provide feedback on the writing quality of submissions. Collectively, all of this detail provides students with insights into the basis of their overall grade.

Specific weights are omitted from this example, as the grading expectations in preparing a Scorecard and accompanying report will differ from an introductory managerial accounting course to upper division or graduate-level accounting courses. Consequently, instructors should select grading

Table 3. Sample Grading Worksheet.

	Maximum Points	Points Awarded
Content and quality of analysis		
(1) Appropriate Coverage of Scorecard Dimensions		
(a) Clarity and appropriateness of financial measures		
(b) Clarity and appropriateness of customer measures		
(c) Clarity and appropriateness of process measures		
(d) Clarity and appropriateness of learning and growth measures		
(2) Discussion clearly details and justifies recommended measures		
(3) Assertions are substantiated with relevant data and examples		
(4) Balanced Scorecard implementation hurdles and pitfalls outlined in Ittner and Larcker (2003) are specifically discussed and applied		
(a) Identifies store strategy and links measures		
(b) Discusses importance of statistical validation of measures		
(c) Details importance of performance targets		
(d) Highlights importance of measurement reliability		
(e) Applies findings to campus store context		
(5) Utilization of external research resources		
(a) Cites and applies Scorecard literature (i.e., Kaplan and Norton)		
(b) Cites and applies college store industry resources (i.e., NACS)		
Writing quality		
(1) Uses correct grammar, spelling, and punctuation		
(2) Appropriate professional tone and language (lack of clichés, etc.)		
(3) Overall clarity and word choice		
(4) Sentences and paragraphs are concise and understandable		
Organization		
(1) Includes clear and concise introduction and conclusion paragraphs		
(2) Body of report contained well-labeled sections and paragraphs		
(3) Appropriate transitions and labeling of appendices and figures		
(4) Text adequately references and describes content of all supporting tables and figures		
Overall presentation		
(1) Polished, proofread, and professional appearance of document		
(2) Meets overall assignment objectives		
Total points awarded		

scales or weights that reflect their own unique educational objectives and course administration standards. Additionally, the instructor may employ a peer evaluation component to reward teamwork, individual contribution, and cooperation.

This feedback also may be useful for accreditation purposes and assessment reviews, since the grading worksheet is consistent in nature with the assessment rubrics that accreditation agencies are encouraging business school faculty to employ (Suskie, 2004). For example, the AACSB provides rubric guidance and examples from selected schools on its website (www.aacsb.edu/resource_centers/assessment/rubric.asp).

ASSESSMENT

Consistent with Barton, MacArthur, and Moore (2005), we conducted a brief student survey to evaluate student perceptions of this educational activity. After submitting their final consulting report, students were asked to respond anonymously to 11 survey questions. Twenty-one graduate and 28 undergraduate students completed the survey. Mean responses and significance levels for difference in group means tests are reported in Table 4.

Both graduate and undergraduate students viewed visiting "live" businesses as an effective way for business students to learn (question 11). They also indicated that the assignment helped them apply what they learned about performance measurement (questions 1 and 3). Additionally, students in both groups generally considered the Scorecard a valuable management tool (question 5). However, only the graduate students found the assignment to be an effective way to learn technical material (question 2). Graduate students also perceived the exercise to be challenging (question 8), and judged Scorecard design and implementation to be a difficult process (questions 6 and 7). Difference in means tests suggest that graduate students felt more strongly about the Scorecard assignment. Graduate student age and maturity levels, as well as professional work experience, may have contributed to this greater appreciation of this active learning activity. While graduate student perceptions were stronger in response to some questions, the undergraduate means indicate positive (at worst, neutral) feedback to each of the questions. These results highlight the importance of explicitly emphasizing and reinforcing key learning points to less experienced undergraduates as they are introduced to and complete this experience.

We also asked students if they found anything in the consulting exercise to be unclear or unrealistic, and whether they would recommend that instructors at their institution or other universities use this assignment. Seventy-one percent of surveyed students indicated that the Scorecard exercise was clear and that the assignment was realistic, and 93% recommended that instructors at other universities utilize it.

Table 4. Student Survey Responses.

Survey Question	Mean Responses			Difference in Group Means
	Undergraduate ($n = 28$)	Graduate ($n = 21$)	Total ($n = 49$)	
1. This assignment helped me to apply what I have learned about developing performance measurement systems.	4.14	4.48	4.29	$t = 1.24$ n/s
2. Group exercises are an effective way to learn technical material.	3.25	4.48	3.78	$t = 5.19^{***}$
3. Visiting the campus store and meeting with management was worthwhile for completing this assignment.	4.29	4.76	4.49	$t = 2.40^{*}$
4. This project was a realistic simulation of business consulting.	3.93	3.81	3.88	$t = 0.64$ n/s
5. Based on this experience, I believe that the Balanced Scorecard can be a valuable management tool.	4.32	3.95	4.16	$t = 1.27$ n/s
6. Designing an effective Balanced Scorecard is not difficult.	3.75	2.24	3.10	$t = 5.32^{***}$
7. Implementing an effective Balanced Scorecard is not difficult.	3.21	1.81	2.61	$t = 6.32^{***}$
8. This assignment was challenging.	3.04	4.00	3.45	$t = 4.53^{***}$
9. Ambiguity and uncertainty do not bother me when I am asked to solve a problem.	3.29	2.57	2.98	$t = 2.09^{*}$
10. Generally, I would prefer to have more assignments of this nature in my classes.	2.86	3.62	3.18	$t = 3.42^{**}$
11. Visiting "live" businesses is an effective way for business students to learn.	4.25	4.67	4.43	$t = 2.25^{*}$

Scale: 1, strongly disagree; 2, disagree; 3, neutral; 4, agree; 5, strongly agree.
$^{*} = p < .05$;
$^{**} = p < .01$;
$^{***} = p < .001$.

Finally, students were asked to provide any other comments, suggestions, or ideas that they might have regarding the bookstore assignment. A representative sample of student responses is provided in Table 5. Some students, particularly undergraduates, found it hard to work without financial statements. Others expressed difficulty in dealing with the

Table 5. Student Comments.

Positive Feedback
Undergraduate students
I think you learn more and what you do learn stays with you longer.
The case was very realistic and didn't require much background research because we were familiar with the campus store.
It was pretty interesting and applied the textbook to real life.
This assignment helped me gain a better understanding of how the balanced scorecard could help a business.
Group projects and meeting outside professionals is beneficial.
Graduate students
The bookstore is a familiar organization, so developing the Balanced Scorecard was interesting and useful.
This was a great way to apply what we learned in class.
It gives practical real-world experience.
The case was a good way to introduce the class to actual consulting.
It incorporates many different aspects of learning.
I enjoyed the assignment because it helped me to better grasp the ideas of the Balanced Scorecard.
It's good to do real-world work in business school since it is more interesting and intellectually stimulating.
Suggestions for Improvement
Undergraduate students
While completing this assignment I had a feeling of vagueness.
Maybe review what a memo is next time you assign the project.
Graduate students
It was hard not working with real company financials/statistics.
I understand that time is a constraint, but it would have been nice to have more time at the bookstore, or even a chance to return with follow-up questions.
It is difficult to set measures and objectives when the bookstore doesn't have the technology to do so.
Spend more time in smaller groups for the bookstore visit.
More structured guidelines.

assignment's ambiguity and uncertainty. It is interesting to note that the students did not equate ambiguity and uncertainty with the "real world," as they expressed preferences for situations with clear-cut, objective answers.

Overall, students agreed that this experiential learning project was a clear and realistic application of preparing a Scorecard, which also introduced them to a consulting perspective. Student responses indicated that the assignment succeeded in linking textbook theory with the "real world."

LIMITATIONS AND CONCLUSIONS

Naturally, several limitations exist and should be recognized. One is that the assignment may not be reusable every semester due to potential leakage of the solution. Instructors can overcome this problem by using other university business operations (i.e., food services, athletics, copy center) for the assignment, instead of relying solely on the campus bookstore. Another possible limitation is the time burden that the bookstore manager may face if multiple course sections within one university use this activity in the same semester. Finally, class size also can limit use of this tool since large classes make the campus store tour difficult and also reduce the students' interaction with the store manager during the interview phase.

Conversely, this instructional tool can easily be adapted to introductory management accounting courses at both the graduate and undergraduate level. The strength of this assignment is its use of an experiential learning approach that integrates both verbal and written communication requirements to learn about the Scorecard. Given recent calls that experiential learning be adopted by business school curricula (McCarthy & McCarthy, 2006), this assignment provides a convenient and tractable option for most accounting instructors. This assignment also supports Stocks et al.'s (1992) argument that the "writing to learn" approach "can be effectively used as a means for helping students understand accounting issues, concepts, and procedures while reinforcing writing skills taught in the English composition and Business Communication courses" (p. 195). Instructors will find this tool to be a convenient, direct, efficient, and inexpensive way to teach the Balanced Scorecard in either the cost or managerial accounting course.

ACKNOWLEDGMENTS

The authors wish to thank Sheela Bhagat, Michael Krause, Shelley Rhoades-Catanach, the meeting participants of the American Accounting Association's 2006 Mid-Atlantic Regional and Annual Meetings, and two anonymous reviewers for comments and suggestions received on earlier drafts of this paper, and store managers at our institutions for their time, input, and support.

REFERENCES

Barsky, N. P., & Catanach, A. H., Jr. (2005). Motivating student interest in accounting: A business planning approach to the introductory management accounting course. *Advances in Accounting Education: Teaching and Curriculum Innovations*, *7*, 27–63.

Barton, T. L., MacArthur, J. B., & Moore, R. L. (2005). BuyGasCo corporation: The use of alternative costing methods in a predatory pricing lawsuit. *Issues in Accounting Education*, *20*(4), 341–357.

Brewer, P. C. (2000). An approach to organizing a management accounting curriculum. *Issues in Accounting Education*, *15*, 211–235.

Catanach, A. H., & Rhoades, S. C. (1997). A practical guide to collaborative writing. *Issues in Accounting Education*, *12*(2), 521–536.

Grove, H, Cook, T., & Richter, K. (2000). The Coors case, balanced scorecard. *Institute of Management Accountants, IMA publication number 00355*, 17–25.

Grove, H., & Rudebusch, T. (2004). Westlake bookstore case. *The Journal of Accounting Case Research*, *8*, 105–118.

Ittner, C. D., & Larcker, D. F. (2003). Coming up short on nonfinancial performance measurement. *Harvard Business Review*, *81*(11), 88–95.

Kaplan, R. S., & Tempest, N. (2001). Wells Fargo online financial services (A). *Harvard Business School*. Product Number: 9-198-146.

McCarthy, P. R., & McCarthy, H. M. (2006). When case studies are not enough: Integrating experiential learning into business curricula. *Journal of Education for Business*, *81*(4), 201–204.

Schofield, B. W., & Combes, L. (1993). Designing and managing meaningful writing assignments. *Issues in Accounting Education*, *8*, 71–85.

Stocks, K. D., Stoddard, T. D., & Waters, M. L. (1992). Writing in the accounting curriculum: Guidelines for professors. *Issues in Accounting Education*, *7*, 193–204.

Suskie, L. (2004). *Assessing student learning*. Boston, MA: Anker Publishing.

APPENDIX. THE CAMPUS BOOKSTORE BALANCED SCORECARD ASSIGNMENT

Almost all college campuses have a bookstore that sells textbooks, supplies, clothing, and many other products demanded by college students. Many of these stores face direct competition from other nearby bookshops, as well as the growing presence of online retailers. In this competitive environment, the primary customers (students) rely on these providers to deliver the educational resources needed for their college or university studies.

As a bookstore customer, you may be familiar with its products and services, and may even have some ideas about how the operations and offerings can be improved. On a day selected by your instructor, your class will either: (1) take a "behind the scenes" tour of the bookstore led by the store's general manager to learn more about its operations or (2) the general manager will visit your class for a discussion of the bookstore's operations.

The primary purposes of this learning exercise are to: (1) provide practical experience in developing and designing a Balanced Scorecard for a retail business, (2) illustrate the application of the business value chain, performance measurement, and process improvement in a realistic business setting, and (3) simulate a business consulting experience to emphasize required workplace skills. Your professor, who is serving as the engagement partner, has discussed your assignment with the campus store manager and has obtained the necessary approvals for you to engage in this performance measurement consulting exercise.

BACKGROUND

Prior to visiting your "client," familiarize your team with the Balanced Scorecard and the bookstore's operations. To gain a consultant's perspective, explore the store's website, search for industry articles and websites about college bookstores, and reflect on your experiences as a customer at the store. Next, develop a list of questions for store management. As a team, consider the following questions in developing a list of data that you need to gather from your store tour or store manager meeting.

- What is the store's business strategy? How does the store create value for its customers? What kind of products or services does the company offer? How does the operation differentiate itself from the competition?
- What does the store's "business value chain" look like? Do all products and services require the same set of business value chain processes or are they different? Why?
- Which business structural forces (i.e., technology, customer expectations, globalization) affect the way the store conducts its business?
- Are there any industry trends that the consultant and/or manager should consider?
- Is there an industry association for college bookstores and what type of performance data does it offer about the industry?
- Who owns the bookstore and how are employees evaluated and rewarded?
- What specific financial and non-financial measures might be useful to the store in measuring its performance? How do these measures fit into the four dimensions of the Balanced Scorecard?
- How might the store develop meaningful targets and benchmarks for each dimension of the Balanced Scorecard?

These questions are designed to prepare you for your visit to the client. Do not prepare a memo that simply answers these questions. Remember that your assignment will require you to develop a Balanced Scorecard for the campus bookstore. To do so, you will need to ask insightful questions and take detailed notes when visiting the store. After collecting your responses, your team should reevaluate these questions before drafting your report.

REQUIREMENTS

(1) Based on your responses to the above questions, create a Balanced Scorecard (with the measures that you selected) to include as an appendix to your final manager report. For each of the four Balanced Scorecard dimensions, identify at least three potential strategic objectives for the bookstore and at least one specific measure that relates to each objective. The last page of this assignment provides an example of the three-column Scorecard that your team should complete and attach to the manager report as an appendix.

(2) Write a report (two to three pages, single-spaced) to the store managers that describes how the Balanced Scorecard might help the store. Since your final report will be shared with the store manager, prepare it in a manner that is consistent with what a professional consulting firm would provide to a real client (i.e., correct spelling, grammatically correct, clear and concise writing, and active voice).

   (a) Your first paragraph should describe the purpose of the report, the nature of your assignment, and the scope of your work (i.e., how and when were your data collected). You also should provide some general background on the Balanced Scorecard as well as a specific recommendation about its applicability to this context.

   (b) Next discuss each dimension of the Balanced Scorecard (created in requirement 1). For each dimension, provide from one to three paragraphs that describe and justify your recommended strategic objectives and related measures. Carefully consider the key bookstore stakeholders (i.e., the University, students, faculty, employees, and suppliers) and explain the importance and applicability of each measure.

   (c) There are many articles that identify barriers to successfully implementing the Balanced Scorecard. According to an article in the *Harvard Business Review* entitled "Coming Up Short on

Nonfinancial Performance Measurement," by Ittner and Larcker (2003), companies often make four common mistakes when implementing non-financial performance measurements. Your memo should discuss these common mistakes and provide specific suggestions about how the store manager may overcome each of these pitfalls when implementing the Balanced Scorecard.

(d) Since the store manager is likely to implement some of your suggestions, conclude your report by discussing any relevant limitations of your work and recommendations.

THE CAMPUS BOOKSTORE BALANCED SCORECARD ASSIGNMENT BALANCED SCORECARD TEMPLATE

Scorecard Dimension	Strategic Objectives	Performance Measures
Financial		
Customer		
Internal business process		
Learning and growth		

Note: The Balanced Scorecard consists of four dimensions. Each is briefly described below, beginning with the Learning & Growth dimension which serves as the foundation for the Scorecard framework.

The first dimension of the Balanced Scorecard is the Learning and Growth dimension which helps managers focus on the employees of the business. Strategic objectives of this dimension should focus on improving the skills of their employees which translates into improved business processes.

The second dimension of the Balanced Scorecard is the Internal Business Process dimension which focuses managers on those issues most important to meeting customer demands. Strategic objectives of this dimension should focus on efficient and effective business processes which improve customer satisfaction.

The third Balanced Scorecard dimension is the Customer dimension which focuses managers on what it takes to satisfies customers. Strategic objectives of this dimension should focus on achieving customer satisfaction, which leads to increased sales and achievement of financial goals. The fourth Balanced Scorecard dimension is the Financial dimension which focuses on achieving financial goals. Strategic objectives of this dimension should focus on improving the financial performance of the company.

For each of the balanced scorecard dimensions students need to identify 2–3 strategic objectives for each dimension, and there should be at least one performance measure linked to each strategic objective.

A PRELIMINARY STUDY OF LEARNING OBJECTIVES ACROSS THE CURRICULUM: AN ANALYSIS OF VARIOUS ACCOUNTING TEXTBOOKS

Leonard Stokes

ABSTRACT

This study examines 117 verbs associated with 2,872 learning objectives, and 377 questions taken from 24 textbooks across the accounting curriculum. To determine the level of cognitive ability associated with the individual learning objectives I analyzed the verbs based upon Bloom's Taxonomy. To reach across the accounting curriculum I chose texts from Financial Accounting, Intermediate Financial Accounting, Advanced Financial Accounting, Managerial Accounting, Cost Accounting, and Auditing. Results of the analysis found that the authors used verbs at the lower learning levels of the cognitive domain. The verbs used by the author teams depend upon individual preference rather a specific segment of the cognitive domain. In addition, as the student progresses through the accounting curriculum some topics in upper level textbooks use learning objectives at the same level as in introductory level textbooks.

Advances in Accounting Education: Teaching and Curriculum Innovations, Volume 9, 307–326

ISSN: 1085-4622/doi:10.1016/S1085-4622(08)09015-9

Accounting professionals and academics have expressed concerns about the future direction of accounting education for decades. The then 'Big 8' issued their White Paper 'Perspectives on Education' (Arthur Andersen & Co et al., 1989) to begin a dialog about a change in training professional accountants. In 'Reorienting Accounting Education', Schultz (1989, p. 22) stated that a widespread adoption of restructuring cannot take place without textbook and classroom material development. These earlier calls for change did not overcome a pessimistic attitude as Albrecht and Sack (2000, p. 52) continued to express concerns about the future of accounting education.

With many of these earlier calls for action still unanswered the AICPA, AACSB, and the regional accrediting bodies are calling for an increased measure of the effectiveness of education. In response to these outside pressures program administrators are trying to quantify the results of learning. Learning objectives appear in many accounting textbooks. Evaluating the construction of the learning objectives included in accounting textbooks is beyond the scope of this chapter.

This study examines 24 textbooks from across the accounting curriculum. Not all textbook author teams use learning objectives. In the sample, 117 verbs are associated with 2,872 learning objectives. Bloom's Taxonomy (1956) was the basis to analyze the verbs in determining the level of cognitive ability associated with the individual learning objectives. The sample includes texts from six accounting curriculum categories. Various author teams and a variety of publishers provide participant diversity.

This chapter begins with a summary of some research on valuing textbooks. It continues with a discussion of learning objectives from the viewpoint of the textbook author and the student. The analysis of learning objectives in the accounting texts involves evaluating the learning objective's primary verb. I based a comparison of the verbs used to the learning levels promulgated in Bloom's Taxonomy (1956), upon McBeath's (1992) listing of 'Verbs Applicable to the Cognitive Domain'. The chapter concludes with an analysis of findings, and a discussion of limitations and future research.

BACKGROUND ON ANALYZING ACCOUNTING TEXTBOOKS

Smith and DeRidder (1997, p. 373) conducted a survey related to the textbook adoption process. They found that in general textbook adoption decisions rely on key adoption criteria such as comprehensibility, timeliness, and exposition quality. Their study did not examine the role of learning objectives in the textbook selection process.

Davidson and Baldwin (2005) used Bloom's Taxonomy to analyze the cognitive demands inherent in the end-of-chapter material in intermediate textbooks from 1934 to 2004. One of their concerns was to develop the intellectual skills outlined by the 1989 'Big 8' White Paper. They state 'students must therefore have exposure to levels 5 and 6 items so they can develop the intellectual skills needed for today's accounting career' (Davidson & Baldwin, 2005, p. 83). They found that 86% of the end-of-chapter items 'do not include a meaningful concentration of items that focus on the two highest levels of learning' (Davidson & Baldwin, 2005, p. 89).

Davidson and Baldwin's argument is that end-of-chapter material should be at the higher levels of learning. This assumption regarding learning levels implies that the end-of-chapter material should be consistent with the author's stated learning objectives. Some texts relate the end-of-chapter material to the specific chapter's learning objectives. Edmonds, Edmonds, Tsay, Olds, and Schneider (2006a), *Managerial Accounting*, cross-refers the learning objectives directly within the end-of-chapter materials. Other texts such as Nikolai, Bazley, and Jones (2007), *Intermediate Accounting*, provide the cross-references in the supplemental material solution manual.

In this study the majority of stated learning objectives were associated with the lower levels within the cognitive domain. If Davidson and Baldwin's assumption that the end-of-chapter material relates to the learning objectives then this material should be consistent with the specific chapter's learning objectives. A preponderance of the learning objectives being at the lower learning levels unexpectedly result in the end-of-chapter material not containing issues at the higher levels of learning.

BLOOM'S TAXONOMY

Bloom's Taxonomy (1956) is an important educational work that is cited hundreds of times a year (Brazelton, 2000, p. 61). The taxonomy is based upon the concept that learning occurs cumulatively over time. The six levels of cognitive development assume that a student progresses from recall or memorization at the lower levels to more abstract and complex level of evaluation. The levels are commonly referred to as (McBeath, 1992, p. 166): Knowledge, Comprehension, Application, Analysis, Synthesis, and Evaluation. The classroom can create an arena where the thought processes that instructors use at one level become the building blocks for the next level (Brazelton, 2000, p. 60).

The paradigm supporting these building blocks allows the students to develop skills necessary to support critical thinking. Students must have an organized thought process to support critical thinking. Brazelton (2000, pp. 62–63) believes that instructors can use Bloom's framework in the classroom to help accomplish the educational goals that the accounting profession advocates. In addition she states (Brazelton, 2000, p. 82):

> If students taking sequentially-ordered courses are not exposed to communication at higher cognitive levels throughout the curriculum, those skills learned in the early courses never are developed fully.

Brazelton's thoughts are a challenge to faculty members teaching a course to provide similar cognitive demands. I believe that the textbooks used in the course should aid the instructor in pushing the cognitive demands on the students. To me no one portion of the curriculum is solely responsible for developing higher level learning and critical thinking skills.

AUTHOR'S STATEMENTS REGARDING LEARNING OBJECTIVES

Some textbook authors mention learning objectives in their preface or description of the text. They write preface sections that focus on learning objectives predominately for the faculty members assigning the text in the course, not specifically the students reading the text. Some selected comments include:

> Each chapter has an Understanding the Learning Objectives section. These "summaries" enable the student to determine how well the Learning Objectives were accomplished. We were the first authors (1974) to ever include Learning Objectives in an accounting text. These objectives have been included at the beginning of the chapter, as marginal notes, within the chapter, at the end of the chapter, and in supplements such as the Test Bank, Instructors' Resource Guide, Computerized Test Bank, Instructors' Resource Guide, Computerized Test Bank, and Study Guide. The objectives are also indicated for each exercise and problem. (Hermanson, Edwards, & Maher, 1995)

> Traditionally, skill development in introductory accounting has been focused at a relatively low level, concentrating primarily on comprehension and recall. Accounting education has traditionally emphasized content. Rigor has been measured by the quantity of content covered. Authors and educators have added more and more topics to the curricula and accounting textbooks have grown ever larger. This model provides little opportunity to help students develop the skills that the modern

> business environment they will face demands. (Edmonds, Edmonds, Olds, & Schneider, 2006b)
>
> Clear Objectives:
> Objectives at the beginning of each chapter prepare students for what they will be studying. We list each objective in the margin beside the topical coverage to reinforce students' learning. (Nikolai et al., 2007)

The authors mention learning objectives in a very positive manner. Also, according to Hermanson et al. (1995), learning objectives have been part of some accounting textbooks since 1974. Author teams mentioning learning objectives would give the appearance that they believe the use of learning objectives is important in their textbook. The above comments related to learning objectives do not express any concrete basis for how the individual author teams determined the definition of the learning objectives. By examining the learning objectives currently in use I hope to begin a discussion to create learning objectives that will aid in creating a continuum from the lower to higher learning levels within the accounting curriculum.

The lack of clarity in choice and definition for individual learning objectives could impact textbook readers. The majority of textbook readers and users are the students. Challenging students to progress through the cognitive levels requires the cooperation of all facets of the educational team, including all faculty members teaching a course as well as textbook authors. Students appear to take a passive approach to learning which may cause a conflict with Brazelton's (2000) desire for a more challenging and active learning environment in the classroom.

STUDENTS' USE OF TEXTBOOKS

Issit (2004, p. 689) discusses textbooks as being a major part of the educational process. He states that

> Textbooks function to some extent as the voices of the disciplines – as such they have a key function as building blocks in the architecture of knowledge. They present both the discipline's internal workings and its sense of self-identity as a coherent domain of study.

He also suggests that 'the traditional form of the textbook is largely one that assumes and perpetrates a "received knowledge, passive consumption" pedagogical model' (Issit, 2004, p. 683). Sikorski et al. (2002, p. 313) encourages professors to promote frequent and critical reading of textbooks, through either the use of quizzes or calling on students in class. They also claim that

> Students who succeed in introductory level college courses without critically reading their texts would seem less likely to excel in future individual learning endeavors in college and beyond.

Wandersee's findings (1988, p. 73) are consistent with the concept of a passive perception of textbook use in education. In studying 133 undergraduates from a private four-year college in the Midwest he found that 'only 6% of the students queried make a conscious effort to link new concepts in the text to prior knowledge'.

Phillips and Phillips (2006, p. 31) provided a look at student motivation for reading a textbook. Their study included 172 undergraduate students in introductory financial accounting using learning journals. They found that academically strong students appear to read with the primary goal of developing an understanding of the assigned material. On the other hand, academically weak students appear to read with the primary goal of reducing anxiety.

Phillips and Phillips recommended that professors take an active role in advising students on how to read the text. This advice encourages students to avoid reading chapters later. Also, students should attempt to identify and resolve issues that seem confusing to them. They also found that only some students read learning objectives. Of those that do read the learning objectives 39% were in the top quartile and 27% were in the second quartile of academic ability as measured in the study. They found that most students who skipped the learning objectives were in the fourth and third quartiles (33% and 30%, respectively).

Brazelton (2000, pp. 74–81) encourages faculty to use a variety of techniques in the classroom. These techniques provide the student assistance in developing tools necessary to be a critical thinker. Her lists ignore the textbook. This lack of attention to the textbook could imply it is of minimal value to the learning process and should be discarded. Instead, as recommended by Phillips and Phillips the faculty member might take an active role in advising how to use the text. Eide (2000, p. 39) also suggests that providing the students with learning strategies helps the students to process information becoming active participants in the learning process.

Due to the difficulty in reading accounting textbooks she recommends the use of the PQ4R method (Eide, 2000, p. 49). This process suggests reading the objectives as a first step. Learning objectives written at a higher cognitive level could then be considered a step in the critical thinking learning process. Proper utilization of the textbook and its learning objectives would appear to be an important part of the student's total learning experience.

EVALUATING LEARNING OBJECTIVES

This study looks at the learning objectives stated in accounting textbooks. The sample of texts is a cross-section within the accounting curriculum (Table 1). In addition, a section of this chapter will trace textbook learning objectives through different levels of the curriculum.

The goal of selecting four texts from each curriculum category is to obtain a variety of approaches to creating and stating learning objectives within this category. In selecting a variety of author teams the lead author of a set of teams included both a Financial (Edmonds et al., 2006b) and Managerial Text (Edmonds et al., 2006a). In addition, lead authors in both Financial

Table 1. Listing of Textbooks Used in the Study by Curriculum Category.

Category	Text	Edition	Publisher
Financial	Edmonds, Edmonds, McNair, Olds	5th	McGraw-Hill/Irwin
	Kimmel, Weygandt, Kieso	4th	Wiley
	Libby, Libby, Short	5th	McGraw-Hill/Irwin
	Albrecht, Stice, Stice	10th	Thomson/Southwestern
Managerial	Edmonds, Edmonds, Tsay, Olds	3rd	McGraw-Hill/Irwin
	Jackson, Sawyers, Jenkins	3rd	Thomson/Southwestern
	Hilton	6th	McGraw-Hill/Irwin
	Horngren, Sunden, Stratton	13th	Pearson/Prentice Hall
Intermediate	Norton, Diamond, Pagach		Houghton Mifflin
	Kieso, Weygandt, Warfield	12th	Wiley
	Spiceland, Sepe, Tomassinni	4th	McGraw-Hill/Irwin
	Nikolai, Bazley, Jones	10th	Thomson/Southwestern
Advanced	Beams, Anthony, Clement, Lowensohn	9th	Pearson/Prentice Hall
	Fischer, Taylor, Cheng	8th	Thomson/Southwestern
	Baker, Lembke, King, Jeffrey	7th	McGraw-Hill/Irwin
	Hoyle, Schaefer, Doupnik	8th	McGraw-Hill/Irwin
Cost	Hansen, Mowen	5th	Thomson/Southwestern
	Eldenberg, Wolcott		Wiley
	Kinney, Prather-Kinsey, Raiborn	6th	Thomson/Southwestern
	Horngren, Datar, Foster	12th	Pearson/Prentice Hall
Auditing	Arens, Elder, Beasley	11th	Pearson/Prentice Hall
	Messier, Glover, Prawitt	5th	McGraw-Hill/Irwin
	Ricchute	8th	Thomson/Southwestern
	Boynton, Johnson	8th	Wiley

and Intermediate (Kieso), and in Managerial and Cost (Horngren) were the same. The sample includes texts with longevity such as Kieso's 12th edition, and Horngren's 13th edition and first edition texts such as Eldenberg and Wolcott (2005), and Norton, Diamond, and Pagach (2006).

By having a variety of editions I was hoping to include learning objectives from authors of well-established texts as well as new writing teams. In this manner I was trying to include a broad cross-section of contributors to the accounting curriculum.

Table 2 contains a summary of the number of learning objectives for each curriculum category. The process involves selecting a primary verb for every learning objective in each textbook. Typically, the textbook authors began the learning objective with a verb. For this chapter that verb is considered the primary verb. For example, 'define' is the primary verb in Learning Objective 1 from Libby, Libby, and Short (2007), *Financial Accounting*, Chapter 2:

> Define the objectives of financial reporting, the elements of the balance sheet, and the related key accounting assumptions and principles.

Since there are many more learning objectives (2,872) than primary verbs (117), most learning objectives use the same primary verb. The number of primary verbs, 276, results from counting each verb an author team used to describe the learning objectives. Therefore, some of the verbs count more than once. For instance, Albrecht, Stice, and Stice (2008), *Financial Accounting*, uses 'describe' as the primary verb for two different learning objectives in Chapter 1.

Table 3 lists the verbs the author teams select most often. Table 4 lists the most often used verbs based upon accounting curriculum category. The verbs most often used represent over 50% of the learning objectives. The other verbs have minimal usage and are not in a separate list.

Table 2. Number of Learning Objectives.

Curriculum Category	Number of Learning Objectives	Number of Primary Verbs Used
Financial	372	38
Managerial	509	54
Intermediate	731	43
Advanced	319	52
Cost	297	45
Auditing	644	44
Total	2,872	276

Table 3. Primary Verbs Used Most Often in a Learning Objective.

Non-Accounting Specific Primary Verbs		Accounting Specific Verbs	
Explain	17.1%	Account	29.5
Understand	15.6	Record	13.3
Describe	12.6	Apply	8.9
Identify	9.6	Report	6.3
All others	44.1	All others	42
Total	100%	Total	100%

Table 4. Percentage of Learning Objectives Covered by the Same Verb within Each Curriculum Category.

	Explain	Understand	Identify	Describe	Accounting Specific
Financial	21.8%	5.1%	9.7%	12.1%	13.2%
Managerial	19.1	2.0	5.3	12.4	3.5
Intermediate	21.9	9.7	12.4	16.3	11.4
Advanced	9.9	9.0	2.8	3.5	15.9
Cost	9.5	3.2	3.4	8.6	3.8
Auditing	1.9	38.8	10.2	6.1	4.8

Table 5. Percentage of Accounting Specific Learning Objectives Covered by the Same Verb within Each Curriculum Category.

	Account	Record	Apply	Report
Financial	30.6%	28.6%	0.0%	28.6%
Managerial	0.0	22.2	0.0	0.0
Intermediate	49.4	18.1	2.4	3.6
Advanced	24.6	7.2	20.3	0.0
Cost	33.3	0.0	0.0	0.0
Auditing	0.0	0.0	44.4	0.0

I determined some of the verbs to be accounting specific (Table 5). The use of these verbs in the learning objectives is not common usage for the manner utilized in textbooks other than accounting. For example, Albrecht et al. (2008), *Financial Accounting*, Chapter 6, Learning Objective 7 is:

Reconcile a checking account.

This use of 'reconcile' is accounting specific. The accounting specific use of the word 'account' from Albrecht et al. (2008), *Financial Accounting*, Chapter 9, Learning Objective 9 is:

> Account for changes in depreciation estimates and methods.

Some verbs were used in the primary sense as they might be found in other textbooks and in an accounting specific sense, such as 'apply'. Beams, Anthony, Clement, and Lowensohn (2006), *Advanced Accounting,* Chapter 2, Learning objective 5 is:

> Apply the equity method to purchase price applications.

Horngren et al. (2005), *Managerial Accounting,* Chapter 5, Learning Objective 2 is:

> Apply the decision process to make business decisions.

The Beams' use of 'apply' is accounting specific and the use by Horngren is common in textbooks other than accounting.

ASSOCIATING LEARNING OBJECTIVES WITH BLOOM'S TAXONOMY

McBeath (1992, p. 11) produced a guidebook on learning outcomes that includes a list of 'Verbs Applicable to the Cognitive Domain'. This listing provides a summary of some verbs based upon the six levels of Bloom's Taxonomy (1956). The first step was matching the primary verb in the learning objectives to McBeath's list. If a primary verb match did not appear in McBeath's list, then I used Roget's Thesaurus (1990) to find a synonym for the verb which I matched to the list. The Thesaurus was a source to determine a use for those verbs not matched directly in this manner. Once I chose a synonym for this deemed use, this synonym became the match to the Taxonomy. For instance the word 'integrate' lead to 'aggregate', which lead to 'assemble', which is a synthesis verb. Therefore, I deemed 'integrate' to be at the synthesis level. Table 6 contains the most commonly used verbs and their respective cognitive domain.

The majority of verbs belong to the knowledge and comprehension levels, the lower levels of learning. The focus of each textbook appears to be on the lower levels of learning. Table 7 summarizes by the six cognitive domains the learning objectives' primary verbs and accounting specific verbs. Table 8

Table 6

Panel A: Most Commonly Used Verbs per Cognitive Domain

Bloom's taxonomy	Explain	Understand	Identify	Describe
Knowledge		X		
Comprehension	X		X	X
Application				
Analysis				
Synthesis				
Evaluation				

Panel B: Most Commonly Used Accounting Specific Verbs per Cognitive Domain

Bloom's taxonomy	Account	Record	Apply	Report
Knowledge	X	X		
Comprehension				
Application			X	
Analysis				
Synthesis				X
Evaluation				

Table 7

Panel A: Percentage of Learning Objectives per Cognitive Domain Primary Verbs

	Knowledge	Comprehension	Application	Analysis	Synthesis	Evaluation
Total (%)	29.5	45.4	7.5	9.7	6.7	1.2

Panel B: Percentage of Learning Objectives per Cognitive Domain Accounting Specific Verbs

	Knowledge	Comprehension	Application	Analysis	Synthesis	Evaluation
Total (%)	47.8	1.2	14.1	19.9	9.6	7.4

summarizes for the six cognitive domains the primary verbs and accounting specific verbs from the learning objectives for each curriculum category.

Overall, the three higher levels of the cognitive domain, (analysis, synthesis, and evaluation) total less than 18% of all of the learning objectives using primary verbs and 36.9% of the learning objectives using accounting specific verbs. The verbs 'compute' or 'calculate' represent the majority of primary verbs at the analysis level. Auditing (10.2%) and intermediate accounting (11.1%) have the lowest percentage of learning objectives that use primary verbs at the highest levels of the cognitive domain. Intermediate accounting (24%) texts have the lowest percentage of

Table 8

	Knowledge	Comprehension	Application	Analysis	Synthesis	Evaluation	Total
Panel A: Percentage of Learning Objectives per Cognitive Domain by Curriculum Category Using Primary Verbs							
Financial	14.2	57.3	5.9	15.2	6.2	1.2	100
Managerial	9.0	45.1	10.8	19.8	12.2	3.1	100
Intermediate	20.1	62.3	6.5	7.4	3.7	0.0	100
Advanced	31.2	32.0	22.8	5.2	8.8	0.0	100
Cost	21.7	57.2	5.4	9.1	5.8	.7	100
Auditing	66.5	21.7	1.	3.3	5.1	1.8	100
Panel B: Percentage of Learning Objectives Per Cognitive Domain by Curriculum Category Using Accounting Specific Verbs							
Financial	59.2	0.0	0.0	8.2	30.6	2.0	100
Managerial	22.2	0.0	16.7	50.0	11.1	0.0	100
Intermediate	69.9	2.5	3.6	8.4	8.4	7.2	100
Advanced	39.2	1.5	24.6	27.5	1.4	5.8	100
Cost	38.1	0.0	4.8	52.4	4.8	0.0	100
Auditing	12.9	0.0	45.2	12.9	0.0	29.0	100

learning objectives that use accounting specific verbs at the highest levels of the cognitive domain.

Author Team Verb Preference

The textbook author teams' preference for certain words appears to govern the word usage. I was not able to determine a discernable pattern to the verb selection between author teams. The auditing text authors began 644 learning objectives with 44 different verbs. One auditing author team used 'know' 17 times, and 'determine' 54 times, another author team used 'know' 40 times and 'determine' 11 times. The other auditing author team that used learning objectives did not use these verbs at all. With the advanced texts, one author team used 'determine' 25 times and another author team used the term once. In the intermediate accounting texts one author team used 'understand' 50 of the 71 total instances.

AUTHOR'S USE OF ALTERNATIVE TO LEARNING OBJECTIVES

Not all author teams use learning objectives. Table 9 provides a summary of approaches within the various curriculum categories. One of the author

Table 9. Author Team's Use of Learning Objectives or an Alternative.

	Learning Objective	Questions	Neither	Total
Financial	4	0	0	4
Managerial	4	0	0	4
Intermediate	4	0	0	4
Advanced	2	1	1	4
Cost	2	2	0	4
Auditing	3	0	1	4

Table 10. List of Question Words Used by Curriculum Classification.

Question	Cost	Advanced	Total
Does	0	1	1
How	112	3	115
Should	0	1	1
What	123	3	126
When	2	41	43
Where	0	0	0
Which	2	1	3
Who	0	1	1
Why	24	62	86
Will	0	1	1
Total	263	114	377

teams in each of the advanced and audit series did not use learning objectives nor questions to guide their readers. Questions alone guide the reader in some advanced and cost texts sampled.

Some author teams like to use specific question words to guide their reader (Table 10). The cost author teams both like 'how' and 'what'. The advanced team preferred 'when' or 'why'. All questions included in the author's list were included in the count. For instance Kinney, Prather-Kinsey, and Raiborn (2006), *Cost Accounting: Foundations and Evolutions*, Chapter 2, for objective 2 states:

> How costs are classified and why are such classifications useful?

I counted them as two questions one 'how' and the other 'why'.

In this chapter I did not evaluate whether the learning objectives or questions achieved their intended goal in the textbook. In addition, I did not analyze the questions to see how I could categorize them under Bloom's Taxonomy. The goal of this chapter is to begin a discussion on the appropriateness of how the learning objectives are written. Further research can evaluate the inclusion and writing of questions. This chapter is only pointing out that the use of questions appears to be an alternative to explicitly stating learning objectives used in some of the upper level accounting curriculum categories.

DISCUSSION AND ANALYSIS

Prior textbook evaluation studies ignored the stated learning objectives. The findings of this chapter appear to be consistent with Davidson and Baldwin's (2005, p. 91) analysis of intermediate textbooks who did not find 'items at the highest learning level'. Although they claim that there does appear 'to have been a general trend toward more computation type questions at the analysis level'.

Learning objectives which contain analysis and synthesis verbs are greater in number than the number of evaluation verbs. Verbs such as 'compare', 'compute', and 'demonstrate' precede learning objectives at the analysis level. Primary verbs such as 'link' and 'prepare' precede learning objectives at the synthesis level. There were only three primary verbs at the evaluation level: 'choose', 'decide', and 'evaluate'. Many of the accounting specific verbs such as 'adjust', 'allocate', and 'defer' are the analysis level. 'Report' is considered to be at the synthesis level. It is not unexpected that these three categories of higher level learning objectives have less than the number of learning objectives using knowledge and comprehension type verbs. However, while progressing through the curriculum the lack of emphasis on higher level verbs being utilized in composing textbook learning objectives is surprising.

Potential Impact on Assessment Initiatives

Based upon comments mentioned previously by authors such as Nikolai et al. (2007) and Hermanson et al. (1995), it would be expected that the majority of end-of-chapter items would be consistent with the learning objectives and therefore, not be at the highest learning levels. The lack of material in the higher learning levels does not mean that Davidson and Baldwin's concerns are misplaced, especially as an individual course professor tries to assess learning in the classroom.

Currently, assessment of the course and program are a major aspect of the higher education process. Ammons and Mills (2005) have emphasized assessment process at the course level. Kimmel, Marquette, and Olsen (1998) and Stivers, Campbell, and Hermanson (2000) have provided information on assessment for Accounting Programs. In addition at the program level AACSB (2007, p. 33) states

> Accounting faculty in different institutions are expected to develop alternate approaches for meeting and assuring educational objectives and delivery of overall high quality.

Producing high quality outcomes assessments would suggest that the inputs to the educational process are important. An assumption, I have heard at my institution regarding assessment practices, is that faculty at the course level, and the institution at the program level are developing critical thinking as an important aspect of the learning process. At some point in the curriculum the learning objectives must correspond to this expected level of learning.

For accounting, Baldwin and Chesser (2003, p. 103) suggest that building a grid and analyzing cases can help the student develop a balance between content complexity and the integration of skill development. Wandersee (1988, p. 78) found that the majority of students, 55%, 'seldom construct organizational tools' while reading textbooks. Organizational tools include such things as outlines, lists, diagrams, and charts. These results suggest that students do not push much beyond the objectives of the text.

Calderon, Green, and Harkness (2005, p. 281) provide a summary of best practices in assessment where they state:

> Effective assessment requires faculty to align learning goals and objectives with the curriculum. This alignment implies that faculty will identify each learning objective and determine the specific courses in the curriculum in which students will learn and develop the underlying skills.

It seems that assessment will require faculty in higher level courses to acknowledge learning from introductory courses. What follows is an example of issues of learning objectives that do not appear to include cumulative learning as the student progresses through the curriculum.

Issues Traced through the Curriculum

Investments' using the fair value and equity methods is a topic that flows through the financial accounting series. Albrecht et al. (2008), in *Financial Accounting*, Chapter 12, uses verbs such as 'understand' at the knowledge level. Kieso, Weygandt, and Warfield (2007), in *Intermediate Accounting*,

Chapter 17 uses 'identify' and 'describe' at the comprehension level. Beams et al. (2006), in *Advanced Accounting*, Chapter 2 uses 'apply' at the comprehension level.

Plant, Property and Equipment is an area studied in both financial and intermediate accounting. Libby et al. (2007) in *Financial Accounting*, Chapter 8, uses 'explain' impairment at the comprehension level. Both Kieso and Nikolai in their separate intermediate accounting texts each use 'explain' related to impairments. Nikolai in Chapter 10 uses 'record acquisition' which is at the knowledge level.

Similar types of concerns arise in the managerial and cost series. Jackson, Sawyers, and Jenkins (2006), *Managerial Accounting*, Chapter 13, wants to 'describe the role of ABC management'. Describe is at the comprehension level. Horngren, Datar, and Foster (2006), *Cost Accounting*, Chapter 5, wants to 'explain how ABC systems are used in ABC Management'. 'Explain' is also at the comprehension level.

A faculty member cannot be dependent upon the text to emphasize higher level thinking skills. However, textbooks that aim at lower levels of learning, then make it difficult for students to move beyond these lower levels and into higher levels. Van Gelder (2005, p. 42) emphasizes that for students to improve their critical thinking skills 'they must engage in critical thinking itself'. Davidson and Baldwin (2005, p. 89) suggest a professor's reliance on textbook end-of-chapter items that are at the lower levels of learning will not automatically expose students to materials that require methods of thinking and learning at the highest levels. Faculty may need to create exercises that stress and assess critical thinking without depending upon the textbook.

Brazelton (2000) provides guidance for faculty who want to develop materials to aid in improving critical thinking. Bayou and Reinstein (2000, p. 8) emphasize that effective accounting knowledge utilization requires developing accounting graduates' reasoning, evaluative, and self-reflective skills. They again argue for a switch from passive teaching to what they refer to as 'dynamic knowledge acquisition'. Massey and Van Hise (2003) advocate that since accounting texts do not keep abreast of changes in accounting education then maybe faculty should create a custom-published text.

LIMITATIONS AND FURTHER RESEARCH

This study is a first attempt at analyzing accounting textbook learning objectives based upon Bloom's Taxonomy. The purpose of this study is not to criticize any author team or publisher. I did not attempt to verify that the list of learning objectives is actually covered in the text. Evaluation of the construction of the learning objectives in all business disciplines, not just accounting, is a further step in this line of research. Also, I only sampled some textbooks from each curriculum category.

Additionally, I did not attempt to quantify a specific mix of learning objectives nor establish a required number of lower level or higher level learning objectives. Continued research in this area is encouraged by both academics and accounting professionals.

The accounting profession may want to emulate the IMA's cognitive expectations for the CMA Examination. These cognitive skills, based upon Bloom's Taxonomy, are stated in the content specification outlines (2004, p. 3). The cognitive skill expectations of the different professional organizations can be a significant contribution to an ongoing dialog with professors, textbook authors, and publishers.

CONCLUSION

Textbooks form a significant part of the preparation of accountants. The accounting profession wants individuals to enter the profession who can think critically. Textbooks focus the majority of the learning objectives at the lowest levels of learning. The accounting profession and the professoriate can not expect all of the critical thinking to be accomplished exclusively in the class room, especially using materials focused at the lower levels of learning.

Faculty members concerned about integrating the textbook learning objectives into course and program assessment may want to seriously consider the level of the learning objectives when selecting a textbook. If the textbook authors and publishers do not take writing learning objectives at higher learning levels seriously, then the accounting faculty may develop their own materials and forgo the use of an expensive text that does not meet their needs.

REFERENCES

AACSB Eligibility Procedures and Standards for Accounting Accreditation Standards, revised April 23, 2007.

Albrecht, W. S., & Sack, R. J. (2000). *Accounting education: Charting the course through a perilous future* (Vol. 16), Accounting Education Series, Sarasota, FL: American Accounting Association.

Albrecht, W. S., Stice, E. K., & Stice, J. D. (2008). *Financial accounting* (10th ed.). Mason, OH: Thomson/Southwestern.

Ammons, J. L., & Mills, S. K. (2005). Course-embedded assessments for evaluating cross-functional integration and improving the teaching-learning process. *Issues in Accounting Education, 20*(1), 1–20.

Arens, A. A., Elder, R. J., & Beasley, M. (2006). *Auditing and assurance services: An integrated approach* (11th ed.). Upper Saddle River, NJ: Pearson/Prentice Hall.

Arthur Andersen & Co, Arthur Young, Coopers & Lybrand, Deloitte Haskins & Sells, Ernst & Whinney, Peat Marwick Main & Co., Price Waterhouse, and Touche Ross. (1989). *Perspectives on education: Capabilities for success in the accounting profession.*

Baker, R. E., Lembke, V. C., King, T. E., & Jeffrey, C. G. (2008). *Advanced financial accounting* (7th ed.). New York, NY: McGraw-Hill/Irwin.

Baldwin, J. N., & Chesser, D. L. (2003). An approach to integrating accounting courses. *Journal of Accounting Education, 21*, 101–126.

Bayou, M. E., & Reinstein, A. (2000). The dual role of critical thinking in accounting education. In: B. N. Schwartz & E. Ketz (Eds), *Advances in accounting education teaching and curriculum innovations* (Vol. 2, pp. 1–20). Stamford, CT: JAI Press.

Beams, F. A., Anthony, J. H., Clement, R. P., & Lowensohn, S. H. (2006). *Advanced accounting* (9th ed.). Upper Saddle River, NJ: Pearson/Prentice Hall.

Bloom, B. (Ed.) (1956). *Taxonomy of educational objectives: The classification of educational goals: Handbook I, Cognitive Domain.* New York, Toronto: Longmans, Green.

Boynton, W. C., & Johnson, R. N. (2006). *Modern auditing: Assurance services and the integrity of financial reporting* (8th ed.). Hoboken, NJ: Wiley.

Brazelton, J. K. (2000). Students may blossom using Bloom's Taxonomy in the accounting curriculum. In: B. N. Schwartz & E. Ketz (Eds), *Advances in accounting education teaching and curriculum innovations* (Vol. 2, pp. 57–85). Stamford, CT: JAI Press.

Calderon, T., Green, B. P., & Harkness, M. (2005). Best practices in accounting program assessment: Executive summary, AAA teaching and curriculum committee on best practices in accounting program assessment. In: B. N. Schwartz & E. Ketz (Eds), *Advances in accounting education teaching and curriculum innovations* (Vol. 5, pp. 277–306). Stamford, CT: JAI Press.

CMA Content Specification Outline (effective 7/1/2004).

Davidson, R. A., & Baldwin, B. A. (2005). Cognitive skills objectives in intermediate accounting textbooks: Evidence from end-of-chapter material. *Journal of Accounting Education, 23*(2).

Edmonds, T. P., Edmonds, C. D., McNair, F. M., Olds, P. R., & Schneider, N. W. (2006a). *Fundamental financial accounting concepts* (5th ed.). New York, NY: McGraw-Hill/Irwin.

Edmonds, T. P., Edmonds, C. D., Tsay, B.-Y., Olds, P. R., & Schneider, N. (2006b). *Fundamental managerial accounting concepts* (3rd ed.). New York, NY: McGraw-Hill/Irwin.

Eide, B. J. (2000). Integrating learning strategies in accounting courses. In: B. N. Schwartz & E. Ketz (Eds), *Advances in accounting education teaching and curriculum innovations* (Vol. 2, pp. 37–55). Stamford, CT: JAI Press.

Eldenberg, L. G., & Wolcott, S. (2005). *Cost management: Measuring, monitoring, and motivating performance*. Hoboken, NJ: Wiley.

Fischer, P. M., Taylor, W. J., & Cheng, R. H. (2006). *Advanced accounting* (9th ed.). Mason, OH: Thomson/Southwestern.

Hansen, D. R., & Mowen, M. M. (2006). *Cost management: Accounting and control* (5th ed.). Mason, OH: Thomson/Southwestern.

Hermanson, R. H., Edwards, J. D., & Maher, M. W. (1995). *Accounting a business perspective* (6th ed.). New York, NY: Irwin.

Hilton, R. W. (2005). *Managerial accounting: Creating value in a dynamic business environment* (6th ed.). New York, NY: McGraw-Hill/Irwin.

Horngren, C. T., Datar, S. M., & Foster, G. (2006). *Cost accounting: A managerial emphasis* (12th ed.). Upper Saddle River, NJ: Pearson/Prentice Hall.

Horngren, C. T., Sundem, G. L., & Stratton, W. O. (2005). *Introduction to management accounting* (13th ed.). Upper Saddle River, NJ: Pearson/Prentice Hall.

Hoyle, J. B., Schaefer, T. F., & Doupnik, T. S. (2007). *Advanced accounting* (8th ed.). New York, NY: McGraw-Hill/Irwin.

Issit, J. (2004). Reflections on the study of textbooks. *History of Education*, *33*(5), 683–696.

Jackson, S., Sawyers, R., & Jenkins, G. (2006). *Managerial accounting* (3rd ed.). Mason, OH: Thomson/Southwestern.

Kieso, D. E., Weygandt, J. J., & Warfield, T. D. (2007). *Intermediate accounting* (12th ed.). Hoboken, NJ: Wiley.

Kimmel, P. D., Weygandt, J., & Kieso, D. E. (2007). *Financial accounting: Tools for business decision making* (4th ed.). Hoboken, NJ: Wiley.

Kimmel, S. L., Marquette, R. P., & Olsen, D. H. (1998). Outcomes assessment programs: Historical perspective and state of the art. *Issues in Accounting Education*, *13*(4), 851–869.

Kinney, M. R., Prather-Kinsey, J., & Raiborn, C. (2006). *Cost accounting: Foundations and evolutions* (6th ed.). Mason, OH: Thomson/Southwestern.

Libby, R., Libby, P., & Short, D. G. (2007). *Financial accounting* (5th ed.). New York, NY: McGraw-Hill Irwin.

Massey, D., & Van Hise, J. (2003). Creating a custom-published textbook to facilitate curriculum change: An example from advanced accounting. In: B. N. Schwartz & E. Ketz (Eds), *Advances in accounting education teaching and curriculum innovations* (Vol. 5, pp. 243–261). Stamford, CT: JAI Press.

McBeath, R. J. (Ed.) (1992). *Instructing and evaluation in higher education: A guidebook for planning learning outcome*. Education Technology Publications.

Messier, W., Glover, S. M., & Prawitt, D. F. (2008). *Auditing and assurance services: A systematic approach* (5th ed.). New York, NY: McGraw-Hill/Irwin.

Nikolai, L. A., Bazley, J. D., & Jones, J. P. (2007). *Intermediate accounting* (10th ed.). Mason, OH: Thomson/Southwestern.

Norton, C. L., Diamond, M. A., & Pagach, D. P. (2006). *Intermediate accounting: Financial reporting and analysis*. Boston, MA: Houghton Mifflin.

Phillips, B. J., & Phillips, F. (2006). Sink or skim: Textbook reading behaviors of introductory accounting students. *Issues in Accounting Education*, *22*(1), 21–44.

Ricchiute, D. N. (2006). *Auditing* (8th ed.). Mason, OH: Thomson/Southwestern.

Roget's Thesaurus of English Words and Phrases. (1990). Portland House, New York.

Schultz, J. J. (1989). *Reorienting accounting education: Reports on the environment, professoriate, and curriculum of accounting* (Vol.10), Accounting Education Series, Sarasota, FL: American Accounting Association.

Sikorski, J. F., Rich, K., Saville, B. K., Buskist, W., Drogan, O., & Davis, S. F. (2002). Student use of introductory texts: Comparative survey findings from two universities. *Teaching of Psychology*, *29*(4), 312–313.

Smith, K. J., & DeRidder, J. J. (1997). The selection process for accounting textbooks: General criteria and publishers incentives – A survey. *Issues in Accounting Education*, *12*(2), 367–384.

Spiceland, J. D., Sepe, J., & Tomassinni, L. (2007). *Intermediate accounting* (4th ed.). New York, NY: McGraw-Hill/Irwin.

Stivers, B. Pl., Campbell, J. E., & Hermanson, H. M. (2000). An assessment program for accounting: Design, implementation, and reflection. *Issues in Accounting Education*, *15*(4), 553–572.

Van Gelder, T. (2005). Teaching critical thinking: Some lessons from cognitive science. *College Teaching*, *53*(1), 41–46.

Wandersee, J. H. (1988). Ways students read texts. *Journal of Research in Science Teaching*, *25*(1), 69–84.